南方軍政関係史料㊶

第二次世界大戦期東ティモール文献目録

Materials on East Timor during World War II

東ティモール日本占領期史料フォーラム編

edited by
The Forum for Historical Documents on
East Timor during the Japanese
Occupation Period

龍 溪 書 舎

Published by
Ryukei Shyosha

Tokyo 2008

目　　　次

まえがき（Preface） ··· 3
解説（Introduction） ··· 11
凡例（Explanatory Note） ··· 31
日本語文献（Japanese Language Publications）
　Ⅰ．単行書（Monographs） ···35
　　戦前・戦中篇［Prewar-Wartime Materials］ ··35
　　戦後篇［Postwar Writings］ ···46
　Ⅱ．雑誌論文（Periodical Articles） ··79
　　戦前・戦中篇［Prewar-Wartime Materials］ ··79
　　戦後篇［Postwar Writings］ ···86
　Ⅲ．地図類（Maps） ···89
　Ⅳ．戦友会誌（Veteran's Organization Newsletters） ·································93
外国語文献（Foreign Language Publications）
　Ⅰ．English Language Publications ···95
　Ⅱ．Portuguese Language Publications ··107
　Ⅲ．Dutch Language Publication ···127
　Ⅳ．中国語文献（台湾） ···133
公文書（Public Records）
　Ⅰ．日本所蔵史料（Materials in Japanese Archives） ······························139
　　1．解説（Explanation） ··141
　　2．外務省外交史料館所蔵史料（The Diplomatic Records Office of
　　　　Ministry of Foreign Affairs） ···142
　　3．防衛省防衛研究所所蔵史料（The National Institute for
　　　　Defense Studies of the Ministry of Defense） ·····························172
　　4．国立公文書館所蔵史料（The National Archives） ··························180
　Ⅱ．ポルトガル所蔵史料（Materials in Portuguese Archives） ················197

1．Libraries and Archives in Portugal and Macau ……………… 199
　　　2．A Brief List of Useful Documents and Archival Sources in Portugal… 203
　　　3．Arquivo Histórico Militar（AHM）……………………………… 207
Ⅲ．オーストラリア所蔵史料（Materials in Australian Archives）……………… 211
　　　1．Australian Archives …………………………………………… 213
　　　2．National Archive of Australia-Canberra Holdings ……………… 220
　　　3．National Archive of Australia-Melbourne Holdings …………… 228
　　　4．Australian War Memorial ……………………………………… 246
Ⅳ．イギリス所蔵史料（Materials in British Archives）…………………………… 277
　　　1．United Kingdom [London Archives] …………………………… 279
　　　2．Files and Items in the Public Records Office Collection of
　　　　　the National Archives…………………………………………… 289
Ⅴ．オランダ所蔵史料（Materials in the Archives of the Netherlands）……… 301
　　　1．Archives in the Netherlands …………………………………… 303

ま え が き

　東ティモール日本占領期史料フォーラムは、第2次世界大戦中日本軍が実質的に統治した東ティモール（当時の呼称はポルトガル領ティモール）における占領政策の実際、それに対する東ティモール社会の対応、さらには豪亜地中海と呼ばれたこの地域の国際関係を学術的に考察するための基礎作業として、上記テーマにかかわる「資料・文献・口述調査」の実施を目的に発足した。（財）トヨタ財団の研究助成を得て2003年7月から4年2ヵ月にわたり調査活動を行ってきた本フォーラムは、以下の3点を基本目的として設定した。
1．日本占領期東ティモールに関する関係諸国の一次史・資料および文献の所在を明らかにし、それを日本語・英語2ヵ国語で「文献目録」として刊行すること。
2．戦時期の東ティモールとさまざまなレベルでかかわった関係各国の当事者からの聞き取り調査を実施し、その成果を「証言集」として記録に残すこと。
3．調査活動の過程で入手した学術価値を有する一次資料を、所蔵機関の承認を得た上で刊行すること。

　今回、刊行することとなった文献目録は、上記3目的のうち本フォーラムが最も重視したものであり、当時の錯綜した国際関係における東ティモールの微妙な立場あるいは戦略的な重要性を反映して、きわめて多岐にわたる公文書、出版物、学術論文・一般論文、戦友会記録等が対象となっている。具体的な編纂作業を進めるにあたっては、とりわけ文献掲載資料の選別に関しては、吉久明宏委員を中心としメンバーのいずれかが現物の確認作業を行うことで、確実な情報を提供できるよう留意した。公文書に関しても基本的に同様の手続きを踏み、日本および旧宗主国ポルトガルといった直接当事国のみならず、第2次世界大戦中の東ティモールにかかわった他の関係諸国として、東ティモールに近接するオーストラリア、西ティモールを植民地として領有したオランダ、さらにはこの地域の国際秩序に重大な関心を有していたイギリスでも調査を行った。このような国際的な規模での広範多岐にわたる調査を限られた期間内で完了するため、本フォーラムでは編集作業の主担当者を決め――日本：吉久明宏、高橋茂人、大庭定男、ポルトガル：ジェフリー・ガン（Geoffrey Gunn）、高橋茂人、オーストラリア：ブラッド・ホートン（Brad Horton）、山本まゆみ、イギリス：ブラッ

ド・ホートン——調査活動の効率化を図る努力をした。

　しかしながら、調査にあたっては関係諸国の公文書館、図書館等の諸機関、さまざまな形でご支援を頂いた研究者、司書、アーキビストおよび戦友会の方々のお力添えなしには、こうした地道な作業を進めることはできなかったであろう。特に、国立オランダ戦争史資料研究所（NIOD）の元研究員マリスカ・ヘイマンス（Mariska Heijmans）夫人にはオランダ公文書館での調査を、そして外務省外交史料館の高橋和宏氏には、外交史料館での調査に多大のご協力をいただいた。また外国語文献のネイティブ・チェックにあたっては、ピーター・ポスト氏（Dr. Peter Post、オランダ語）、マリア・マヌエラ・アルバレス夫人（Maria Manuela Alvares、ポルトガル語）、紀旭峰氏（中国語）のご協力をいただいた。

　なお本フォーラムの第2の課題である「証言集」に関しては、すでに日本人、東ティモール人、オーストラリア人、そして台湾人当事者からの聞き取り調査を完了しており、テープ起こし作業を終了後、具体的な刊行準備に入る予定である。③に関しては、ポルトガル政府から派遣され日本軍支配下に置かれた植民地ティモールの事情調査を行ったマカオ政庁秘書長コスタ（Silva e Costa）大尉、及びそれに同行した外務省政務局第2課長曾禰益の報告書を収録した『日本占領下の東ティモール視察復命書——日本・ポルトガル両国当事者の記録——』を公刊済みである（龍溪書舎、2005年）。

　本文献目録の刊行にあたっては、研究助成と同じくトヨタ財団より出版助成を受けることができ、また龍溪書舎の北村正光社長、長島大樹氏からは厳しい出版状況の中、暖かいご配慮をいただくことができた。本フォーラム発足以来、トヨタ財団のプログラム・オフィサー川崎恵津子氏、姫本由美子氏からは、さまざまな形で力強いご協力を頂いた。ここにフォーラム・メンバー一同心から御礼を申し上げたい。

　最後になったが、この4年間余、苦楽を共にした本フォーラム・メンバーは以下（次頁）のとおりである。文献目録公刊の最終段階においては、とりわけ高橋茂人、ブラッド・ホートン、山本まゆみ、吉久明宏の諸委員には多大なご負担をおかけすることとなった。また、フォーラムの活動が順調に運営されたことは、本格的な東ティモール研究を志す大学院生高橋茂人委員の熱意と誠実さの賜であったことを付言させていただきたい。

大庭定男（現代史研究者、戦時期ジャワ軍政に関与）
ガン・ジェフリー（長崎大学経済学部教授）
倉沢愛子（慶応義塾大学経済学部教授）
髙橋茂人（早稲田大学大学院アジア太平洋研究科博士後期課程）
塩崎弘明（長崎純心大学人文学部教授）
ホートン、ウィリアム・ブラッドリー（拓殖大学商学部講師）
山﨑功（佐賀大学教育文化学部准教授）
山本まゆみ（早稲田大学文学部講師）
吉久明宏（元国立国会図書館司書）
後藤乾一（早稲田大学大学院アジア太平洋研究科教授）

フォーラム代表者　後藤乾一
2008年初夏

Preface

The Forum for Historical Documents on East Timor during the Japanese Occupation Period [Higashi Timōru Nihon senryō-ki shiryō fōramu] was established to provide basic data on East Timor during World War II especially when the Japanese military governed—publications, documents, and interviews—and so facilitate more substantial scholarly exploration. More specifically, the forum has been hoping to assist in the unearthing of facts about occupation policy, the reaction of different societies in the colony of Portuguese Timor, and on the international relations of this region of Australia and the Asian mediterranean sea. For the last four years and two months since being awarded a Toyota Foundation Initiative Grant in July 2003, the forum has engaged in research guided by the following three fundamental project goals:

1. To find primary sources and publications related to Japanese occupied East Timor, and compile a Japanese and English language bibliography.
2. To interview individuals from different countries who experienced the war in East Timor at different levels, and insofar as possible to preserve records of the interviews in a "collection of memories."
3. To publish a selection of academically valuable primary documents.

The production of this bibliographical publication has been the Forum's most highly prioritized goal. The diverse combination of archival documents, monographs, academic articles, and other periodicals like veterans' newsletters which we have sought to catalog reflect the sensitive position and strategically important location of East Timor in international relations at that time. Wherever possible materials in our bibliography have been directly examined by Akihiro Yoshihisa or other Forum members, a challenge given the wide scope of the project. In our search for important archival documents, we have covered not only Japan and the former metropole Portugal, but also Australia, the Netherlands (the former colonial ruler of west Timor), as well as England which was greatly interested in maintaining order in this area. Despite the need to conduct research in various countries during a limited period, we have strived to be as meticulous as possible in creating this bibliography. Accordingly, one or two researchers have been assigned primary responsibility for work in each country, a system which has helped us to complete the project in a timely manner. The majority of research in Japan was completed by Akihiro Yoshihisa and Shigehito Takahashi. Research in Portugal was conducted by Geoffrey Gunn and Shigehito Takahashi. Research in England was undertaken by Brad Horton, while he also undertook most research in Australia in conjunction with Mayumi Yamamoto. On the course of the research, we received warm support from each country's archives, libraries, museums, and research institutions. Besides, we also received various forms of cooperation and help from researchers, librarians, archivists such as Ms. Mariska Heijmans (then at the Netherlands Institute for War Documentation) who compiled the initial list of Dutch materials, and Dr. Kazuhiro Takahashi at the Diplomatic Record Office of the Ministry of Foreign Affairs of Japan. Without their support and cooperation, it would have been difficult to complete this bibliography.

The second goal of this project is to compile a "collection of memories," a set of interviews with East Timorese, Japanese, Australians, a Taiwanese, and an individual born in Java, all of whom had substantial experiences of "war" in East Timor. After the process of transcribing is completed, we will make a concrete schedule for the publication of these testimonies. With respect to the third goal, this forum has already published *Nihon-gun senryō-ki no Higashi Timōru shisatsu fukumeisho— Nihon・Porutogaru ryōkoku tōjisha no kiroku* [Reports on the Inspection Mission to Japanese Military Occupied East Timor: The Records of both Japanese and Portuguese Parties] (Ryukei Shyosha, 2005). The book contains official instructions and a report by Captain Silva e Costa who was dispatched by the Portuguese government to investigate the actual situation in its colony of Portuguese Timor then under Japanese military control, as well as a report of the Head of the Second Section of the Bureau of Political Affairs in the Japanese Ministry of Foreign Affairs, Eki Sone, who accompanied Captain Costa.

Since the launch of this project, the Toyota Foundation has provided both financial and moral support to this forum, and during the research period, program officers Ms. Etsuko Kawasaki and Ms. Yumiko Himemoto offered important encouragement and advice allowing the project to efficiently move forward. The Toyota Foundation has also generously offered a publication grant to defray the costs of this bibliography. As Forum members, we all would like to express our heart-felt appreciation. Additionally, despite the difficult situation of the publication industry, the president of Ryukei Shyosha, Mr. Masamitsu Kitamura, has generously offered his assistance in our project.

For the last three years, Shigehito Takahashi has borne the especially heavy job of facilitating communication between Forum members, as well as maintaining contact with potential informants and other interested parties. In the final stage of producing this bibliography, Akihiro Yoshihisa, Brad Horton, Mayumi Yamamoto, and Shigehito Takahashi shouldered particularly heavy burdens. Finally, throughout the course of our work over the last four years, the following members of this forum have shared the joys, sorrows, and frustrations of research on this fascinating subject:

Aiko Kurasawa (Professor, Faculty of Economics, Keio University)
Akihiro Yoshihisa (Former librarian of the National Diet Library)
William Bradley Horton (Lecturer at the Faculty of Commerce, Takushoku University)
Geoffrey Gunn (Professor, Faculty of Economics, Nagasaki University)
Hiroaki Shiozaki (Professor, Faculty of Humanities, Nagasaki Junshin Catholic University)
Isao Yamazaki (Associate Professor, Faculty of Culture and Education, Saga University)
Mayumi Yamamoto (Lecturer, School of Letters, Arts, and Sciences, Waseda University)
Sadao Ōba (Contemporary Japanese historian, and a participant of the Japanese military government in Java during World War II)
Shigehito Takahashi (Ph.D. student, Graduate School of Asia-Pacific Studies, Waseda University)
Ken'ichi Goto (Professor, Graduate School of Asia-Pacific Studies, Waseda Univeristy)

Forum Organizer　Ken'ichi Goto
Summer 2008

解　説

　2002年5月に独立した東ティモールは、複数の国による支配の歴史を持つだけではなく植民地支配から独立を果たした国インドネシアによる支配を経験したという稀有な歴史を持っている。さらに、第2次世界大戦期、ポルトガル領であった東ティモールには、中立国領土であるにもかかわらず、1941年12月17日に連合軍のオランダ領東インド軍とオーストラリア軍が進攻し、またそれを口実に1942年2月20日には日本軍が侵攻するという戦禍にさらされた経験をも持つ。

　このように、多数の国々から介入を受けた東ティモールは、その歴史を辿る上で関わった国々から史・資料を収集する必要がある。特に、第2次大戦期に関しては、植民地宗主国ポルトガルの史・資料のみならず、戦争中東ティモールに侵攻したオランダ、オーストラリア、イギリス、日本等の史・資料が、その歴史を知る上で必須となる。

　東ティモール全般に関する総合的な文献目録としては、Sherlock[1980]、Rowland[1992]が広範な文献を網羅している。戦時期ティモールについての主要文献はSherlock[1985]にまとめられており、英語圏の研究者・読者になじみの薄いポルトガル語の文献も含めて取り上げているが、日本語文献には触れられていない。そこで東ティモールの歴史経験から、本文献目録は、アジア太平洋戦争期の東ティモール[1]（蘭領西ティモールも含む）に関する日本語、英語、ポルトガル語、オランダ語、中国語の書籍（学術書、一般書、回想録など）、雑誌論文、評論、随想など文献および日本、オランダ、オーストラリア、イギリス、ポルトガルの公文書館所蔵の東ティモールに関わる文書を収録した[2]。

　当解説では収録した主要な史・資料を紹介しつつ、未だ研究途上にある第2次世界大戦期の東ティモールの歴史を紐解いていくこととする。

---

[1] アジア太平洋戦争期の東ティモールは、正確にはポルトガル領ティモールと表記するべきだが煩雑さをさけるため、本文献目録では書名や引用以外は原則として東ティモールで統一した。

[2] 日本語文献は、単行書、雑誌論文、地図を収録した。このうち、単行書および雑誌論文は戦前・戦中と戦後の二つに分類して収録している。

資料集・公文書

戦時期ティモールに関連した外交文書は、オーストラリア側のものがDepartment of Foreign Affairs and Trade(1975-1993)に、ポルトガル側のものがMinistério dos Negociós Estrangeiros(1961-1980)、イギリス側についてはMota(1997)にそれぞれ公刊されている。条約関係の文書は日本外務省条約局が1941年、1942年に編纂、一部収録されている。また、オーストラリアの戦争戦略に関する基本文書は、Robertson and McCarthy（1985）に採録されている。各文書館で一次資料を検索するための案内としては、本文献目録の各文書館紹介に加え、ポルトガルのサラザール文書館についてはGarcia（1992）を、カエタノ文書館はFrazão and Filipe（2005）を利用できる。

戦時中、実質的に日本軍占領下にあった東ティモールではポルトガルの主権が制限された形となっており、これに対しポルトガル本国は視察員の派遣を日本側に要求していた。軍事的観点からこの視察を一蹴してきた日本側だったが、戦局が次第に悪化する中、対ポルトガル宥和政策の一環として1944年3月に要求を受け入れるにいたった。この現地視察に関係した日本・ポルトガル両国当事者の報告書は［東ティモール日本占領期史料フォーラム編 2005］に復刻されている。

戦前の東ティモールに関する基礎情報

当時の地誌に関しては、日本語文献では［朝日新聞社中央調査会編 1941；1942］［日本国際問題調査会編 1942；1943］［台湾総督府編 1937；1943］などにポルトガル領ティモールについての章や節があるが、［ドゥアルテ 1942］［日葡協会編 1942］がより包括的で詳細に記述している。前者は元ティモール総督ドゥアルテ（1926-28）の著作を抜粋整理再編したものである。その他、現地調査を踏まえた報告書が、［南洋興発内SAPT.LDA東京事務所編 1937］［熱帯文化協会編 1937］［熱帯文化協会企画部調査課編 1941］など各種刊行されている。英語文献では［Allied Mining Corporation and Asia Investment Company 1937］［Gutterres 1942］で、ポルトガル語文献では［Carvalho 1947］の第1部や［Oliveira 2004］で、開戦前の概要を知ることが出来る。

1936年の政庁調査によるとアジア太平洋戦争開戦前の東ティモールの人口は460,588人、そのうち「土着民」は456,723人であった。ヨーロッパ人510人のうちポルトガル人は約490人で、官吏、農園主、商人、神父およびその家族と流刑人などからなっていた。華僑・インド人・アラビア人など東洋人は2,587人、主として商業に従事し、華僑は約2,500人とその大半を占めていた。メスティーソは610人で、下級官吏、農園、商店の従業員などの職業に就き、またポルトガルのアフリカ植民地モザンビーク出身

の黒人兵も158人いた［日葡協会編 1942：26-40］。一方、隣接する蘭領西ティモールの人口は、約40万人のティモール人のほか、オランダ人・華人・アラブ人などが4〜5千人であった［Wigmore 1957：466］。

　開戦直前に東ティモールに滞在していた日本人の数は資料により差異があり、正確な数を確定することは困難であるが、領事館、大日本航空、南洋興発などの職員、関係者を中心に20から30名ほどいたようである［Carvalho 1947：59；南洋庁内務部企画課 1942：9-10；日葡協会 1942：39-40；川淵龍彦1942：50；Lee 2000ほか］。

　植民地の統治機構として総督府以下、内務部、財務部、農務部、国防部、海防部、司法部の6部が設けられ、植民地行政を分掌していた。戦時中の総督はカルヴァーリョ大尉（Manuel de Abreu Ferreira de Carvalho、1940–1945年）であった。東部蘭領ティモールは、首府ディリ市（Concelho de Díli）に加えフロンテイラ、スーロ、マナトゥトゥ、サンドミンゴス、ラウテン5郡の行政区に分割していた［南洋庁内務部企画課 1942：11-12］[3]。

　同植民地の防衛には、正規軍はわずか軽歩兵1中隊と騎兵1小隊が配置されているのみであった[4]。正規軍を補うために、予備役としてモラドーレスと呼ばれたティモール人の志願兵部隊が存在した［Estado-Maior do Ecercito 1994: 497-498］。

　首府ディリには、開戦直前の1941年10月に日本領事館（黒木時太郎領事、10月18日ディリ着任）が開設された。これに対し、英・豪政府は対抗措置としてオーストラリア人民間航空局責任者デヴィッド＝ロスを英国領事として任命し1941年4月からディリに駐在、同年12月10日ポルトガル総督によって正式に承認した[5]。

地図

　地図に関しては、外邦図を中心に19点を採録した。外邦図とは第二次世界大戦終結までに日本がアジア太平洋地域で作成した地図のことであるが、近年その基礎的研究や学術資料としての利用方法についての研究が行なわれるようになった[6]。これら外邦図のコレクションは大阪大学、お茶の水大学、京都大学、東北大学、岐阜県図書館

---

[3] 行政区は戦後すぐに再編が行なわれ、ディリ市と9郡（ラウテン、バウカウ、ヴィケケ、マナトゥトゥ、アイナロ、エルメラ、ボボナロ、コヴァリマ、オエクシ）に増加した［Felgas 1956: 320］。

[4] 国際連盟への報告によれば、予算が確保された時点でティモールには軽歩兵2中隊、工兵1中隊、砲兵1中隊が配備される計画であった。League of Nations. 1940. *Armaments Year-book*, pp. 287-289.

[5] National Archives of Australia, "Agency notes for agency CA3217". ロスは戦時下の1942年7月10日ダーウィンに避難し、東ティモールにおける英豪の外交代表は消失することになる。オーストラリア領事館は戦後1946年1月1日にディリで開設された。

[6] 小林茂　2006「近代日本の地図作成と東アジア−外邦図研究の展望−」『E-journal GEO』vol. 1 (1), pp. 52-66.

世界分布図センター、国立国会図書館などに収蔵されている。

　一方、外邦図の中でも兵要地誌図は特別のカテゴリーを構成しており、その多くが「一般図に軍用車両の通過可能性など、各種軍事情報を記入したもので、基本的に多色刷りとなっている[7]。」東ティモールについての兵要地誌図を見てみると、参謀本部作成の1943年版とその1年後に作成された岡第一六〇一部隊[8]作成のものを比較することにより、その間に蓄積した現地事情・兵要地誌の情報量の増加をうかがうことができる。衆知のように、地図は地域研究その他を進める上で最も基礎的な資料の一つであり、当時の状況を知る上で第一級の資料である。

連合軍側部隊の戦史と回想録

　1939年9月、第二次世界大戦の開戦にともないポルトガルは中立を宣言していた。しかし、アジア太平洋戦争開戦（1941年12月8日）により、日本軍の南進政策を憂慮していたオーストラリア・オランダ領東インド（蘭印）軍が、1941年12月17日、蘭領西ティモールのクーパンからディリに侵攻する。侵攻作戦に従事したのは、オーストラリア軍が2／2独立中隊（約250人、司令官：スペンスSpence少佐）とファン・ストラーテンvan Straten大佐が指揮をとる蘭印軍約260人であった。これに先立ち、豪軍2／40大隊と2／2独立中隊からなるスパロー部隊（司令官：レガットLeggatt中佐、将校70名、約兵1,330名）が、約500名の蘭印軍（司令官：デティガーDetiger中佐）を援助するため12月12日にクーパンに派兵されており[9]、その一部がディリに侵攻した。クーパンの蘭印軍には、ジャワからの増援約100名に先んじて、同月15日ファン・ストラーテンvan Straten大佐が西ティモール蘭印軍指揮官として着任した。

　東ティモールでゲリラ戦を展開していた豪・蘭印軍であったが、日本軍の掃討作戦によって情勢が不利になり、2／2独立中隊と蘭印軍は1942年12月10日から16日にかけてオーストラリアに撤退した。2／4独立中隊（ウォーカーWalker大佐、9月12日～、P. 611）も翌43年1月9日に撤退し、これ以降、東ティモールには特務機関Service Reconnaissance Department（SRD、通称Z Special Forces）の小部隊を残すのみであった。2／2独立中隊の副司令官Callinanの著作は、英語圏における戦時期ティモールの歴史認識に多大な影響を与えており、最も重要な基礎資料の一つである。また、1940年代～50年代に発足した2／2独立中隊、および2／4独立中隊戦友会の

---

[7] 「「兵要地誌図」（大阪大学文学研究科人文地理学教室所蔵）目録」『外邦図研究ニュースレター』No. 1 (2003), p. 43.

[8] 岡第一六〇一部隊は南方軍総司令部の通称号。

[9] The Japanese Thrust, p. 467.

会誌は、現在も発行され続けている。その他、2／2独立中隊については［Campbell 1995］［Doig 1986］、2／4独立中隊は［Lambert 1997］［Lipman 1983］、SRDは［Courtney 1993］［Holland 1999］［Powell 1996］などが参考になる。

日本軍占領部隊の戦史と回想録

一方、蘭印侵攻作戦を展開中の日本軍は、予定していた蘭領西ティモールの侵攻時に東ティモールに不法駐留している豪・蘭印軍に背後から攻撃される可能性があること、東ティモールの中立性は豪・蘭印軍の侵攻によって実質的に破棄されていることなどを理由として、翌1942年2月20日、西ティモールの首府クーパンに加えて東ティモールのディリに同時侵攻した[10]。陸軍の東方支隊（支隊長：伊東武夫少将）[11]が上陸部隊の中心となり、支隊主力に加えて海軍の横須賀鎮守府第三特別陸戦隊（約300名）、佐世保連合特別陸戦隊（2小隊）がクーパンを攻撃、陸軍歩兵第二百二十八連隊（連隊長：土井定七大佐）の第二大隊を中心とした部隊がディリを攻撃した。上陸作戦にあたって海軍は、クーパンに対して東方支援隊・第二護衛隊の主力が、ディリに対しては第七駆逐隊の第一小隊（潮、漣）が援護した。

歩兵第二二八連隊の部隊史としては［歩兵第二二八連隊史編纂委員会編 1973］がある。その他回想録は［片桐 1968］［川井〔2000〕］などが刊行されている。海軍将兵による回想録類は、残念ながら現時点では見つけることができなかった。

ティモール侵攻作戦に先立ち、同侵攻作戦への妨害を阻止するためポートダーウィンに対して2月19日に奇襲攻撃を行い、豪軍の戦闘機・艦船・陸上施設などを破壊した［防衛庁防衛研修所戦史室1969『蘭印・ベンガル湾方面海軍進攻作戦』：342-353］。これは豪本土がはじめて経験した空爆であった。

南方要域防衛に関する陸海軍中央協定（1942年6月29日）により、ティモール島の防衛は海軍の担当とされていた。しかし、ミッドウェー敗戦以降の日本海軍の戦力低下を背景として、同年8月21日陸海軍中央協定の改定が示達され、同島の防衛が陸軍の担当に変更となった。東方支隊の後任として、ジャワ島に駐留していた第四十八師団（師団長：土橋勇逸中将）が派遣されることになった。

こうして、ティモール島を占領していた東方支隊は、第四十八師団歩兵団司令部および歩兵第四十七連隊を中心とする安部支隊（支隊長：安部孝一少将）に任務を引き

---

10 この間の作戦計画策定過程に関しては防衛庁防衛研修所戦史室編 1967『蘭印攻略作戦』pp. 394-401、より詳細な分析は［Frei 1996］を参照。
11 東方支隊は第三十八歩兵団司令部、歩兵第二百二十八連隊、山砲兵第三十八連隊第二大隊を中心として編成された。防衛庁防衛研修所戦史室編 1969『豪北陸軍作戦』p. 16。

継ぎ、翌1943年1月までの間に第四十八師団（歩兵第四十七連隊、台湾歩兵第一連隊、台湾歩兵第二連隊を中心として編成）が漸次ティモール島に移駐した[12]。ティモール島の「防衛」区分は3区に分割され、このうち東ティモールは歩兵第四十七連隊、台湾歩兵第二連隊が駐留した。

憲兵隊に関しては、1943年2月第五野戦憲兵隊第一分隊（隊長：油谷清憲兵少佐）が第四十八師団に配属され、クーパンに本部を、ソエ（西ティモール）、ディリ、ラウテンに分遣隊を、アタンブア（西ティモール）に分駐所を設置した[13]。

第四十八師団の戦友会である南星会は、部隊史［南星会編 1967］に加え、1977年から1995年まで戦友会誌を発行している。回想録は、二人の師団長［土橋 1985］［山田 1979］、歩兵第四十七連隊の主計将校［竹林 1988］、台湾歩兵第二連隊の各部隊［台歩二会編 1977-81］［十中隊史編集事務局編 1982］［台湾歩兵第二連隊第九中隊編 1981］［立川編 1977］などによって刊行されている。また、歩兵連隊以外にも捜索連隊［捜索第四十八連隊戦友会編 1982］、山砲兵［熊本蓬莱山吹会編 1960］［蓬莱山吹会編 1984；1987］、工兵［潮谷編 1982］、輜重兵［幸田編 1965］［輜重兵第四十八連隊誌刊行会編 1988］など第四十八師団を構成していた各部隊の回想録が出版されている。軍医による回想録は［高木〔n.d.〕；1975］、［久金 1984；1985；1987］などがある。［西村 1979］

その他、戦前・戦中期の東ティモールにかかわった団体・人物によるものとして、南洋興発に関しては［栗林商会編 1970］、大日本航空に関しては［日本航空協会 1966；1975］［大日本航空社史刊行会編 1975］などの単行書に加え、雑誌論文として浅香良一、川淵龍彦、長谷川直美、松永寿雄、松原晩香の論考や座談会の記録など多数存在する。

ポルトガル人による記録

カルヴァーリョ（Carvalho）総督はアジア太平洋戦争開戦前の1940年にディリに着任し、終戦後の1945年12月に後任のルアス（Oscar Freire de Vasconcelos Ruas）大尉に総督の任務を引き継いだ。この間の出来事を綴った報告書［Carvalho 1947；2003］が植民地省から刊行されたが、サラザール首相により発行中止に追い込まれた。2003年にカルヴァーリョ報告書は復刻され、戦時期東ティモールを研究する上で最も基本的な文献・資料になった。ティモール人コミュニティは本国ポルトガルの中立政

---

[12] 第四十八師団（通称号は海兵団）の構成部隊詳細は、［厚生省援護局編 1961］を参照。

[13] 第五野戦憲兵隊は1943年1月4日に東京で編成され、同年2月22日スラバヤに上陸、第十九軍司令官の隷下に入った。［全国憲友会連合会編纂委員会 1976：1064］

策に従う人びとと連合国軍に協力したグループ、日本軍に協力した人びとに分裂した。騎兵隊司令官のリベラート（Antonio Oliveira Liberato）中尉はカルヴァーリョ総督に従った中心人物の一人であり、2点の回想録［Liberato 1947; 1951］を刊行している。これに対し、フロンテイラ郡長ソウザ＝サントス（Antonio Policarpo de Sousa Santos）や国外追放者で弁護士のブランダウン（Carlos Cal Brandão）は連合国軍に協力し、後に連合国軍が東ティモールから引揚げる際には共にオーストラリアへ避難した。ブランダウンは戦後すぐに［Brandão 1946］を刊行し、血を流しながら歩くしかばねの様な兵士を表紙とした衝撃性もあってか、本国ポルトガルで5刷りを超えるベストセラーとなった。ソウザ＝サントスはリベラート中尉の著作に反論するため、［Sousa Santos 1947; 1973］を刊行した。その他、医療・保健状況を記述した［Carvalho 1972］などもある。

　ティモール人による記憶

　最後に、ティモール人自身による戦時期に関する記録であるが、これは残念ながら非常に限られている。ラモス・ホルタRamos Horta大統領やベロBelo司教など戦後生まれのティモール人指導者たちの回想録で、両親や兄弟から聞かされた話を部分的に言及している[14]。ミッシェル・ターナーMichelle Turnerは難民としてオーストラリアに渡ったティモール人7人[15]にインタビューをおこない、戦時期の経験を記録している［Turner 1992］。また、ポルトガルでも高い評価を得ているティモール人作家カルドーゾは、戦時期を主題とした小説を描いている［Cardoso 2007］。このようにティモール人による戦時期の記録は非常に限られており、今後ティモール人自身の手による記録・研究が進められることが期待される。

　研究書・論文

　戦時期東ティモールの研究は、大きく3つの流れにまとめることが出来る。すなわち軍事史からのアプローチ、国際関係史としての研究、および東ティモール史の一部としての研究である。
　軍事史からのアプローチでは、戦闘の経過、特に侵攻時の作戦経過を中心とした「公認の歴史」叢書が、オーストラリアおよび日本で刊行されている。すなわち、オース

---

[14] Ramos-Horta, José. 1996. *Funu: the unfinished saga of East Timor*, Lawrenceville, NJ; Asmara, Eritrea: the Red Sea Press (First printing in 1987), pp. 5-8, 20-21, Kohen, Arnold. 1999. *From the place of the dead: Bishop Belo and the struggle for East Timor*, Oxford: Lion Publishing, pp. 62-63.

[15] ただし、うち2人は両親から聞いた話を語っている。

トラリアのそれはAustralia in the War of 1935-1945シリーズであり、東ティモールは主としてWigmoreとMcCarthyの2巻で取り上げられている。日本側では防衛庁防衛研修所戦史室が編纂した「戦史叢書」(全102巻、1966－1980年)において、『蘭印攻略作戦』(1967)、『豪北方面陸軍作戦』(1969)、『南西方面陸軍作戦：マレー・蘭印の防衛』(1976)の3巻で東ティモールが扱われている。また、防衛研究所戦史部の野村佳正の研究では、軍事占領政策を取り上げている[17]。

日本軍は1942年、台湾で陸軍特別志願兵制度を導入した[16]。東ティモールを占領していた第四十八師団は台湾守備隊の流れを引いており(1940年11月30日、台湾混成旅団を母体として編成)、同制度導入後に台湾人特別志願兵約450人が配属された。これら台湾人特別志願兵に関しては、兵士本人による回想録［鄭 1998］や回想小説［陳 2000］のほか、日本人研究者による聞き取り［林 2000；後藤編 2005］が刊行されている。

国際関係史としての研究では、戦前・戦中期の日本が東ティモールに対して向けた関心を二つの国策会社(南洋興発と大日本航空)の動きを中心に、関係国、すなわち日・葡・豪・蘭・英間の国際関係を分析したものとして、［後藤 1999; Goto 2003］がある。先述したように、ポルトガルは400年以上にわたるイギリスとの同盟関係にもかかわらず、第二次世界大戦では中立を宣言していた。しかし、大西洋に浮かぶポルトガル領アソーレス諸島は、ヨーロッパとアメリカをつなぐ要衝として重要な位置にあり、ポルトガルとイギリスの間でアソーレス協定が調印(1943年6月)され、英米による軍事基地の使用とポルトガル植民地の主権尊重が取引された経緯は、［Gunn 1988］および［Bessa 1992］が明らかにしている。

アジア太平洋戦争を東ティモール史の一部として位置づける試みは、［Boxer 1960］［Oliveira］［Gunn 1999］などで見ることが出来る。

なお、以下に掲げる文献は、他の文献などで言及もしくは参考文献として挙げられているものの、本フォーラムの調査では実物の確認が取れなかったものである。今後の調査活動や他の研究者などにより発見される可能性もあることから、その際の参考として記しておく。

16　台湾における陸軍特別志願兵制度の概略については、近藤正己　1996『総力戦と台湾：日本植民地崩壊の研究』刀水書房、pp. 46-60を参照。

17　野村佳正　2004「軍事作戦と軍事占領政策―第2次世界大戦期東チモールの場合」『戦史研究年報』(7)：2004.3, p47-68.

会計分析研究所南洋調査部（Kaikei Bunseki Kenkyūjo Nan'yō Chōsabu）編
　葡領チモール島産業状況（Poryō Chimōrutō sangyō jōkyō）会計分析研究所南洋調査部　1941　27p（南方産業関係資料）
　　Title translation: The industrial situation on Portuguese Timor Island

才木一兼（SAIKI Kazukane）著
　ダラバイ工作（Darabai kōsaku）〔n.p.〕〔n.d.〕
　　Title translation: Darabai opearation

参謀本部（Sanbō Honbu）編
　葡領殖民地要覧（Poryō shokuminchi yōran）参謀本部　1912
　　Title translation: Overview of Portuguese colonies

台湾拓殖株式会社調査課（Taiwan Takusyoku Kabushiki Kaisha Chōsaka）編
　チモール島の鉱産資源（Chimōrutō no kōsan shigen）台湾拓殖株式会社調査課　1942　28p　（台調資B17-6）
　　Title translation: Mining resources on Timor Island

〔農林省〕南方資源調査室（Nanpō Shigen Chōsashitsu）編
　蘭領ニューギニア及チモール島事情に就て（Ranryō Nyūginia oyobi Chimōrutō jijō ni tsuite）〔農林省〕南方資源調査室〔n.d.〕17p
　　Titile translation: On the conditions in Dutch New Guinea and Timor Island

南洋興発株式会社東京事務所（Nan'yō Kōhatsu Kabushiki Kaisha Tōkyō Jimusho）編
　葡領チモール調査報告（Poryō Chimōru chōsa hōkoku）池上隆訳　南洋興発株式会社東京事務所　1937
　　Title translation: A research report on Portuguese Timor

　チモールへの日本航空路線（Chimōru e no Nihon kōkū rosen）南洋経済研究所　1942
　　Title translation: The Japanese airline route to Timor

ポルトガル領チモール鉱山法（Porutogaruryō Chimōru kōzanhō）〔n.p.〕 1936
Title translation: Portuguese Timor's legal regulations for mining

ポルトガル領ティモールの地質と鉱産（Porutogaruryō Chimōru no chishitsu to kōsan）L.C. David等著　台湾南方協会訳　台北〔1941〕5p（南支南洋　第191号抜刷）
Title translation: The geology and mining industry of Portuguese Timor

蘭領「チモール」貿易の進展と民族自決（Ranryō "Chimōru" bōeki no shinten to minzoku jiketsu）〔n.p.〕〔n.d.〕
Title translation: Development of the Dutch Timor trade and national autonomy

Introduction

East Timor[1] has a long complicated history of foreign control. Then known to the world as Portuguese Timor, along with the entire Portuguese empire, it was a neutral territory at the start of World War II. Tragically, from the early days of the Pacific War, Timor was drawn into the conflict, first by an invasion of a combined Australian-Netherlands East Indies force on December 17, 1941, then further by the Imperial Japanese forces invasion on February 20, 1942, a combination which led to a prolonged conflict and widespread devastation.

Research on the history of East Timor thus potentially requires access to materials from a number of different countries involved—directly or indirectly—in its history. For the period covering World War II, documents produced by the belligerent parties (Australian, Dutch and Japanese) are of obvious importance, as are documents of the British and Portuguese governments.

A pair of English language bibliographies have long provided valuable general introductions to East Timor and materials about its history, Kevin Sherlock (1980) and Ian Rowland (1992). An additional discussion of materials related to Portuguese Timor during World War I and II was presented in a bibliographical article of *Kabar Seberang* in 1985. Although this article did not cover Japanese language publications, it is especially useful for its coverage of Portuguese language publications that might be less familiar to both researchers and general readers from English speaking countries. The absence of other research tools for Timor during this period is particularly glaring since East Timor became an independent country in 2002.

---

[1] Although East Timor during the Pacific War was known to all parties as Portuguese Timor, the terms are interchangeable for this period.

Materials on East Timor during World War II covers monographs, journal articles, essays and memoirs written in Japanese, English, Dutch, Chinese, and also tries to provide access to materials deposited in archives in Japan, the Netherlands, Australia, UK, and Portugal, wherever possible by presenting lists of documents.[2]

While the bibliography is categorized by language and country housing the archives, this brief introduction provides an integrated discussion of publications in the context of the history of East Timor during World War II.

Official Documents

Selections of diplomatic documents relating to wartime Timor have been reproduced by the Department of Foreign Affairs and Trade (Australian documents), Ministério dos Negociós Estrangeiros (Portuguese documents), and Mota (British documents). Some relevant treaties and agreements have been published by the Ministry of Foreign Affairs (Gaimushō Jōyakukyoku 1941, 1942), while Robertson and McCarthy (1985) have reproduced basic documents on war strategies of Australia. For archival guidance in accessing primary sources, in addition to the archival sections of this bibliography, see Garcia (1992) for the Salazar Archives and Frazão and Filipe (2005]) for the Caetano Archives of Portugal.

Basic Data and Information on Wartime East Timor

Regarding topography, various editions of almanacs (Asahi Shinbunsha Chūō Chōsakai [1941, 1942], Nihon Kokusai Mondai Chōsakai [1942, 1943], and Taiwan Sōtokufu [1937, 1943]) have entries on Portuguese Timor, but Duarute (1942) and

---

[2] Japanese language publications are divided into works published in monograph form, journal articles, and maps. Monographs and journal articles are further divided into pre-war/war-time and post-war sections.

Nippo Kyōkai (1942) have more detailed comprehensive descriptions in Japanese. Duarute (1942) is an abridged translation of a book written by Teofilo Duarte, the governor of Timor between 1926-1928. Nan'yō Kōhatsu SAPT.LDA Tōkyō jimusho (1937), Nettai Bunka Kyōkai (1937), and Nettai Bunka Kyōkai Kikakubu Chōsaka (1941) are each based on field research. Surveys produced during the prewar period by the Allied Mining Corporation and Asia Investment Company (1937) and Gutterres (1942) in English and Chapter I of Manuel de Abreu Ferreira de Carvalho (1947) and Luna de Oliveira (2004) in Portuguese.

According to the 1936 census, the total population was 460,588. Of these, 456,723 were natives, while Portuguese who made up about 490 out of the 510 Europeans, were bureaucrats, plantation owners, merchants, and missionaries, as well as dependants and deportees. The "Asian" population, that is the Chinese, Indians and Arabs totaled 2,587. These were mainly engaged in commerce, especially the approximately 2,500 Chinese. There were 610 mestizos working as low-ranking officials, plantation officials and shop clerks. Additionally there were 158 Mozambican soldiers (Nippo Kyōkai 1942: 26-40). In Dutch West Timor, there were about 400,000 native Indonesians and 4,000-5,000 Dutch, Chinese and Arabs (Wigmore 1957: 466). The number of Japanese reportedly living in East Timor before the war varied from source to source, but was probably 20-30, comprising of staff and dependants of the Consulate, Dai Nippon Airlines and the Nan'yō Kōhatsu K. K.

The administration of Portuguese Timor included the Governor's office, the Department of Internal Affairs, the Department of Treasury, the Department of Agriculture, the Department of Defense, the Department of the Navy, and the Department of Justice. The eastern part of Portuguese Timor was divided into Municipal Dili and five districts, Fronteira, Suro, Manatuto, San Domingos and Lautem. The Governor of Timor during the war was Captain Manuel de Abreu Ferreira de Carvalho (1940-45).[3]

Only one company of light infantry and one platoon of cavalry were deployed in Timor, but these were augmented by Timorese volunteers called *Moradores*

[Estado-Maior do Exército 1994: 497-498].[4]

Japan opened a consulate in October 1941, just before the start of the war, with Consul KUROKI Tokitarō arriving in Dili on October 18. This led to the appointment of a consul for Britain. David Ross, an Australian Civil Aviation official stationed in Dili as Qantas representative since April 1941, was selected by the governments of the United Kingdom and Australia and officially approved by the Portuguese Government on December 10, 1941.[5]

Maps

This bibliography includes a list of 18 Gaihōzu and other maps. Gaihōzu are maps on Asia Pacific region, produced by Japan until the end of the war.[6] Collections of these Gaihōzu are held in the libraries of Osaka University, Ochanomizu University, Kyoto University, Tohoku University, Gifu Prefectural Library World Distribution Map Center, and the National Diet Library.

Heiyōchishizu is a special category of Gaihōzu, and many are "multi-color" maps reproduced from ordinary maps, indicating various military information, such as roads which can be used for military vehicles."[7] Heiyōchishizu on East Timor were produced by Sanbōhonbu and Oka Dai 1601 Unit,[8] in 1943 and 1944 respectively, and comparisons of these provides an indication of the increased information about

---

[3] The colonial administration was reorganized after the war. In the new system, Portuguese Timor was divided into Municipal Dili and 9 districts (Lautem, Baucau, Vieque, Manatuto, Ainaro, Ermera, Bobonaro, Cova-Lima and Oe-Cussi) [Felgas 1956: 320].

[4] According to a report to the League of Nations, there would be two light infantry companies, one engineer company and one artillery company deployed in Timor once the budget was approved (League of Nations, *Armaments Year-book* [1940], pp.287-289).

[5] National Archives of Australia, "Agency notes for agency CA3217". Ross was evacuated to Darwin on July 10, 1942. An Australian Consulate opened in Dili on January 1, 1946.

[6] 小林茂2006「近代日本の地図作成と東アジア―外邦図研究の展望―」『E-journal GEO』vol.1 (1), pp. 52-66.

[7] 「兵要地誌図」(大阪大学文学研究科人文地理学教室所蔵) 目録」『外邦図研究ニュースレター』No. 1 (2003), p.43.

[8] Oka 1601 Unit was a pseudonym for the Southern Army General Headquarters.

the situation and topography in one year. These maps are potentially important materials for research about the situation on the ground during this period.

War History and Memoirs of the Allied Forces

Portugal declared itself neutral at the beginning of World War II in September 1939. However, with the advent of the Pacific war on December 8, 1941, a combined Australia-Netherlands East Indies force invaded Dili from Kupang, West Timor, as a response to an anticipated Japanese invasion. On December 12, Australia had deployed a special force of around 1,330 men to Kupang to support the 500 man Dutch East Indies Army force under Lt. Col. Detiger. The Australian Sparrow Force was comprised mainly of the 2/40 Battalion and the 2/2nd Independent Company, under the initial overall command of Lt. Col. Leggatt. Col. van Straten was appointed to be KNIL Commander at Kupang, arriving on December 15, prior to the arrival of another 100 soldiers from Java. For the occupation of Dili, a part of this force was detached, the 250 man 2/2nd Independent Company, initially commanded by Major Spence, and around 260 troops from the Dutch East Indies Army, under the overall command of Col. Van Straten.

Following the arrival of Japanese troops and the surrender of the main body of Allied troops in West Timor, the remaining units of the Sparrow Force fought a prolonged guerilla war and were finally evacuated in late 1942-early 1943 (including the 2/4th Independent Company which had been introduced in September). After February 1943, only small special force units of the Service Reconnaissance Department (SRD) visited Timor.

A number of former soldiers have published works based on their own experiences, for example the 2nd commander of the 2/2nd Independent Company, Bernard Callinan, whose book has had a great influence on the views of English-speaking audiences, and been utilized as the main source for other publications. Other officers who wrote about their experiences include former platoon commander Archie Campbell's narrative related to the 2/2nd Independent Company and Lt. Rex Lipman's narrative of his experiences with the 2/24th Company. Both independent companies have also published monographs, compiled largely out of the experiences of their members. Furthermore, the veterans associations of 2/2nd and 2/4th Independent Companies have published newsletters since the later 1940s or early 1950s, which sometimes include their experiences. One SRD member's experiences were published after his death (Holland 1999).

War History and Memoirs of the Japanese Occupation Military

The Japanese Military landed in Dili and West Timor simultaneously on February 20, 1942. The decision to enter Portuguese Timor was not taken lightly, and was finally accepted because the neutrality of Portuguese Timor had already been violated by Allied entry into Dili in December 1941, and because of possible counter attacks by the combined Australian-Dutch East Indies forces in East Timor if left alone.[9] The main landing force in Timor was the Eastern Detachment (commanded by Maj. Gen. ITO Takeo), a detachment built around the 38th Infantry group, and supported by the 3rd Yokosuka Special Naval Landing Force and 2 platoons of the Sasebo Combined Special Landing Force.[10] Col. DOI Sadashichi was to occupy Dili with his 2nd Battalion of the 228th Infantry Regiment as the main assault unit. The Navy covered the landing operations; the main component of the Eastern Support Fleet and the 2nd Guard Fleet for Kupang, and the Ushio and the Sazanami of the 7th Destroyer Fleet for Dili.

The 228th Infantry Regiment unit history is compiled in *A history of the 228th Infantry Regiment* [Hohei Dainihyaku-nijūhachi Rentai shi], but several memoirs

---

[9] For process of decision-making on operation policy, see Frei (1996) and 防衛庁防衛研修所戦史室編 1967『蘭印攻略作戦』pp. 394-401.

[10] The 38th Infantry Group was largely made up of the 228th Infantry Regiment and the 2nd Battalion of the 38th Mount Artillery Regiment. See 防衛庁防衛研修所戦史室編1969『豪北陸軍作戦』p.16 and Ambon and Timor Invasion Operations.

also exist, such as that of Katagiri (1968) and Kawai (2000). No memoirs of the Navy personnel engaged in the invasion have been found.

On February 19, prior to the invasion of Timor, a bombing raid was conducted on Port Darwin resulting in the destructions of fighters, ground facilities, and the ships of the Australian Military. This attempt to prevent a counterattack against Japanese forces in Timor was the first bombing of the Australian continent.

Under the Army-Navy Central Agreement on the Important Southern Area Defense (June 29, 1942), the defense of Timor Island was assigned to the Navy. The defeat at Midway and the decrease in Navy's war capabilities after that led to a transfer of responsibilities for the island's defense to the Army, by way of an order revising the Army-Navy central agreement on August 21, 1942 of the same year. The Eastern Detachment was thus gradually replaced by the 48th Division, commanded by Lt. Gen. TSUCHIHASHI Yuitsu, then based on Java.

Thus, the Eastern Detachment occupying Timor Island was partially replaced by the Abe Detachment (Commander Maj. Gen. ABE Koichi), comprised mainly of 48th Division Infantry Group Headquarters and 47th Infantry Regiment, leading to complete replacement with 48th Division (comprised mainly of the 47th Infantry Regiment, the 1st Taiwanese Infantry Regiment, and the 2nd Taiwanese Infantry Regiment) by January 1943.[11] Timor was divided into three districts for defense purposes, and the 47th Infantry Regiment and 2nd Taiwanese Infantry Regiment were stationed in East Timor. Of special interest is the 1st Platoon of the 5th Field Military Police (Commander Maj. YUTANI Kiyoshi) which was assigned to the 48th Division in February 1943. The Platoon Kenpeitai HQ was established in Kupang, with detachments located in Soë (West Timor), Dili and Lautem, and a substation in Atambua (West Timor).[12]

---

[11] For details of components of the 48th Division (pseudonym: Umi Group), see Kōseishō Engokyoku (1961).

[12] The 5th Field Military Police was formally established in Tokyo on January 4, 1943, and landed in Surabaya on February 22 of the same year. It was placed under the command of the 19th Army (Zenkoku Ken'yūkai Rengōkai Hensan Iinkai 1976: 1064).

Numerous materials have been published by members of these units. Nanseikai, the veterans' association of the 48th Division published a unit history (1967) and newsletters from 1977 to 1995. Two division commanders, TSUCHIHASHI Yūitsu and YAMADA Kunitarō wrote memoirs, but numerous other memoirs and unit histories have been published and are included in the bibliography. To mention only two, the surgeons TAKAGI Hideo and HISAKANE Akira have published their recollections of this period.

Records of the Portuguese

Governor Carvalho arrived in Dili in 1940, just before the start of the Pacific War, and remained there until handing over the reigns of authority to his successor, Captain Oscar Freire de Vasconcelos Ruas, in December 1945. His report (Carvalho 1947; 2003) was published by Ministry of Colonies, but was suppressed by Prime Minister Salazar. This report is one of the most basic documents for the study of wartime East Timor. The Portuguese in East Timor were divided into those who remained loyal to the metropolitan policy of neutrality, those who allied with the Allied Forces, and those who collaborated with the Japanese Military. Lt. Antonio Oliveira Liberato of the Cavalry Company (*Companhia de Caçadores*) was one of loyalists to Governor Carvalho, and following the war he published two memoirs (Liberato 1947; 1951). On the other hand, the administrator of Fronteira district, Antonio Policarpo de Sousa Santos, and a deportee lawyer, Carlos Cal Brandão, chose to collaborate with the Allied Forces, and were evacuated to Australia when the troops retreated from East Timor. Brandão published a memoir soon after the war (Brandão 1946), and it became best seller, going through at least 5 printings. Its cover, a color drawing of a bleeding, zombie-like soldier might have contributed to its popularity. Sousa Santos published his writings as refutations of Lt. Liberato's works. Doctor Carvalho (different from Governor Carvalho) wrote about the medical and health situation [Carvalho 1972].

Memories of the Timorese

Publications of the Timorese themselves on the war period are, regrettably, very limited. Timorese leaders born after the war, such as the future president of the Democratic Republic of Timor-Leste, Jose Ramos-Horta, and Bishop Carlos Belo, both Nobel Peace Prize laureates, sometimes describe stories told by their parents and brothers/sisters in their memoirs.[13] An Australian woman, Michelle Turner (1992) interviewed 7 Timorese refugees in Australia and recorded their stories.[14] A Timorese writer, Luís Cardoso, highly praised in Portugal, recently published a novel about the war-time period [Cardoso 2007]. Thus, Timorese records on war period have been very limited and it is much hoped that the Timorese people will develop an interest in recording and studying their history.

On the Historiography of Timor in the War

Studies on war-time East Timor can be divided into three categories: military history, international relations, and the history of East Timor.

Studies of military history mainly deal with battles, especially invasion operations, and official histories have been published in various countries. In "Australia in the War of 1935-1945," East Timor was discussed at length in two volumes, those written by Lionel Wigmore and David McCarthy. The Japanese National Institute for Defence Studies compiled a "Military History Series" (*Senshi Sosho*) and East Timor was dealt mainly in three volumes. NOMURA Yoshimasa of the War History Department of the National Institute for Defense Studies has studied military occupation policy in East Timor.

A small number of works related to Taiwanese involvement in Timor have been

---

[13] Ramos-Horta, Jose. 1996. *Funu: The unfinished saga of East Timor*, Lawrenceville, NJ; Asmara, Eritrea: The Red Sea Press (First printing, 1987), pp.5-8, 20-21, Arnold Kohen, *From the place of the dead: Bishop Belo and the struggle for East Timor*, Oxford: Lion Publishing, 1999, pp. 62-63.

[14] Two of them, though, told stories heard from their parents.

published. In 1942, the Japanese Military introduced the Army Special Volunteers system in Taiwan. The 48th Division was assigned around 450 Taiwanese Special Volunteers. One Taiwanese Special Volunteer has written a memoir (Zheng 1998), another a memorial novel (Chen 2000), and some interviews have also been published (e.g. Hayashi 2000).

Focus of international relations studies are prewar/war-time activities of two Japanese national policy companies, i.e. the Nan'yō Kōhatsu and Dai Nippon Kōkū, and relations between Japan, Portugal, Australia, the Netherlands and Britain (e.g. Goto 1999, 2003). Though Portugal had been a faithful ally of Britain for over 400 years, it declared itself neutral in World War II. The Portuguese Azores Islands in the Atlantic Ocean were located in a strategic position, connecting America and Europe. The Azores Agreement was signed between Portugal and Britain in June 1943, which led its use as a military base by America and Britain and recognition of Portuguese sovereignty in its colonies. This has been the focus of studies by Gunn (1988) and Bessa (1992).

凡　例

1．排列

　各部における文献の排列は著者あるいは編者の「あいうえお順」に行い、著者あるいは編者が同一の場合には出版年順に排列した。また、著者あるいは編者がない場合には書名の「あいうえお順」に排列した。

2．記載内容

　単行書は、著者あるいは編者名、書名（：副書名）、出版地（東京の場合には省略）、出版社、出版年、ページ数、（シリーズ名）、注記の順で記した。著者あるいは編者名、出版年等が図書に明記されていない場合でも、内容から判断可能であれば［　］を付記し記載した。

　一冊のすべて（もしくは大部分）がティモール関係でない場合には、内容細目として当該部分の章（節）名とページを記載した。

3．表記方法

　漢字の旧字体は基本的に新字体に統一した。漢数字を算用数字に変更した場合もある。

　ティモール（チモール）の表記は文献資料に表記されているとおりに記載した。

　日本語のローマ字表記はAmerican Library Association-Library of Congress）の指針（*ALA-LC Romanization Tables: Transliteration Schemes for Non-Roman Scripts, 1997 edition*）に従った。

　人名のローマ字表記は氏・名の順で記載し、氏はすべて大文字で表記した。

4．所蔵機関

　現在、インターネットによる各図書館の蔵書検索（OPAC）が可能な状況にあるが、本文献目録では利用者の利便性を考慮し、所蔵機関が限られている一部の文献はその所蔵機関を各文献の最後に表示した。

　各所蔵機関の表示は、次ページのとおりである。

〔気象庁〕：気象庁図書館
〔岐阜県〕：岐阜県立図書館
〔熊本県〕：熊本県立図書館
〔研究会〕：東ティモール日本占領期史料フォーラム
〔昭和館〕：昭和館図書室
〔台湾分館〕：国立中央図書館台湾分館
〔東大経〕：東京大学経済学部図書館
〔内閣〕：内閣文庫
〔農総研〕：農業総合研究所
〔宮崎県〕：宮崎県立図書館
〔民博〕：国立民族学博物館図書室

Explanatory Note

1. Order

Items are arranged by author/editor in Japanese alphabetical order, and secondarily by publication year. Items without an author/editor are arranged by title in Japanese alphabetical order.[a/i/u/e/o; ka/ki/ku/ke/ko; sa/shi/su/se/so; ta/chi/tsu/te/to; na/ni/nu/ne/no; ha/hi/hu/he/ho; ma/mi/mu/me/mo; ya/yu/yo; ra/ri/ru/re/ro; wa/wo/wn]

2. Content of Descriptions

Monographs are described with the author/editor, title: subtitle, place of publication (omitted for Tokyo), publisher, year of publication, number of pages, (series title), and supplementary note.

When a substantial portion of a monograph is not related to Timor, the title(s) and pages for the relevant chapter(s) and/or section(s) title and pages are specified.

3. Translations and Romanizations

The names of both corporate and individual authors have been romanized largely for the convenience of foreign researchers, although Japanese readers will also find it convenient to determine the correct reading of some names.

The main titles and the relevant section titles have been translated as well to assist researchers who need to determine which publications are most likely to be of use.

4. Form and Style

Whenever possible, old Chinese characters (*kanji*) have been changed into their newer form. In general, Chinese numerals have been converted to Arabic numerals.

Romanization of Japanese follows the modified Hepburn system described in *ALA-LC Romanization Tables: Transliteration Schemes for Non-Roman Scripts* (1997 edition). For clarity's sake, two points need to be explicitly mentioned.

Japanese author/editor names are written surname first, followed by the given name, while the surnames have been capitalized.

Timōru/Chimōru are used interchangeably in accordance with the item in question, as dictated by the ALA-LC Hepburn romanization system.

5．Holding Institutes

Although Public Access Catalogs for most libraries are available through the internet, whenever possible this bibliography provides names of libraries holding hard-to-find items.

The most common libraries are designated as follows:

〔気象庁〕：Japan Meteorological Agency
〔岐阜県〕：Gifu Prefecture Library
〔熊本県〕：Kumamoto Prefecture Library
〔研究会〕：The Forum for Historical Documents on East Timor during the Japanese Occupation Period
〔昭和館〕：Showa-kan Library
〔台湾分館〕：National Taiwan Library
〔東大経〕：Faculty of Economics Library, University of Tokyo
〔内閣〕：Cabinet Library
〔農総研〕：National Research Institute of Agricultural Economies
〔宮崎県〕：Miyazaki Prefecture Library
〔民博〕：National Museum of Ethnology (MINPAKU) Library

日本語文献

Japanese Language Publications

48th Division Headquarters

(犬童巳来男氏提供
Reproduced courtesy of Mr. Mikio Indo)

A camoflaged Japanese transport ship being bombed by American planes near Timor.
Courtesy of the Netherlands Institute for War Documentation

I．単行書（Monographs）

戦前・戦中篇［Prewar-Wartime Materials］

朝日新聞社中央調査会（Asahi Shinbunsha Chūō Chōsakai）編
朝日東亜年報：昭和13－16年版（Asahi Tōa nenpō: Shōwa 13-16 nenban）　朝日新聞社　1941　670p
内容細目：チモール　p. 217
Title translation: Asahi East Asia almanac, 1938-1941 edition
Relevant section: Timor, p. 217

朝日新聞社中央調査会（Asahi Shinbunsha Chūō Chōsakai）編
朝日東亜年報：昭和17年版（Asahi Tōa nenpō: Shōwa 17 nenban）　朝日新聞社　1942　727, 24p
内容細目：第1部　東亜諸国の展望　葡領チモール島　pp. 163-167
Title translation: Asahi East Asia almanac, 1942 edition
Relevant section: Part 1. Prospects of East Asian countries, Portuguese Timor, pp. 163-167

飯本　信之（IIMOTO Nobuyuki）、佐藤　弘（SATŌ Hiroshi）編
東印度2（旧蘭印2、旧英領ボルネオ、葡領チモール）（Tōindo 2 (kyū Ran'in 2, kyū Eiryō Boruneo, Poryō Chimōru)）　ダイヤモンド社　1942　421p　（南洋地理大系　第6巻）
内容細目：葡領チモール　pp. 387-417
Title translation: East Indies 2 (former Dutch Indies 2, Former British Borneo, Portuguese Timor) (An overview of South Seas geography, vol. 6)
Relevant section: Portuguese Timor, pp. 387-417

欧文社編集局（Ōbunsha Henshūkyoku）編
大東亜太平洋圏の新展望（Dai Tōa Taiheiyōken no shin tenbō）　欧文社　1942　297p

内容細目：第10章　蘭領東印度諸島　第4節　英領ニューギニア・葡領チモール pp. 204-206

Title translation: New Prospects for the Greater East Asia Pacific Sphere

Relevant section: Chapter 10, The Netherlands East Indies Archipelago, Section 4, British New Guinea, Portuguese Timor, pp. 204-206

海軍省医務局第二課（Kaigunshō Imukyoku Dainika）編

第四南遣艦隊麾下ノマラリアニ就テ（Daiyon Nanken Kantai kika no mararia ni tsuite）　昭和19年3月10日第四南遣艦隊司令部報告　海軍省医務局第二課　1944　1冊

内容細目：「チモール」島のマラリア（内田四警軍医長）

Title translation: Regarding malaria in the 4th Southern Expeditionary Fleet controlled area, March 10, 1944, the 4th Southern Fleet Commander's report

Relevant section: Malaria on Timor Island (UCHIDA, Chief surgeon of No 4 Guard Unit)　〔昭和館〕

海軍有終会（Kaigun Yūshūkai）編

太平洋二千六百年史（Taiheiyō nisen-roppyakunenshi）　海防義会　1940　1086, 38, 50p 図版17枚

内容細目：第2　現勢篇　第9章　葡領各地　第1節　チモール　pp. 1059-1083

Title translation: 2600 years of Pacific region history

Relevant section: Number 2, Current situation issue. Chapter 9, Individual Portuguese territories, Section 1, East Timor.

〔外務省（Gaimushō）〕著

南洋経略論（Nan'yō keiryakuron）　n.p.　〔1936〕　204p

内容細目：葡領チモール　pp. 111-112

対葡政策　pp. 196-198

Title translation: Views on governing the South Seas

Relevant section: Portuguese Timor, pp. 111-112

Policy on Portugal, pp. 196-198　〔早稲田大学〕

〔外務省（Gaimushō）〕著
  南洋経略論：未定稿（Nan'yō keiryakuron: miteikō）　n.p.　〔1936〕　1冊
  内容細目：葡領チモール
  対葡政策
  外務省便箋使用
  Title translation: Views on governing the South Seas: draft
  Relevant section: Portuguese Timor
  Policy on Portugal　　　　　　　　　　　　　　　　　　〔早稲田大学〕
  Using ministry of Foreign Affairs letterhead

外務省条約局（Gaimushō Jōyakukyoku）編
  「オーストラリア」ト「ポルトガル」領「ティモール」トノ間ニ航空業務ヲ開設スルコトニ関スル「オーストラリア」政府「ポルトガル」国政府間交換公文（"Ōsutoraria" to "Porutogaru" ryō "Timōru" to no kan ni kōkū gyōmu o kaisetsusuru koto ni kansuru "Ōsutoraria" seifu "Porutogaru" koku seifu kan kōkan kōbun）　外務省条約局　1941　10p　（条約集　第19集第30巻574）
  Original English title: Exchange of notes between the Australian Government and the Portuguese Government regarding the establishment of an air service between Australia & Portuguese Timor.

外務省条約局（Gaimushō Jōyakukyoku）編
  「パラオ」「ディリー」間航空業務設定ニ関スル日本国政府「ポルトガル」国政府間協定（"Parao" "Dirī" kan kōkū gyōmu settei ni kansuru Nihonkoku seifu "Porutogaru" koku seifu kan kyōtei）　外務省条約局　1941　6, 5p　（条約集　第19集第37巻581）
  Original French title: Accord entre les gouvernements Japonais et Potugais pour l'establissement d'un service aérien entre Palao et Dili.
  Title translation: Agreement between the Japanese and Portuguese governments for the establishment of an air service between Palau and Dili.

外務省条約局（Gaimushō Jōyakukyoku）編
  東「インド」諸島関係条約集（Higashi "Indo" shotō kankei jōyakushū）　外務省条約局　1942　9, 369p

I．単行書（Monographs）

内容細目：14.「チモール」及「ソロル」群島ニ於ケル「オランダ」国及「ポルトガル」国属地ノ境界ニ関スル「オランダ」国「ポルトガル」国間条約

15.「チモール」及「ソロル」群島ニ於ケル各自ノ属地ニ関スル通商（火器其ノ他ノ貿易）、航海、国境及相互先買権ニ関スル「ポルトガル」国「オランダ」国間条約

16.「チモール」島ニ於ケル「オランダ」国及「ポルトガル」国属地確定ニ関スル属地ノ境界確定ニ関スル「オランダ」国「ポルトガル」国間条約　pp. 239-275

Title translation: A Collection of treaties related to the East Indies archipelago

Relevant section: 14. Treaty between the Netherlands and Portugal regarding the border between Dutch territories and Portuguese territories in the Timor and Solor archipelago

15. Treaty between the Netherlands and Portugal regarding trade (firearms and other trading), navigation, the border and mutual first refusal on lands in each territory in the Timor and Solor archipelago

16. Treaty between the Netherlands and Portugal regarding finalization of the border in the course of finalizing Dutch and Portuguese territories on Timor Island, pp. 239-2751

外務省通商局（Gaimushō Tsūshōkyoku）編
葡萄牙植民地事情（Porutogaru shokuminchi jijō）　外務省通商局　1929　68p
内容：「ティモール」県　pp. 59-63
Title translation: Conditions in Portuguese colonies
Relevant section: Timor province, pp. 59-63

外務省通商局（Gaimushō Tsūshōkyoku）編
葡領「チモール」植民地事情（Poryō "Chimōru" shokuminchi jijō）　外務省通商局　1934　2, 30p
Title translation: Conditions in the Portuguese colony of Timor

〔逓信省〕航空局国際課（Kōkūkyoku Kokusaika）編
葡領「チモール」、蘭印資料（Poryō "Chimōru," Ran'in shiryō）〔n.p.〕〔逓信省〕航空局国際課　1940　1冊
内容細目：葡領「チモール」植民地概要（外務省通商局）、チモール島の現状（松

江浩正)、葡領「チモール」植民地事情、葡萄牙領「チモール」ノ資源、蘭領印度ニ於ケル飛行場調、蘭印東部諸島の交通事情（航空局国際課)、蘭領東印度に於ける石油鉱業、ニュー・ギニー航空事情（航空局国際課)、台拓、南拓、南興の概要

Title translation: Documents on Portuguese Timor and the Netherlands Indies

Relevant section: A brief description of the Portuguese colony of Timor（Ministry of Foreign Affairs, Bureau of Commerce), The current conditions of Timor island （MATSUE Hiromasa), Conditions in the Portuguese colony of Timor, The resources of Portuguese Timor, Research on airfields in the Netherlands Indies, Transportation situations in the Dutch Indies' eastern archipelago（International Section in Aviation Bureau), Oil and mining industry in the Netherlands East Indies, The situation of aviation in New Guinea（International Section in Aviation Bureau), A brief description of the Taiwan Colonization Company, South Seas Colonization Company, and South Seas Development Company.

第三気象隊（Daisan Kishōtai）編

「クーパン」「チモール海」「ダーウィン」雨期天候予察参考資料（"Kūpan" "Chimōru-kai" "Dāwin" uki tenkō yosatsu sankō shiryō）1943　1冊（三気機密参考資料）

Title translation: Reference documents on the prediction of weather in the rainy season for Kupang, the Timor Sea, and Darwin　　　　　　　　　〔気象庁〕

大日本航空株式会社（Dai Nihon Kōkū Kabushiki Kaisha）編

デリー基地調査報告（Derī kichi chōsa hōkoku）浅香良一担当〔n.p.〕1940　13p（企画資料　第306号）

Title translation: An investigation report on the Dili base　　　　　　　〔内閣〕

太平洋協会（Taiheiyō Kyōkai）編

大南洋：文化と農業（Dai Nan'yō: bunka to nōgyō）河出書房　1941　496, 12, 23p
内容細目：紅頭嶼生物地理と新ワーレス線北端の改訂（鹿野忠雄）

Original English title: Greater South Seas: Its Culture and Its Soil

Relevant section (original English title): Biogeography of the Island of Kotosho（Botel Tobago）with Special Reference to the Neo-Wallace Line（KANŌ Tadao）

大本営海軍報道部（Daihon'ei Kaigun Hōdōbu）編
　大東亜戦争と帝国海軍：第１集（Dai Tōa Sensō to Teikoku Kaigun: dai 1 shū）
　興亜日本社　1942　223, 21p 図版
　内容細目：海軍落下傘部隊の攻略戦　pp. 86-93
　チモール島攻略記（○○特務少尉）pp. 94-101
　Title translation: The Greater East Asia War and the Imperial Navy. The first collection
　Relevant section: Naval paratroopers' victorious battles, p. 86-93.
　　The story of the conquest of Timor island（○○ special mission naval ensign）, pp. 94-101.

台湾総督府官房外事部（Taiwan Sōtokufu kanbō Gaijibu）編
　南洋年鑑：第３回版（Nan'yō nenkan: dai 3 kaiban）台北　南洋協会台湾支部　1937　1707p
　内容細目：蘭領印度　附　蘭領チモル　pp. 1555-1566
　Title translation: The South Seas almanac: Third edition
　Relevant section: Dutch Indies, Attachment, Portuguese Timor, pp. 1555-1566

台湾総督府外事部（Taiwan Sōtokufu Gaijibu）編
　東印度：附　葡領チモール（Tōindo: Fu Poryō Chimōru）台北　台湾総督府外事部　1943　450p（外事部調査　157）
　Title translation: East Indies. Attached, Portuguese Timor　　〔台湾分館〕

台湾総督府外事部（Taiwan Sōtokufu Gaijibu）編
　南洋年鑑：第４回版（Nan'yō nenkan: dai 4 kaiban）下巻　台北　南方資料館　1943　1294, 13p
　内容細目：〔附〕葡領チモール　pp. 829-840
　Title translation: The South Seas almanac: Fourth edition
　Relevant section: Attachment, Portuguese Timor, pp. 829-840

土屋　賢一（TSUCHIYA Ken'ichi）著
　無敵陸戦隊（Muteki rikusentai）郁文社　1943　280p
　内容細目：チモール島空からの奇襲　pp. 153-169

Title translation: Invincible marines
Relevant section: Sudden attack from the Timor skies, pp. 153-169 〔昭和館〕

ドゥアルテ、テオフィーロ（DUARUTE Teofiro）著
葡萄牙領チモール概観（Porutogaruryō Chimōru gaikan） Teofilio DUARTE著
西村朝日太郎訳　東亜研究所　1942　5, 116, 35p　（資料丙　第243号C）
Original Portuguese title: Timor, ante-camara do inferno?（1930）
Title translation: A survey of Portuguese Timor

東京日日新聞社（Tōkyō Nichinichi Shinbunsha）、大阪毎日新聞社（Ōsaka Mainichi Shinbunsha）編
ジャワ作戦（Jawa sakusen）　東京日日新聞社　1942　4,282p　（大東亜戦史）
内容細目：第3章　東方諸島の攻略（セレベス・アンボン・チモール・バリー）
チモールへ再び空から進撃　pp. 80-84
Title translation: The Java operation,（History of the Greater East Asia War）
Relevant section: Chapter 3, The capture of the eastward archipelago（Celebes, Ambon, Timor, Bali）, Once more an attack from the air on Timor, pp. 80-84

中山　信夫（NAKAYAMA Nobuo）著
クーパン飛行場：海軍落下傘部隊手記（Kūpan hikōjō: Kaigun rakkasan butai shuki）　高橋亮絵　海洋文化社　1943　297p
Title translation: Kupang airfield: The journal of a Navy paratrooper unit

南方問題研究所（Nanpō Mondai Kenkyūjo）
南方問題と国民の覚悟（Nanpō mondai to kokumin no kakugo）　南方問題研究所　1941　340p　改訂増補
内容細目：葡領チモール　pp. 263-278
Title translation: The southern problem and the people's determination
Relevant section: Portuguese Timor, pp. 263-278

南洋興発内SAPT. LDA 東京事務所（Nan'yō Kōhatsu SAPT. LDA Tōkyō jimusho）編
**葡領チモール調査報告書：「アライド・マイニング・コーポレーション」ノ「アジア・

I. 単行書 (Monographs)

インヴェストメント・コンパニー」ニ対スル（Poryō Chimōru chōsa hōkokusho: "Araido Mainingu Kōporēshon" no "Ajia Invesutomento Konpanī" ni taisuru）〔n.p.〕 南洋興発内SAPTL東京事務所　1937　212p

Title translation: Research report on Portuguese Timor: the Allied Mining Corporation to the Asian Investment Company

南洋庁内務部企画課（Nan'yōchō Naimubu Kikakuka）編
葡領チモール島事情（Poryō Chimōrutō jijō）〔n.p.〕 南洋庁内務部企画課　1942　30p（企画課資料　第19集）

Title translation: Conditions in Portuguese Timor

日葡協会（Nippo Kyōkai）編
葡領チモールの全貌（Poryō Chimōru no zenbō）　協和書房　1942　6, 3, 142p（葡萄牙叢書　第3集）

Title translation: Survey of Portuguese Timor

日本外事協会（Nihon Gaiji Kyōkai）編
南方政策を現地に視る（Nanpō seisaku o genchi ni miru）　日本外事協会　1936　393p
内容細目：チモール　p. 261

Title translation: Field investigations on southern policy
Relevant section: Timor p. 261

日本国際問題調査会（Nihon Kokusai Mondai Chōsakai）著
世界年鑑：昭和17年版（Sekai nenkan: Shōwa 17 nenban）　創美社　1942　76,1546,14p
内容細目：第2篇　39　葡領チモール　pp. 672-674

Title translation: World almanac, 1942 edition.
Relevant section: Vol.2, 39, Portuguese Timor, pp. 672-674.

日本国際問題調査会（Nihon Kokusai Mondai Chōsakai）著
世界年鑑：昭和18年版（Sekai nenkan: Shōwa 18 nenban）　創美社　1943　1495p
内容細目：36　葡領チモール　pp. 579-582

Title translation: World almanac, 1943 edition.

Relevant section: 36, Portuguese Timor, pp. 579-582.

日本油脂株式会社企画部調査課（Nihon Yushi Kabushiki Kaisha Kikakubu Chōsaka）編

大南洋共栄圏之産業全貌：英領北ボルネオ、サラワク、ブルネイ並ニ葡萄牙領チモール之部（Dai Nan'yō Kyōeiken no sangyō zenbō: Eiryō Kitaboruneo, Sarawaku, Burunei narabini Porutogaruryō Chimōru no bu）〔n.p.〕 日本油脂株式会社 1941　69p　（調査報告　120号）

Title translation: Survey of industries in the Greater South Sea Co-prosperity Sphere: The British North Borneo, Sarawak, Brunei and Portuguese Timor sections

日本油料統制株式会社南方油脂資源調査室（Nihon Yuryō Tōsei Kabushiki Gaisha Nanpō Yushi Shigen Chōsashitsu）編

南太平洋諸島ニ於ケル油脂資源：附　葡領チモール（Minami Taiheiyō shotō ni okeru yushi shigen Fu Poryō Chimōru）　日本油料統制株式会社南方油脂資源調査室　1942　9p　（南方油脂資源資料　第8号）

Title translation: The oil and fat natural resources of the Southern Pacific Islands

熱帯文化協会（Nettai Bunka Kyōkai）編

葡領「チモール」植民地調査報告書（Poryō Chimōru shokuminchi chōsa hōkokusho） 熱帯文化協会　1937　72p　葡萄牙領チモール地図（50万分1）

Title translation: A research report on the colony of Portuguese Timor Attached, a Portuguese Timor map, Scale 1:500,000

熱帯文化協会（Nettai Bunka Kyōkai）編

葡萄牙領チモール島に於ける石油開発に関する総督令抄訳（Porutogaruryō Chimōrutō ni okeru sekiyu kaihatsu ni kansuru sōtoku-rei shōyaku）〔n.p.〕〔n.d.〕 27p

Title translation: An abridged translation by the order of the Governor-general on oil development in Portuguese Timor Island　　　　　　　　　　〔拓殖大〕

I. 単行書 (Monographs)

熱帯文化協会企画部調査課（Nettai Bunka Kyōkai Kikakubu Chōsaka）編
 葡領チモール植民地調査報告書（Poryō Chimōru shokuminchi chōsa hōkokusho）
 〔熱帯文化協会企画部調査課〕〔1941〕　110p
 Title translation: A research report on the colony of Portuguese Timor

能仲　文夫（NONAKA Fumio）著
 南洋と松江春次（Nan'yō to Matsue Haruji）　時代社　1941　534,12p
 内容細目：葡領チモール島　pp. 419-442
 Title translation: The South Seas and Matsue Haruji
 Relevant section: Portuguese Timor Island, pp. 419-442

野村合名会社海外事業部（Nomura Gōmei Gaisha Kaigai Jigyōbu）著
 葡領チモール概説（Poryō Chimōru gaisetsu）　野村合名会社海外事業部　1941　19枚
 Title translation: Outline of Portuguese Timor

浜松市商工課（Hamamatsu-shi Shōkōka）編
 大東亜共栄圏南方諸領事情：第1　蘭印・チモール・ニューギニア（Dai Tōa Kyōeiken nanpō shoryō jijō: dai 1, Ran'in, Chimōru, Nyūginia）　浜松　浜松市商工課　1942　40,3,22p
 Title translation: Conditions in individual southern territories in the Greater East Asia Co-prosperity Sphere: Number 1, Netherlands Indies, Timor, New Guinea

三吉　朋十（MIYOSHI Tomokazu）著
 パラワン・チモール・セレベス探検記（Parawan, Chimōru, Serebesu tanken-ki）
 刀江書院　1942　528p
 内容細目：東印度チモール島探検　pp. 197-260
 Title translation: An account of an expedition to Palawan, Timor and Celebes
 Relevant section: Expedition to the East Indies' Timor Island, pp. 197-260

本内　達蔵（MOTOUCHI Tatsuzō）著
 陸戦隊と落下傘隊（Rikusentai to rakkasantai）　大東亜社　1944　171p　（海軍叢書）

内容細目：クーパン飛行場占領　pp. 160-165

Title translation: Marines and paratroops

Relevant section: The occupation of the Kupang airfield, pp. 160-165　〔昭和館〕

山口　喜代松（YAMAGUCHI Kiyomatsu）著

　日本海軍陸戦隊史（Nihon Kaigun rikusentai shi）　大新社　1943　306p

　内容細目：大東亜戦争（2）　4、バリ島及びチモール島占領　pp. 284-286

　Title translation: History of the Japanese Naval Brigade

　Relevant section: Greater East Asia War（2）4, The occupation of Bali Island and Timor Island, pp. 284-286

横浜商工会議所（Yokohama Shōko Kaigisho）編

　蘭領東印度篇：附　葡領チモール篇（Ranryō Tōindo hen: fu Poryō Chimōru hen）

　横浜　横浜商工会議所　1942　236, 29p　（大東亜共栄圏資源図絵　第2集）

　Title translation: Dutch East Indies, Attached, Portuguese Timor（A sketch of Greater East Asia Co-prosperity Sphere resources, Second issue）

米田　正武（YONEDA Masatake）著

　葡領チモール（附ニューギニア）（Poryō Chimōru（Fu Nyūginia））〔n.p.〕〔拓殖奨励館調査部〕　1937　26丁

　Title translation: Portuguese Timor, Attached, New Guinea

チモール地方税関報告（Chimōru chihō zeikan hōkoku）〔n.p.〕〔1913〕240p

　Title translation: A report on customs in the Timor area　〔農総研〕

ポルトガル領チモール州土地租借認可に関する一般法及特別法の編纂（Porutogaruryō Chimōru-shū tochi soshaku ninka ni kansuru ippanhō oyobi tokubetsuhō no hensan）〔n.p.〕　1936　494p

　Title translation: A compilation of general and special laws regarding authorization of land leasing in the province of Portuguese Timor　〔研究会〕

Ⅰ．単行書（Monographs）

戦後篇（Postwar writings）

秋本　実（AKIMOTO Minoru）著
　落下傘部隊（Rakkasan butai）　R出版　1972　273p　（空の戦記）
　内容細目：第5章　クーパン降下作戦　pp. 101-116
　Title translation: Paratroop units
　Relevant section: Chapter 5, The landing operation in Kupang, pp. 101-116

アクティブ・ミュージアム「女たちの戦争と平和資料館」（Akutivu Myūjiamu "Onna tachi no Sensō to Heiwa Siryōkan) 編
　東ティモール・戦争を生きぬいた女たち：日本軍とインドネシア支配の下で（Higashi Timōru, sensō o ikinuita onna tachi: Nihongun to Indoneshia shihai no moto de）
　アクティブ・ミュージアム「女たちの戦争と平和資料館」　2007　48p
　Original English title: East Timorese Women Speak Out: Sexual Violence under Japanese and Indonesian Occupation

朝日新聞社（Asahi Shinbunsha）編
　敵は日本人だった（Teki wa nihonjin datta）　朝日新聞社　1991　271p　（女たちの太平洋戦争2）
　内容細目：強制労働・慰安所の開設－南の楽園汚した軍隊（揚田明夫）　pp. 146-147
　Title translation: Enemies were the Japanese
　Relevant section: Forced labor/opening of a comfort house－troops violated the paradise in the South（AGETA Akio）

アムネスティ・インターナショナル日本支部（Amunesuti Intānashonaru Nihonshibu）編
　小さな島の大きな戦争：東チモール独立運動をめぐる大規模人権侵害（Chiisana shima no ōkina sensō: Higashi Chimōru dokuritsu undō o meguru daikibo jinken shingai）　第三書館　1989　310p
　内容細目：私の東チモール（貴島　正道）　pp. 106-119
　Title translation: Big war on a small island: The large scale violation of human

rights in connection with the East Timor independence movement.
Relevant section: My East Timor (KIJIMA Masamichi), pp. 106-119

粟屋　憲太郎（AWAYA Kentarō）、中園　裕（NAKAZONO Hiroshi）編集・解説
内務省新聞記事差止資料集成：第9巻（Naimushō shinbun kiji sashitome shiryō shūsei: dai 9 kan）　日本図書センター　1996　339p（国際検察局押収重要文書3）
内容細目：1941年1月20日　我が南洋委任統治地パラオと葡領チモールのデリー間に於ける第3回目試験飛行に関する件　pp. 315-318
Title translation: A collection of documents related to newspaper prohibitions by the Home Ministry, Volume 9.
Relevant section: January 20, 1941, Regarding the third test flight between our mandated territory Palau and Portuguese Timor, pp. 315-318.

伊藤　玉男（ITŌ Tamao）編
チモールの逆無電（Chimōru no gyakumuden）　新居浜　心友一同　1983　134p
Title translation: Deceptive radio operation of Timor

稲葉　通宗（INABA Michimune）著
海底十一万浬（Kaitei jūichiman kairi）　朝日ソノラマ　1984　477p（航空戦史シリーズ46）
内容細目：第2章　インド洋を征く　チモール水道　pp. 104-113
Title translation: 110 thousand nautical miles under the sea
Relevant section: Chapter 2, Advance to Indian Sea, the Timor channels, pp. 104-113

岩川　隆（IWAKAWA Takashi）著
孤島の土となるとも：BC級戦犯裁判（Kotō no tsuchi to narutomo: bīshīkyū senpan saiban）　講談社　1995　830p
内容細目：クーパン裁判　pp. 347-362
Title translation: Despite becoming the soil of a desert island: The B-C class war tribunals
Relevant section: The Kupang tribunals, pp. 347-362.

インドネシア日本占領期史料フォーラム（Indoneshia Nihon Senryōki Shiryō Fōramu）編

証言集：日本軍占領下のインドネシア（Shōgenshū: Nihongun senryōka no Indoneshia）龍溪書舎　1991　760p

内容細目：陸軍主計中尉としてみた東ティモール（貴島　正道）pp. 717-747

Title translation: A collection of testimonies: Japanese military occupied Indonesia

Relevant section: Observation of East Timor as an Army accounting lieutenant (KIJIMA Masamichi), pp. 717-747

沖縄インドネシア友好協会（Okinawa Indoneshia Yūkōkyōkai）編

Sahabat：沖縄インドネシア友好協会記念誌（Sahabat: Okinawa Indoneshia Yūkōkyōkai kinenshi）沖縄　沖縄インドネシア友好協会　1999　173p

内容細目：忘れられないできごと　嘉数正夫（聞き取り　平良次子）pp. 45-49

Title translation: Sahabat: Okinawa-Indonesia Friendship Association commemorative publication

Relevant section: Unforgettable events, KAKAZU Masao (interviewer, TAIRA Tsugiko) pp. 45-49

沖縄海友会（Okinawa Kaiyūkai）編

沖縄海軍物語：海友会員回想録（Okinawa kaigun monogatari: Kaiyū kai'in kaisōroku）沖縄　沖縄海友会　1985　299,34p

内容細目：チモール島警備隊（与儀　幸雄）p. 106

Title translation: The story of the Okinawan naval story: Recollections of the Naval Friends Association members.

Relevant section: The Timor Island guard (YOGI Yukio), p. 106

尾辻　昇（OTSUJI Noboru）著

南方戦線わが一すじ（Nanpō sensen wagahitosuji）〔牧園町（鹿児島県）〕〔尾辻昇刊〕〔1984〕308p

内容細目：蘭領チモール駐留　pp. 140-229

Title translation: The Southern front: My destiny

Relevant section: Stationed in Dutch Timor, pp. 140-229　〔宮崎県〕

海軍落下傘会（Kaigun Rakkasankai）編
  落下傘奇襲部隊：海軍落下傘部隊生存者の手記（Rakkasan kishū butai: kaigun rakkasan seizonsha no shuki）　叢文社　1990　298p
  Title translation: an ambush paratroop unit, memorirs of naval paratroop unit survivers

外務省（Gaimushō）編
  政府公表集：対外関係　昭和17年度（Seifu kohyoshū: Taigai kankei Shōwa 17 nendo）　佐藤元英監修　クレス出版　1993　1冊　（外務省公表集　第11巻）
  内容細目：「チモール島ノ作戦ニ関スル帝国政府声明」（英）　pp. 3-4
  Statement of the Government Concerning the Operation of Japanese Forces in Dutch Timor（Feb. 20）pp. 7-8
  Title translation: A collection of government public announcements: foreign relations, 1942 fiscal year（A collection of the Ministry of Foreign Affairs' public announcements, volume 11）
  Relevant section: Statement of the Government concerning the operation of Japanese forces in Dutch Timor（Feb. 20）, pp. 3-4 reproduce the statement in Japanese and pp. 7-8 in English.

外務省亜米利加局（Gaimushō Amerikakyoku）編
  外務省執務報告：亜米利加局　第3巻　昭和14年～17年（Gaimushō shitsumu hōkoku: Amerikakyoku, dai 3 kan, Shōwa 14-17 nen）　クレス出版　1994　1冊
  内容細目：昭和十四年度執務報告（第三課関係）　第1章　邦人海外渡航関係　第1節　邦人ノ海外渡航取締及旅券下付ノ一般的方針　第3款　各国別取扱状況　葡領「チモール」　pp. 7-8
  第2節　渡航許可又ハ旅券下付ニ関スル取締方針　第12款　葡領「チモール」渡航者ニ対スル制限　pp. 83-84
  昭和十五年度執務報告（第三課関係）　第1章　邦人海外渡航関係　第2節　各国別海外渡航取扱状況　「ポルトガル」領「チモール」　p. 4
  第3節　渡航許可又ハ旅券下付ニ関スル取締及制限　第8款　「ポルトガル」領「チモール」渡航者ニ対スル制限　p. 58
  昭和十六・十七年度執務報告（第三課関係）　第1章　邦人海外渡航関係　第2節　各国別海外渡航取扱状況　第1款　大東亜戦争勃発前迄ノ取扱状況　「ポルトガル」

領「チモール」 p. 5

第3節　渡航許可又ハ旅券下付ニ関スル取締及制限　第7款　「ポルトガル」領「チモール」渡航者ニ対スル制限　pp. 60-61

Title translation: The Ministry of Foreign Affairs' Executive Office report: American Bureau volume 3, 1939-1942

Relevant section: 1939 annual office report (Regarding the third section). Chapter 1, Section 1, Part 3, Treatment of conditions in various countries, Portuguese Timor, pp. 7-8

Part 12, Portuguese Timor travel restrictions, pp. 83-84

1940 annual office report (Regarding the third section). Chapter 1, Section 2, Treatment of conditions for overseas travel to various countries, Portuguese Timor, p. 4

Part 8, Portuguese Timor travel restrictions, p. 58

1941/1942 annual office report (Regarding the third section). Chapter 1, Section 2, Part 1, Treatment of conditions for overseas travel to various countries, Portuguese Timor, p. 5

Part 7, Portuguese Timor travel restrictions, pp. 60-61

外務省欧亜局 (Gaimushō Ōakyoku) 編

外務省執務報告：欧亜局　第1巻　昭和11年度 (Gaimushō shitsumu hōkoku: Ōakyoku, dai 1 kan, Shōwa 11-nendo)　クレス出版　1994　1冊

内容細目：第3編　第1章　蘭領印度　第8節　葡領「チモール」島　pp. 123-125

Title translation: The Ministry of Foreign Affairs' office reports: European and Oceanic Affairs Bureau, vol. 1, from April 1936 to March 1937

Relevant section: Volume 3, Chapter 1. Netherlands Indies, Section 8, Portuguese Timor Island, pp. 123-125

外務省欧亜局 (Gaimushō Ōakyoku) 編

外務省執務報告：欧亜局　第2巻　昭和13年度 (Gaimushō shitsumu hōkoku: Ōakyoku, dai 2 kan Shōwa 13 nendo)　クレス出版　1994　1冊

内容細目：第6章　其ノ他ノ地域　第3節　葡領「チモール」　葡領「チモール」ニ於ケル日葡合弁事業ニ関スル件　pp. 188-193

Title translation: The Ministry of Foreign Affairs' office reports: European and

Oceanic Affairs Bureau, vol. 2, from April 1938 to March 1939

Relevant section: Chapter 6, Other areas, Section 3. Portuguese Timor, Regarding Japanese-Portuguese joint enterprise in Portuguese Timor, pp. 188-193

外務省通商局（Gaimushō Tsūshōkyoku）編

外務省執務報告：通商局　第3巻　昭和12年度（Gaimushō shitsumu hōkoku: Tsūshōkyoku, dai 2 kan, Shōwa 12 nendo）　クレス出版　1995　1冊

内容細目：第4編　第145　葡領「チモール」　pp. 758-760

Title translation: The Ministry of Foreign Affairs' office reports: The Bureau of Commerce, vol. 2, from April 1937 to March 1938

Relevant section: Volume 4, No. 145. Portuguese Timor, pp. 758-760

外務省通商局（Gaimushō Tsūshōkyoku）編

外務省執務報告：通商局　第3巻　昭和13年度（Gaimushō shitsumu hōkoku: Tsūshōkyoku, dai 3 kan, Shōwa 13 nendo）　クレス出版　1995　1冊

内容細目：第6編　第135　葡領「チモール」　pp. 880-882

Title translation: The Ministry of Foreign Affairs' office reports: The Bureau of Commerce, vol. 3, from April 1938 to March 1939

Relevant section: Volume 6, No. 135. Portuguese Timor, pp. 880-882

鹿島平和研究所（Kajima Heiwa Kenkyūjo）編

日本外交史．24（Nihon gaikōshi. 24）　大東亜戦争・戦時外交　太田一郎 監修　鹿島研究所出版会　1971　530,26p

内容細目：第二章　中立国に対する施策　pp. 64-114

第五節　チモール進駐と対ポルトガル措置　（付）マカオ福井領事射殺事件　pp. 83-91

Title translation: Japanese diplomatic history, 24, The Greater East Asia War and war time diplomacy.

Relevant section: Chapter 2, Policy for neutral countries, pp. 64-114

Section 5, Timor station and provisions for Portugal, (Supplement) The assassination of Macao Consul Fukui, pp. 83-91

片桐　克（KATAGIRI Katsumi）著

　黒潮（Kuroshio）　関　片桐克刊　1968　114p

　内容細目：第三章　濠北作戦　pp. 75-87

　第四章　終戦及び転進　pp. 89-93

　Title translation: The Black Current

　Relevant section: Chapter 3, The Northern Australia operation, pp. 75-87

　Chapter 4, The end of the war and changing direction, pp. 89-93　　〔岐阜県〕

鹿沼　次郎（KANUMA Jirō）著

　軍靴の軌跡（Gunka no kiseki）　奈良市　勤通会事務局　1992　95p

　内容細目：チモール島の防衛　pp. 55-62

　Title translation: In the trail of military boots

　Relevant section: The defence of Timor Island, pp. 55-62　　〔竹井氏蔵〕

川井　惣市（KAWAI Sōichi）著

　皇軍チモール島：戦争回想録　歩兵第二二八連隊攻略戦（Kōgun Chimōruto: Sensō kaisōroku, Hohei Dainihyaku-nijūhachi Rentai kōryaku sen）〔岐阜〕〔川井惣市刊〕〔2000〕　11p

　内容細目：昭和17年2月20日チモール島上陸

　Title translation: The Imperial Army on Timor: The book of war reminiscences, The 228th infantry regiment's capturing strike

　Relevant section: February 20, 1942: Landing on Timor Island

〔岐阜県〕〔奈良県〕

許　玉蘭（KYO Gyokuran）

　玉蘭の移り香（gyokuran no utsurika）れんが書房新社　2006　165p

　内容細目：「東ティモールの話」pp. 69-76

　Title translation: Scent of magnolia conspicus

　Relevant section: Story of East Timor, pp. 69-76

極東国際軍事裁判所（Kyokutō Kokusai Gunji Saibansho）編

　極東国際軍事裁判速記録（Kyokutō Kokusai Gunji Saiban sokkiroku）　第3巻

　第107号－第146号　雄松堂書店　1968　826p

　内容細目：pp. 707-710

Title translation: The International Military Tribunal for the Far East, shorthand notes, vol. 3

Relevant section: pp. 707-710

熊本兵団戦史編さん委員会（Kumamoto Heidan Senshi Hensan Iinkai）編
  熊本兵団戦史（Kumamoto Heidan senshi）〔第3〕 太平洋戦争編　熊本　熊本日日新聞社　1965　405p
  内容細目：第13章　豪北作戦（第四十六師団、第四十八師団）　pp. 188-201
  Title translation: A war history of the Kumamoto Army Corps, [No. 3] Pacific War
  Relevant section: Chapter 13, Northern Australia operations (46th Division, 48th Division) pp. 188-201

熊本蓬莱山吹会（Kumamoto Horai Yamabukikai）編
  台湾山砲之歴史（Taiwan sanpō no rekishi）〔熊本蓬莱山吹会〕 1960 85p
  Title translation: The history of Taiwan mountain guns　〔熊本県〕

栗林商会（Kuribayashi Shōkai）編
  栗林七十五年（Kuribayashi nanajūgonen）　室蘭　栗林商会　1970　318p
  内容細目：第2章　南洋興発会社の経営　第2節　外南洋事業の検討　pp. 97-102
  Title translation: Kuribayashi 75 years' history
  Relevant section: Chapter 2, The management of Nan'yō Kōhatsu K.K.; Volume 2, A review of business in the outer South Seas, pp. 97-102.

軍人会館図書部（Gunjin Kaikan Toshobu）編
  陸海軍軍事年鑑7：昭和18年版（Rikukaigun gunji nenkan 7: Shōwa 18 nenban）
  日本図書センター　1989　998p
  軍事会館図書部昭和18年刊の複製
  内容細目：大東亜戦　二月二十日　チモール島上陸　p. 113
  大東亜戦　三月三十一日　英機我病院船を襲ふ　p. 123
  外交　チモール作戦通告（一七、二、二〇）　p. 823
  Title translation: Army-Navy military almanac, 7. 1943 edition.
  Relevant section: Greater East Asia War, February 20, The landing on Timor

Island, p. 113

Great East Asia War, March 31, British airplanes attacked our hospital ship, p. 123

Diplomacy, Informing about the Timor operation (February 20, 1942), p. 823

厚生省援護局（Kōseishō Engokyoku）編
インドネシヤ方面部隊略歴：スマトラ方面・ジャワ方面・小スンダチモール方面・セラム方面・アンボン方面・セレベス方面・ハルマヘラ方面（Indonesiya hōmen butai ryakureki: Sumatora hōmen, Jawa hōmen, Shō Sunda Timōru hōmen, Seramu hōmen, Anbon hōmen, Serebesu hōmen, Harumahera hōmen）　厚生省援護局　1961　643p

Title translation: Brief histories of Indonesian area units: Sumatra area, Java area, Lesser Sunda-Timor area, Ceram area, Ambon area, Celebes area, Halmahera area.

厚生省援護局（Kōseishō Engokyoku）編
南方・支那・台湾方面陸上部隊（航空・船舶部隊を除く）略歴：第2回 追録（Nanpō, Shina Taiwan hōmen rikujō butai (kōku senpaku butai o nozoku) ryakureki: dai 2 kai tsuiroku）　厚生省援護局　1963　327p
内容細目：小スンダチモール方面部隊　pp. 66-
Title translation: A brief history of the southern area, China, and Taiwan campaign land forces (excluding air and vessel troops), the second appendix.
Relevant section: Lesser Sunda and Timor campaign troops, pp. 66

幸田　録郎（KŌDA Rokurō）編
輜三八追想録（Shi sanhachi tsuisōroku）　タブナ会　1965　292p
内容細目：チモール島の輸送（板垣茂）　pp. 108-111
Title translation: Recollections of the 38th Transport Corps
Relevant section: Transportation on Timor Island (ITAGAKI Shigeru), pp. 108-111

小高　登貫（KODAKA Noritsura）著
わが翼いまだ燃えず（Waga tsubasa imada moezu）　信陽新聞社編　甲陽書房

1965　321p

内容細目：チモール島　pp. 45-48

大久保上飛曹の最後　pp. 49-52

ポートダーウィン攻撃　pp. 53-57

輸送船護衛　pp. 58-61

居眠り飛行　pp. 62-68

Title translation: My wings were yet to be burned

Relevant section: Timor Island, pp. 45-48

The end of Air Sergeant Okubo, pp. 49-52

Attacks on Port Darwin, pp. 53-57

Guarding transportation ships, pp. 58-61

Sleeping flight, pp. 62-68

小瀧　実（KOTAKI Minoru）著

火炎木（Kaenboku）　文芸社　2002　126p

Title translation: A tree in flames

後藤　乾一（GOTŌ Ken'ichi）著

近代日本と東南アジア（Kindai Nihon to Tōnan Ajia）　岩波書店　1995　345p

内容細目：第3章「濠亜地中海」の国際関係

Title translation: Modern Japan and Southeast Asia

Relevant section: International relations in Austro-Asia Mediteranean Sea pp. 119-180

後藤　乾一（GOTŌ Ken'ichi）著

〈東〉ティモール国際関係史：1900－1945（"Higashi" Timōru kokusai kankeishi: 1900-1945）　みすず書房　1999　211, 3p

Title translation: A history of 〈East〉 Timorese international relations: 1900-1945

才木　一兼（SAIKI Kazukane）著

台湾軍第四十八師団：チモール逆無線隊戦記（Taiwangun Daiyonjūhachi Shidan: Chimōru gyaku musentai senki）〔才木一兼〕29p

Title translation: Taiwan Army the 48th Division: war record of Timor deceptive radio operation unit

坂　邦康（SAKA Kuniyasu）編著
蘭印法廷：戦争裁判史実記録1（オランダ軍関係）（Ran'in hōtei: sensō saiban shijitsu kiroku 1 (Orandagun kankei)）　東潮社　1968　171p
Title translation: Dutch Indies' courts: The real historical records of war tribunals. 1 (Dutch military affairs)

笹山　良樹（SASAYAMA Yoshiki）著
思い出の五年間（Omoide no gonenkan）〔出版地不明〕　笹山良樹　1981　108p
Title translation: Five years of memories

笹山　良樹（SASAYAMA Yoshiki）著
チモール島戦記～総集編：及び「従軍慰安婦」について考えてみよう（Chimōrutō senki sōshūhen: oyobi "jūgun ianfu" ni tsuite kangaete miyou）〔川場村（群馬県）〕〔笹山良樹刊〕〔2001〕175p
Title translation: The war on Timor Island, omnibus: and let's think about "military conscripted comfort women"

潮谷　総一郎（SHIOTANI Sōichirō）編著
台湾工兵戦記：台湾工兵四十八連隊戦記（Taiwan kōhei senki: Taiwan Kōhei Yonjūhachi Rentai senki）　北九州市　台工・工四八戦友会　1982　508p
内容細目：第4章　チモール島戡定戦　pp. 281-400
Title translation: A Taiwanese engineer's battle account: The battle stories of the 48th Regiment's Taiwanese engineers
Relevant section: Chapter 4, Mop-up operations in Timor, pp. 281-400

志柿　謙吉（SHIKAKI Kenkichi）著
空母「飛鷹」海戦記（Kūbo "Hidaka" kaisenki）　光人社　2002　246p
内容細目：チモール島視察行　pp. 104-108
デリー訪問　pp. 113-116
Title translation: Naval war record of the carrier *Hidaka*
Relevant section: Inspection trip to Timor Island, pp. 104-108

Visiting Dili, pp. 113-116

輜重兵第四十八連隊誌刊行会（Shichōhei Daiyonjūhachi Rentaishi Kankōkai）編
　追想の戦地：兵站自動車第271・280・281中隊及び輜重兵第四十八連隊部隊史（Tsuisō no senchi: Heitan Jidōsha Dai 271-280-281 Chūtai oyobi Shichōhei Daiyonjūhachi Rentai Butai shi）　吹田市輜重兵第四十八連隊誌刊行会　1988　327p
　Title translation: Recollection of battlefields, the 271st, 280th, and 281st Logistics Automobile Companies and the 48th Transport Regiment military history
〔熊本県〕

従軍回顧録刊行会（Jūgun Kaikoroku Kankōkai）編
　従軍の想い出（Jūgun no omoide）　下巻　岐阜市　従軍回顧録刊行会　1973　432p
　内容細目：南溟の孤島チモール島の現地自活と想い出（片桐　克）　pp. 345-348
　Title translation: Recollections of the conscription of a military, Second volume.
　Relevant section: Memories of self-sufficient local life in the isolated island of Timor in the south seas (KATAGIRI Katsumi) pp. 345-348
〔岐阜県〕

従軍回顧録編纂委員会（Jūgun Kaikoroku Hensan Iinkai）編
　従軍回顧録：第2巻　支那事変・大東亜戦争編（Jūgun kaikoroku: dai 2 kan, Shina Jihen, Dai Tōa Sensō hen）　岐阜市　従軍回顧録編纂委員会　1970　444p
　内容細目：南溟のチモール島における逆無電作戦（片桐　克）　pp. 207-211
　Title translation: Memoirs of military experiences, vol. 2. The China Incident-Greater East Asia War.
　Relevant section: Wireless reversal operation at Timor Island, in the south seas (KATAGIRI Katsumi) pp. 207-211
〔岐阜県〕

史料調査会（Shiryō Chōsakai）編
　大海令：解説（Daikairei: Kaisetsu）　毎日新聞社　1978　295,6p
　内容細目：第2　進攻作戦　1. チモール、アンダマン群島攻略……大海令第14、15号　pp. 96-
　Title translation: The Naval Order. Commentary
　Relevant section: No. 2, Attack strategies 1, the capture of Timor and the Andaman archipelago.....Great Ocean regulations nos. 14, 15, pp. 96-

巣鴨法務委員会（Sugamo Hōmu Iinkai）編

戦犯裁判の実相（Senpan saiban no jissō） 槙書房（発売：不二出版） 1981 700p

内容細目：第2章　裁判其他取扱の不当不法を物語る具体的事例　1．戦争裁判の前後を通じての不当な取扱ひの数々　(6)クーパン　（寺尾　勇太郎）　pp. 55-56　2．取調、裁判、弁護士の活動の不当を物語る事例の数々　(43)クーパン　（下村　侑）　p. 90

Title translation: The real conditions of the war crimes tribunals

Relevant section: Chapter 2, Concrete cases which demonstrate the injustice and illegality of court cases and other treatment, 1. The number of unfair cases of treatment through the pre and post war-tribunal process, (6) Kupang, TERAO Yūtarō, pp. 55-56.

2. A number of cases which tell of the unjustices of the investigations, judicial trials, and attornies' activities (43) Kupang, SHIMOMURA Yū, p. 90

杉村　優（SUGIMURA Masaru）著

日記に見る太平洋戦争（Nikki ni miru Taiheiyō Sensō） 文芸社　1999　441p

内容細目：第3章　チモール海波高し　アンボン、クーパン、ダーウィンは豪洲の生命線　pp. 73-94

Title translation: Seeing the Pacific War in diaries

Relevant section: Chapter 3, High surf on the Timor Sea, Ambon, Kupang, and Darwin are the Australian lifeline, pp. 73-94

関口　精一郎（SEKIGUCHI Seiichirō）著

陸海万里（Rikukai banri） 関口精一郎　1991　275p

内容細目：付　思い出に残る事　pp. 191-203

Title translation: Thousands of miles of land and sea

Relevant section: Attached, Remembering things, pp. 191-203　〔竹井氏蔵〕

関根　精次（SEKINE Seiji）著

炎の翼：海軍陸上攻撃機戦記　九六陸攻・式陸攻・雷爆撃戦（Honoo no tsubasa） 今日の話題社　1976　302p　（太平洋戦争ノンフィクション）

内容細目：クーパン飛行場降下　pp. 61-65

Title translation: Wings of fire: The war narrative of naval land attack airplanes
Relevant section: Dropping to the Kupang airfield, pp. 61-65

全国憲友会連合会編纂委員会（Zenkoku Ken'yūkai Rengōkai Hensan Iinkai）編
　日本憲兵正史（Nihon kenpei seishi）　全国憲友会連合会本部　1976　1450p
　内容細目：第五野戦憲兵隊　pp. 1064-1067
　第五野戦憲兵隊の終戦　pp. 1228-1231
　Title translation: An authentic history of the Japanese military police (Kempeitai)
　Relevant section: The 5th Field Kempeitai, pp. 1064-1067
　The end of the war for the 5th Field Kempeitai, pp. 1228-1231

全国台湾歩兵第一連隊連合会（Zenkoku Taiwan Hohei Daiichi Rentai Rengōkai）編
　軍旗はためくところ：台湾歩兵第一連隊史（Gunki hatameku tokoro: Taiwan Hohei Daiichi Rentai shi）　福岡　台湾歩兵第一連隊史編集部　1988　658p
　内容細目：チモール・スンバ列島・ジャワ篇　pp. 442-490
　Title translation: Military colors fluttering in the wind
　Relevant section: "Timor・Sunda archipelago・Java," pp. 442-490

捜索第四十八連隊戦友会（Sōsaku Daiyonjūhachi Rentai Sen'yūkai）編
　捜索第四十八連隊：汗と硝煙と轟音の記録（Sōsaku Daiyonjūhachi Rentai: ase to shōen to gōon no kiroku）〔捜索第四十八連隊戦友会〕　1982　120p
　Title translation: The 48th Reconnaissance Regiment: A record of sweat, gun smoke and the sounds of aircraft

曽祢　益（SONE Eki）著
　私のメモアール：霞が関から永田町へ（Watakushi no memoāru: Kasumigaseki kara Nagatachō e）　日刊工業新聞社（製作）　1974　274p
　内容細目：無条件降伏への道　帰国、政務局第二課長に　pp. 92-94
　Title translation: My memoirs: From Kasumigaseki to Nagatachō
　Relevant section: The road to unconditional surrender, returning home, becoming the head of second section in the Bureau of Political Affairs, pp. 92-94

60   I．単行書（Monographs）

大日本航空社史刊行会（Dainihon Kōkū Shashi Kankōkai）編
　航空輸送の歩み：昭和二十年迄（Kōkū yusō no ayumi: Shōwa nijūnen made）　日本航空協会　1975　685p
　内容細目：日ポ航空協定とチモール島定期航空　pp. 156-158
　横浜支所の思い出（大堀　修一）　pp. 451-453
　チモール島基地調査行（浅香　良一）　pp. 528-530
　わが青春の基地－チモール島デリーおよびスラバヤ日誌－（橋本　治忠）　pp. 584-593
　チモール島開拓飛行の思い出（川淵　龍彦）　pp. 594-596
　Title translation: Steps in air transport: To 1945.
　Relevant section: The Japan-Portugal aeronautical agreement and regular Timor flights, pp. 156-158
　　　Reminisces of the Yokohama branch office（ŌHORI Shūichi）, pp. 451-453
　　　A Timor Base Research Trip（ASAKA Ryōichi）, pp. 528-530
　　　The base of my youth: A diary of Dili, Timor Island and Surabaya（HASHIMOTO Harutada）, pp. 584-593
　　　Memories of a pioneering flight to Timor Island（KAWABUCHI Tatsuhiko）, pp. 594-596

台歩二会（Taiho Nikai）編
　軍旗と共に幾山河（Gunki to tomoni ikuyakawa）〔正篇〕、〔続編〕〔熊本市〕　台歩二会事務局　1977-81　2冊
　内容細目：(5)　ジャワ・チモール篇　pp. 221-249
　Title translation: Along with the military flag through innumerable mountains and rivers
　　Relevant section: (5) Java, Timor section, pp. 221-249　　　　　　〔熊本県〕

十中隊史編集事務局（Jū Chūtaishi Henshū Jimukyoku）編
　栄光の十中隊（Eikō no Jū Chūtai）〔大分〕　台歩二第十中隊会　1982　442p
　内容細目：第四章　南方編
　Title translation: The glorious 10th Company
　Relevant section: Chapter 4, Southern area

台湾歩兵第二連隊第九中隊（Taiwan Hohei Daini Rentai Daikyū Cuhūtai）編
戦友の碑：私等の小さな戦記（Sen'yū no hi: Watakushira no chiisana senki） 福岡　台湾歩兵第二連隊第九中隊会　1981　300p
Title translation: Monument of battlefield friends: Our little battle memories

高石　末吉（TAKAISHI Suekichi）著
戦費の調達と大陸各地の銀行（Senpi no chōtatsu to tairiku kakuchi no ginkō）
大蔵財務協会　1970　834p　（覚書終戦財政始末　第4巻）
内容細目：第39章　外地の作戦資金と外資金庫・南方開発金庫　6南方開発金庫の実績　pp. 380-392
第44章　南方と枢軸諸国との経済協定　蘭印・比島・チモール島・自由印度仮政府への「借款協定」と「金融協定」　5〔チモール島〕pp. 747-749
Title translation: The procurement of war expenditures and banks in various areas of the mainland China, (Memorandum of the end of war financial management, Volume 4)
Relevant section: Chapter 39, Strategies of outer land capital and foreign capital banks・the Southern Development Bank (Nanpō Kaihatsu Kinko), 6, The accomplishments of the Southern Development Bank, pp. 380-392.
Chapter 44, Economic agreements between the southern area and the Axis countries: "Loan agreements" and "financial agreements" with the Netherlands Indies, the Philippines, Timor island, and the Provisional Government of Free India, 5, [Timor Island], pp. 747-749

高木　秀雄（TAKAGI Hideo）著
南の孤島チモール応召：老軍医の記録（Minami no kotō Chimōru ōshū: rōgun'i no kiroku）〔n.p.〕〔高木秀雄刊〕〔n.d.〕61p
Title translation: The call to go to the solitary southern island Timor: The record of a senior medical doctor　　　　　　　　　　　　　　　　〔宮崎県〕

高木　秀雄（TAKAGI Hideo）著
チモール戦友会：第百九兵站病院（Chimōru sen'yūkai: Daihyaku-kyū Heitan Byōin）〔n.p.〕1975　66p
Title translation: Timor veterans' association: The 109th military hospital

〔研究会〕

高橋　徹（TAKAHASHI Tōru）著

忘れられた南の島（Wasurerareta minami no shima）　朝日新聞社　1963　205p（アサヒ・アドベンチュア・シリーズ）

Title translation: Forgotten southern island

高橋　光夫（TAKAHASHI Mitsuo）編

我等が思い出の記：独立野戦高射砲第三十二大隊部隊史（Warera ga omoide no ki: Dokuritsu Yasen Kōshahō Daisanjūni Daitai Butai shi）〔流山〕　高橋光夫　1991　258p

内容細目：第10章　チモール島の防空勤務　pp. 125-136

第11章　マライラダ河口（第二中隊戦没者追悼記）　pp. 137-146

第12章　クーバン特設高射砲部隊の戦闘（真野　英彦）　pp. 147-151

Title translation: The record of our memories: the history of the 32th independent field antiaircraft artillery battalion

Relevant section: Chapter 10, Air defense service in Timor Island

Chapter 11, Malai Lada river mouth (Memorial notes for the second company war dead)

Chapter 12, The battle of the special antiaircraft artillery troop in Kupang

竹林　良一（TAKEBAYASHI Ryōichi）著

干乾しにやさせない四十七（Hiboshiniya sasenai yonjūshichi）　熊本　竹林良一　1988　326, 5p

内容細目：チモール戦線　pp. 185-297

Title translation: Never let be dried up, the 47th-er

Relevant section: Timor front, pp. 185-297

立川　力造（TACHIKAWA Rikizō）編

回想する足跡（Kaisō suru sokuseki）　熊本市　台湾歩兵第二連隊第七中隊　1977　730p

Title translation: Reminiscences of footprints

〔竹井氏蔵〕

田中　淳夫（TANAKA Atsuo）著
　チモール知られざる虐殺の島（Chimōru shirarezaru gyakusatsu no shima）　彩流社　1988　250p
　Title translation: Timor: An unknown island of massacre

陳　千武（CHIN Senbu）著
　猟女犯：元台湾特別志願兵の追想（Ryōjohan: moto Taiwan tokubetsu shiganhei no tsuisō）　保坂登志子訳　京都　洛西書院　2000　237p
　Title translation: The crime of hunting women: a former Taiwanese special enlisted soldier's reminiscences

土橋　和典（TSUCHIHASHI Kazunori）編
　忠烈抜群・台湾高砂義勇兵の奮戦：台湾・高砂義勇兵に捧ぐ（Chūretsu batsugun, Taiwan Takasago Giyūhei no hunsen: Taiwan Takasago Giyūhei ni sasagu）　戦誌刊行会（発売：星雲社）　1994　357p
　内容細目：第5章　チモール島での台湾特別志願兵（鄭　春河）pp. 277-296
　Title translation: The finest unswerving loyalty-Taiwanese Takasago volunteer soldiers' bravely fighting: Dedicated to Taiwanese-Takasago volunteer soldiers
　Relevant section: Chapter 5, Taiwanese special enlisted soldiers on Timor island (TEI Shunga) pp. 277-296

土橋　勇逸（TSUCHIHASHI Yūitsu）著
　軍服生活四十年の想出（Gunpuku seikatsu yonjūnen no omoide）　土橋弘道編　勁草出版サービスセンター　1985　650p
　内容細目：第6編　大東亜戦争時代　第3節　チモール防衛記　pp. 481-499
　Title translation: Memories of forty years of uniformed life
　Relevant section: Volume 6, Greater East Asia War Period, Secition 3, Defense of Timor, pp. 481-499

鄭　春河（TEI Shunga）著
　台湾人元志願兵と大東亜戦争：いとほしき日本へ（Taiwanjin moto shiganhei to Dai Tōa Sensō: itooshiki nihon e）　展転社　1998　542p
　Title translation: Former volunteer Taiwanese soldiers and the Greater East Asia

I. 単行書（Monographs）

War

豊島　房太郎（TOYOSHIMA Fusataro）、赤塚　正一（AKATSUKA Shōichi）編
　濠北を征く：思い出の記　椰子の実は流れる（Gōhoku o iku: Omoide no ki, yashi no mi wa nagareru）　濠北方面遺骨引揚促進会　1956　530p　附図9枚
　内容細目：チモール島の思い出（依田　潔）pp. 470-473
　Title translation: Advancing towards northern Australia: Writing memories, drifting coconuts
　Relevant section: Recollections of Timor Island（YODA Kiyoshi）pp. 470-473

南星会（Nansei Kai）編
　第四十八師団（台湾混成旅団）戦史（Dai Yonjūhachi Shidan [Taiwan Konsei Ryodan] senshi）　市川市　南星会　1967　210p
　内容細目：第12章　ジャワからチモール島へ
　第13章　チモール島の防衛
　第14章　チモール撤退と白沢部隊の遭難　pp. 159-200
　Title translation: The 48th division (Taiwanese mixed brigade) war history
　Relevant section: Chapter 12: From Java to Timor Island
　Chapter 13: The defence of Timor Island
　Chapter 14: The evacuation of Timor and the Shirasawa unit getting lost
　　　　　　　　　　　　　　　　　　　　　　〔戦史室〕〔九大六〕

中村　泰秀（NAKAMURA Yasuhide）著
　歌集・南十字星（Kashū・Minamijūjisei）　日本放送教育協会　1990　221p
　Title translation: A song book・southern cross

中本　昇（NAKAMOTO Noboru）著
　われら独飛71のあしあと（Warera dokuhi 71 no ashiato）　愛知県稲沢市　家田酉行　1987　466p
　内容細目：独立飛行第71中隊の沿革　pp. 13-17
　地上の楽園ジャワ、チモール島（沢田三夫）pp. 138-139
　ジャワ、チモール島転戦（中西貞之助）pp. 139-140
　濠北チモール島作戦（石倉郁也）p. 147

Title translation: Footsteps of we the 71st Independent Air

Relevant section: Outlines of 71st Independent Air Company, pp. 13-17

Java as the paradise on the earth, Timor Island (SAWADA Mitsuo), pp. 138-139

Battles in Java, Timor Island (NAKANISHI Sadanosuke), pp. 139-140

The North Australia Timor Island campaign (ISHIKURA Ikuya), p. 147

中野校友会（Nakano Kōyūkai）編

陸軍中野学校（Rikugun nakano gakkō）　中野校友会　1978　18, 900p, 図版[8] p

内容細目：第16章　豪北における工作　pp. 592-598

Title translation: Army Nakano School

Relevant section: Chapter 16 North Australia mission, pp. 592-598

西村　庄五郎（NISHIMURA Shōgorō）著

エロマル物語（Eromaru monogatari）　熊本県水俣市　西村庄五郎　1979　78p

Title translation: Iliomar story 〔竹井氏蔵〕

日本航空協会（Nihon Kōkū Kyōkai）編

日本航空史：昭和前期編（Nihon kōkūshi: Shōwa zenki hen）　日本航空協会　1975　982p

内容細目：チモール島への定期航空の開設　pp. 765-768

Title translation: The history of Japanese aviation: Early Showa volume

Relevant section: The establishment of regular flights to Timor Island. pp. 765-768.

日本航空協会（Nihon Kōkū Kyōkai）編

日本民間航空史話（Nihon minkan kōku shiwa）　日本航空協会　1966　554p

内容細目：チモール島開拓飛行の思い出（川渕　竜彦）　pp. 267-269

Title translation: A historical discussion of Japanese civil aviation, pp. 267-269

Relevant section: Memories of frontier aviation on Timor Island (KAWABUCHI Tatsuhiko), pp. 267-269

畠山　清行（HATAKEYAMA Kiyoyuki）著

陸軍中野学校3：秘密戦史（Rikugun Nakano gakkō 3: Himitsu senshi）　番町書房

1973　318p

内容細目：歴史にもない豪州上陸　pp. 109-118

チモール島の混血ゲリラ　pp. 119-126

いっぱい食ったマッカーサー　pp. 126-133

Title translation: Nakano army school 3, Secret military history

Relevant section: The landing at Australia which never became history, pp. 109-118.

The mixed-blood guerillas of Timor Island, pp. 119-26

MacArthur eating well, pp. 126-33

林　えいだい（HAYASHI Eidai）著

台湾の大和魂（Taiwan no yamato damashii）　東方出版　2000　286p

内容細目：第3章　特別志願兵　2．血書志願　(3)　チモール島上陸　pp. 93-98

Title translation: Taiwanese Yamato Spirit

Relevant section: Chapter 3, Special enlisted soldiers, 2, Volunteers' signature in blood, (3) Landing on Timor Island pp. 93-98

林田　安司（HAYASHIDA Yasushi）著

恐竜吠ゆ：野重三大東亜戦史（Kyōryū hoyu: Yajūsan Dai Tōa senshi）　大統書房　1985　428p

内容細目：第7章　豪北方面の作戦　pp. 406-414

Title translation: A dinosaur howling: The Greater East Asia War History of the 3rd Medium Artillery Regiment

Relevant section: Chapter 7, Strategies for the North Australia direction, pp. 406-414

東　秋夫（HIGASHI Akio）著

奇蹟の中攻隊（Kiseki no chūkōtai）：予科練一期生の生還　光人社　1989　270p

内容細目：不死鳥のごとく〔チモール〕　pp. 121-141

Title translation: A miracle in a shock troop unit: The first preparatory military training students returning alive

Relevant section: Like a phoenix [Timor], pp. 121-141

東日本台歩二会連絡所（Higashi Nihon Taiho Nikai Renrakujo）編
榕樹の蔭：台湾歩兵第二連隊靖国大会特集号（Yōju no kage: Taiwan Hohei Daini Rentai Yasukuni taikai tokushuū gō）　三鷹市　東日本台歩二会連絡所　1973　96p
Title translation: The shade of banyan tree, the 2nd Taiwanese Infantry Regiment Yasukuni Shrine convention special issue　　　　〔竹井氏蔵〕

東ティモール日本占領期史料フォーラム（Higashi Timōru Nihon Senryōki Shiryō Fōramu）編
日本軍占領下の東ティモール視察復命書：日本・ポルトガル両国当事者の記録（Nihongun Senryōka no Higashi Timōru shisatsu fukumeisho: Nihon Porutogaru ryōkoku tōjisha no kiroku）　龍溪書舎　2005　178p
Title translation: A report on an inspection mission to East Timor during the Japanese military occupation: Records of both Japanese and Portuguese parties.

久生　十蘭（HISAO Jyūran）著
久生十蘭「従軍日記」（HISAO Jyūran "jūgun nikki"）　小林真二翻刻　講談社　2007　426p
内容細目：第4章　チモール島クーパン警備隊（自7月13日　至8月4日）[昭和18年]　pp. 207-282
Title translation: HISAO Jyūran "war diary"
Relevant section: Chapter 4, Timor Island Kupang Guard Unit (from July 13 to August 4) [1943], pp. 207-282

久金　彰（HISAKANE Akira）著
小スンダの空を行く：クーパン施設隊軍医長の記録　太平洋戦争とチモール島クーパン（Shō Sunda no sora o iku: Kūpan Shisetsutai gun'ichō no kiroku, Taiheiyō Sensō to Chimōrutō Kūpan）　高山　久金彰刊　1984　135p（『高山市医師会報』vol. 33, no. 2 - vol. 34, no. 1別刷）
Title translation: Going to the skies of the Lesser Sundas: The chief medical doctor's memories of the Kupang installation corps. The Pacific war and Kupang on Timor Island.

I．単行書（Monographs）

久金　彰（HISAKANE Akira）著
散華の世代から：太平洋戦争とチモール島クーパン　ある日本人医師の〈戦後の総決算〉（Sange no sedai kara: Taiheiyō Sensō to Chimōrutō Kūpan, aru Nihonjin ishi no "sengo no sōkessan"）　近代文芸社　1985　299p
Title translation: From the generation of fallen flowers. Pacific war and Kupang in Timor Island. One Japanese medical doctor's 〈total settlement in the post war period〉

久金　彰（HISAKANE Akira）著
散華の世代から：太平洋戦争とチモール島クーパン　クーパン海軍施設隊軍医長の記録　ある日本人医師の「戦後の総決算」（Sange no sedai kara: Taiheiyō Sensō to Chimōrutō Kūpan, Kūpan Kaigun Shisetsutai gun'i chō no kiroku, aru Nihonjin ishi no "sengo no sōkessan"）　高山　久金彰刊　1987　180p
Title translation: From the generation of fallen flowers. The record on Pacific war and Kupang on Timor Island by the chief Naval medical doctor; "The post-war total settlement" of a Japanese medical doctor

平松　鷹史（HIRAMATSU Takashi）編
郷土部隊奮戦史：第3（Kyōdo butai funsenshi: dai 3）　大分　大分合同新聞社　1963　525p
内容細目：チモール討伐　pp. 347-371
Title translation: The desperate fighting of a provincial corps
Relevant section: The conquering of Timor, pp. 347-371

平松　鷹史（HIRAMATSU Takashi）編
郷土部隊奮戦史（Kyōdo butai funsenshi）　大分　大分合同新聞社　1983　834p　2版
内容細目：チモール討伐　pp. 705-721
Title translation: The desperate fighting of a provincial corps
Relevant section: The conquering of Timor, pp. 705-721

福山　八郎（FUKUYAMA Hachirō）編
榕樹の蔭（Yōju no kage）　〔n.p.〕　台湾歩兵第二連隊会　1968　236p

内容細目：田中透連隊長追悼篇　pp. 13-54
チモール編、戦友消息編　pp. 101-150
チモール戦線風物点描編（立川　力造）　pp. 151-170
戦後の「チモール」を訪れて（高橋　徹）　pp. 223-224
Title translation: In the shade of the banyan tree
Relevant section: Memorial issue for TANAKA Tōru, regimental commander, pp. 13-54
Timor, veterans' news, pp. 101-150
A sketch of Timor operation line（TACHIKAWA Rikizō）, pp. 151-170
Visiting post-war "Timor"（TAKAHASHI Tōru）, pp. 223-224　　〔熊本県〕

藤山　一郎（FUJIYAMA Ichirō）著
歌声よひびけ南の空に：藤山一郎南方従軍記（Utagoe yo hibike minami no sora ni: Fujiyama Ichirō nanpō jūgunki）　光人社　1986　278p
内容細目：第四章　塹壕の中　最前線の心意気　pp. 121-126
Title translation: A singing voice of hope resonant in southern sky: FUJIYAMA Ichirō southern service account
Relevant section: Chapter 4, In a trench, the spirit of the front line, pp. 121-126

古荘　武雄（FURUSHŌ Takeo）編
高射砲第一〇三連隊史（Kōshahō Daihyaku-san Rentai shi）　稲城　田中書店　1979　463p
内容細目：第8章　第三中隊アンボンからチモールへ　pp. 88-93
Title translation: The history of the 103rd antiaircraft artillery regiment
Relevant section: Chapter 8, The 3rd company from Ambon to Timor, pp. 88-93

閉鎖機関整理委員会（Heisa Kikan Seiri Iinkai）編
閉鎖機関とその特殊清算（Heisa kikan to sono tokushu seisan）　在外活動関係閉鎖機関特殊清算事務所　1954　1626,309p
内容細目：南方開発金庫　pp. 257-263
南洋興発株式会社　pp. 465-474
Title translation: The closing agencies and its special liquidations
Relevant section: The Southern Development Bank（Nanpō Kaihatsu Kinko）, pp.

257-263.

The Nan'yō Kōhatsu K.K., pp. 465-474.

防衛庁防衛研修所戦史室（Bōeichō Bōei Kenshūjo Senshishitsu）著

蘭印攻略作戦（Ran'in kōryaku sakusen） 朝雲新聞社 1967 624p （戦史叢書 第3回配本）

内容細目：第7章 ジャワ外部要域の攻略 5．チモールの攻略 pp. 419-431

Title translation: The Dutch Indies Invasion Campaign（The war history series, distribution vol. 3）

Relevant Section: Chapter 7, The conquering of key areas outside Java, 5, Capturing Timor, pp. 419-431

防衛庁防衛研修所戦史室（Bōeichō Bōei Kenshūjo Senshishitsu）著

豪北方面陸軍作戦（Gōhoku hōmen rikugun sakusen） 朝雲新聞社 1969 675p （戦史叢書 第23回配本）

内容細目：第3章 ソロモン来攻、第16軍東へ延翼 1．チモールまで延翼 2．アラフラ海まで延翼

Title translation: The Northern Australia Area Army Campaign（The war history series, distribution vol. 23）

Relevant section: Chapter 3, Counterattack in the Solomons, The 16th Army extends its wings towards the east, 1. Extending its wings to Timor, 2. Extending its wings to the Arafura Sea

防衛庁防衛研修所戦史室（Bōeichō Bōei Kenshūjo Senshishitsu）著

蘭印・ベンガル湾方面海軍進攻作戦（Ran'in Bengaruwan hōmen kaigun shinkō sakusen） 朝雲新聞社 1969 696p （戦史叢書 第26回配本）

内容細目：第5章 航空基地の推進 14．チモールの攻略 pp. 335-370

Title translation: Naval Advance Campaing in the Dutch Indies・Bay of Bengal Area（The war history series, distribution vol. 26）

Relevant section: Chapter 5, Airfield thrusts, 14. The Timor operation, pp. 335-370

防衛庁防衛研修所戦史室（Bōeichō Bōei Kenshūjo Senshishitsu）著

南西方面陸軍作戦：マレー・蘭印の防衛（Nansei hōmen rikugun sakusen: Marē

Ran'in no bōei）朝雲新聞社　1976　485p　（戦史叢書　第92回配本）

内容細目：チモール陸軍防衛に変更　pp. 44-46

南東方面へ兵力転用相次ぐ　pp. 46-49

第十六軍アラフラ海まで延翼　pp. 49-53

第十九軍の創設　pp. 71-75

Title translation: Army Campaign in the Southwestern Area: The defense of Malaya-Netherlands Indies

Relevant section: Change to Army defense of Timor, pp. 44-46

Successive transfer of military force to the southeast, pp. 46-49

The 16th Army extends its wings to the Arafura Sea, pp. 49-53

The establishment of the 19th Army, pp. 71-75

歩兵第二二八連隊史編纂委員会（Hohei Dainihyaku-nijūhachi Rentaishi Hensan Iinkai）編

歩兵第二二八連隊史（Hohei Dainihyaku-nijūhachi Rentai shi）〔名古屋〕歩兵第二二八連隊史刊行会　1973　474 p

内容細目：第2部　精髄開花　第3章　チモール島攻略戦　pp. 136-162

Title translation: A history of the 228th Infantry Regiment

Relevant section: Part 2, The blooming spirit, Chapter 3, The Timor capturing operation pp. 136-162

蓬莱山吹会（Hōrai Yamabukikai）編

台湾山砲戦記：南十字の星のもと（Taiwan sanpō senki: minami jūji no hoshi no moto）熊本　蓬莱山吹会　1984　947 p. 附図5枚（チモール島図含む）

2版は1987年刊

内容細目：濠北篇　pp. 507-668

Title translation: (Under the southern cross): The military annals of Taiwanese mountain guns, 5 sheets of attached maps, (Map of Timor island included)

Relevant section: Northern Australia section, pp. 507-668

前川　清太郎（MAEKAWA Seitarō）著

ゆりかごの唄：戦時下のある青春（Yurikago no uta: senjika no aru seishun）日本図書刊行会（発売：近代文芸社）　1997　191p

内容細目：8．チモール　pp. 141-171

Title translation: Songs of cradle: A youth in wartime

Relevant section: 8, Timor, pp. 141-171

前田　透（MAEDA Tōru）著

チモール記（Chimōru ki）　蒼土舎（発売：東京音楽社）　1982　260p

Title translation: An Account of Timor

舛田　正義（MASUDA Seigi）著

チモール島宣撫班物語（Chimōrutō senbuhan monogatari）〔n.p.〕〔舛田正義刊〕〔1987〕　223p

Title translation: The story of a Timor Island pacification squad　〔研究会〕

松川　久仁男（MATSUKAWA Kunio）著

独立を忘れた日本（Dokuritsu o wasureta Nihon）　那覇　沖縄経済社　1988　200p

内容細目：チモール島の生活　pp. 143-152

Title translation: The Japan which forgot independence

Relevant section: Life on Timor Island, pp. 143-152　〔沖縄県〕

松井　やより（MATSUI Yayori）ほか編

女性国際戦犯法廷の全記録Ⅰ（Josei Kokusai Senpan Hōtei no zenkiroku I）　緑風出版　2002　352p

内容細目：第1部　ドキュメント女性国際戦犯法廷　第3章　法廷3日目（2000年12月10日）東ティモール　pp. 212-216

［報告］「法廷」とVAWW-NETジャパン調査チーム・ビデオ塾の役割　東ティモール（ポルトガル領ティモール）－はじめて被害を公に（古沢希代子）pp. 276-279

Title translation: Complete records of International Women's War Crime Tribunal I

Relevant section: Part 1 Document of International Women's War Crime Tribunal, Chapter 3 Hearings 3rd day (December 10, 2000), East Timor, pp. 212-216

[Report] "Tribunal" and roles of VAWW-NET Japan Investigation Team・Video Juku, East Timor (Portuguese Timor) － Coming out sufferings for the first time (FURUSAWA Kiyoko), pp. 276-216

松井　やより（MATSUI Yayori）ほか編
女性国際戦犯法廷の全記録 II（Josei Kokusai Senpan Hōtei no zenkiroku II）　緑風出版　2002　443p
内容細目：第 1 部　起訴状　各国起訴状　東ティモール　pp. 67-72
Title translation: Complete records of International Women's War Crime Tribunal II
Relevant section: Part 1 Indictment, Country indictment, East Timor, pp. 67-72

松川　久仁男（MATSUKAWA Kunio）著
補充兵日記（Hojūhei nikki）　泰流社　1979　236p
Title translation: Reinforcement troop's diary　　　　　　　　　　〔沖縄県〕

松野　明久（MATSUNO Akihisa）著
東ティモール独立史（Higashi Timōru dokuritsushi）　早稲田大学出版部　2002　295p
内容細目：ポルトガル領ティモール　pp. 13-15
Title translation: History of East Timorese independence
Relevant section: Portuguese Timor, pp. 13-15

三浦　重介（MIURA Jūsuke）著
チモール逆無電（Chimōru gyaku muden）　自由アジア社　1961　289p
Title translation: Timor deceptive radio operation

湊　集（MINATO Atsumu）著
豪北派遣海部隊防衛作戦従軍記（Gōhoku haken Umi Butai bōei sakusen jūgunki）
ヒューマン・ドキュメント社（発売：星雲社）　1986　87p
Title translation: A military memoir on the defense strategy for the Northern Australia-bound Umi infantry unit

南　不二夫（MINAMI Fujio）著　（本名　山口亘利の項参照）
戦犯六人の死刑囚（Senpan rokunin no shikeishū）　飛鳥書店　1953　227p
Title translation: Six condemned war criminal inmates
Translator's note: See also the republished version under the author's real name, YAMAGUCHI Watari.

I. 単行書 (Monographs)

村上　元三 (MURAKAMI Genzō) 著
思い出の時代作家たち (Omoide no jidai sakka tachi)　文芸春秋　1995　277p
Title translation: Recollection of epoch-creating writers

森　晴治 (MORI Haruji) 著
戦塵 (Senjin)　福岡　葦書房　1978　196p
Title translation: Reminiscenes of War

森島　守人 (MORISHIMA Morito) 著
真珠湾・リスボン・東京：続・一外交官の回想 (Shinjuwan, Risubon, Tōkyō: zoku ichi gaikōkan no kaisō)　岩波書店　1950　179p　(岩波新書)
Title translation: Pearl Harbor・Lisbon・Tokyo: [Continuation] One diplomat's reminiscences.

柳　勇 (YANAGI Isamu) 著
長程万里：回顧録 (Chōtei banri: kaiko roku)　福岡　城島印刷　1989　16, 489p
内容細目：チモール島の戡定戦　pp. 441-460
Title translation: The long great distance: memoirs
Relevant section: Pacification campaign of Timor Island

山口　重晴 (YAMAGUCHI Shigeharu) 著
星ぞらの怪電波：神風は戦後吹いたか (Hoshizora no kaidenpa: kamikaze wa sengo fuita ka)　〔奈良〕〔山口重晴刊〕　1993　242p
Title translation: Mysterious radio waves in the star-filled sky: Divine wind disappointedly blew after the war.

山口　重晴 (YAMAGUCHI Shigeharu) 著
ティモール島星空の勇者たち：輝け南の島の知謀戦 (Timōruto, hoshizora no yūsha tachi: Kagayake minami no shima no chibōsen)　新風舎　2003　241p
Title translation: Timor Island, heroes of the star-filled sky: The glistening brilliant strategic war on a southern island

山口　亘利（YAMAGUCHI Watari）著

南海の死刑囚独房（Nankai no shikeishū dokubō）　国書刊行会　1982　190p　（戦犯叢書4　山下武責任編集）

南不二夫『戦犯六人の死刑囚』改題再刊

Title translation: South seas condemned cell

Notes: The book is a re-titled edition of *Six condemned war criminal inmates* by MINAMI Fujio（pseud.）.

山田　国太郎（YAMADA Kunitarō）著

明治少年の歩み：山田国太郎の一生（Meiji shōnen no ayumi: Yamada Kunitarō no isshō）　愛知県木曽川町　山田国太郎先生「回顧録」を出版する会　1979　344p

内容細目：小スンダ列島、師団初度巡視　pp. 249-252

Title translation: A path of Meiji boy: life of Yamada Kunitarō

Relevant section: The Lesser Sunda archipelago: First Divisional Research

山田　満（YAMADA Mitsuru）編著

東ティモールを知るための50章（Higashi Timōru o shirutame no gojusshō）　明石書店　2006　315p　（エリア・スタディーズ60）

内容細目：第3章　大国のはざまで－日本占領下の東ティモール　pp. 25-30

第4章　性暴力被害者たちの60年－日本軍慰安婦問題　pp. 31-34

Title translation: 50 chapters to understand East Timor

Relevant section: Chapter 3, In between great powers - Japanese occupied East Timor, pp. 25-30

Chapter 4, Sixty years for victims of sexual violence - the issue of Japanese military comofort women, pp. 31-34

山辺　雅男（YAMABE Masao）著

海軍落下傘部隊（Kaigun Rakkasan Butai）　鱒書房　1956　200p　（戦記シリーズ16　海の空挺隊戦記）

内容細目：クーパン降下作戦　pp. 83-114

Title translation: Navy paratroop unit

Relevant section: The Kupang landing operation, pp. 83-114

吉田　千代吉（YOSHIDA Chiyokichi）編
戦史：歩兵第四十七連隊第三大隊第十中隊（Senshi: Hohei Daiyonjushichi Rentai Daisan Daitai Daiju Chutai）　古河市　1981　109p
内容細目：チモール島警備「奇跡の生還」（後藤　実）　pp. 78-80
Title translation: War history, No. 10 Company of the 47th Infantry Regiment, 3rd Battalion
Relevant section: Guarding Timor Island, "miracle return to life" (GOTŌ Minoru), pp. 78-80　　　　　　　　　　　　　　　　　〔戦史室〕

吉田　一（YOSHIDA Hajime）
入道雲は泣いていた（Nyūdōgumo wa naite ita）　弘文堂　1963　236p
内容細目：豪州と対峙するチモール島　pp. 82-88
朝倉中尉の戦死　pp. 89-94
Title translation: Thunderheads were crying
Relevant section: Timor Island confronting Australia, pp. 82-88
Fall in battle of Lieutenant ASAKURA, pp. 89-94

若八会九州支部（Wakahachikai Kyūshū shibu）編
戦塵にまみれた青春：補給戦の真相と陸経幹候隊教育（Senjin ni mamireta seishun: hokyūsen no shinsō to rikukei kanokōtai kyōiku）〔出版地不明〕若八会九州支部　1977　892p
内容細目：あヽチモール島クーパン（長崎道孝）　pp. 62-65
Title translation: Youth covered with the dust of battle: truth of logistics war and education of candidates for senior Army Paymaster unit
Relevant section: Ah, Kupang, Timor Island (NAGASAKI Michitaka)　〔昭和館〕

名鑑台湾歩兵第一連隊（Meikan Taiwan hohei daiichi rentai）〔n.p.〕撰興社　1987 1169p
内容細目：ジャワからチモール島へ、チモール島の防衛　pp. 518-525
Title translation: (A directory)The 1st Taiwan Infantry Regiment
Relevant section: From Java to Timor Island: The defence of Timor Island, pp. 518-525　　　　　　　　　　　　　　　　　〔熊本県〕

台湾歩兵第一連隊第六中隊戦闘小史：太平洋方面（Taiwan Hohei Daiichi Rentai Dairoku Chūtai sentō shōshi: Taiheiyō hōmen） 鹿児島　海の灯会　1979　41p
内容細目：チモール島より引揚まで（岡元藤吉）　pp. 9-13
Title translation: A brief combat history of the 1st Taiwanese Infantry Regiment, 7th Company: The Pacific Campaign
Relevant section: Repatriation from Timor Island（OKAMOTO Tōkichi）, pp. 9-13

II. 雑誌論文（Periodical Articles）

戦前・戦中篇 [Prewar-Wartime Materials]

浅香　良一（ASAKA Ryōichi）
　チモール島に飛びて（Chimōrutō ni tobite）『科学画報』（Kagaku gahō）　30(3)：1941. 3　pp. 52-53
　Title translation: Flying to Timor Island

足立　和雄（ADACHI Kazuo）
　チモール島の王様（Chimōrutō no ōsama）『新青年』（Shin seinen）　24(4)：1943. 4　pp. 62-63
　Title translation: The kings of Timor Island

大久保　武雄（ŌKUBO Takeo）
　太平洋決戦とチモール（Taiheiyō kessen to Chimōru）『太平洋』（Taiheiyō）　5(1)：1942. 1　pp. 50-60
　Title translation: Decisive battles of the Pacific and Timor

大久保　武雄（ŌKUBO Takeo）
　チモールに旅して（Chimōru ni tabishite）『サンデー毎日』（Sandē mainichi）　21(9)：1942. 3. 8　pp. 40-41
　Title translation: Traveling to Timor

金子　光晴（KANEKO Mitsuharu）
　チモール島の日本人酋長（Chimōrutō no Nihonjin shūchō）『婦人子供報知』（Fujin kodomo hōchi）　(137)：1936. 11　pp. 12-13
　Title translation: Japanese tribal chief on Timor Island

川渕　龍彦（KAWABUCHI Tatsuhiko）
　チモール島監禁記（Chimōrutō kankinki）『時局雑誌』（Jikyoku zasshi）　1(5)：

1942　pp. 48-53

Title translation: A journal of imprisonment on Timor Island

齋藤　太郎（SAITŌ Tarō）

葡領チモール島概観（Poryō Chimōrutō gaikan）『太平洋』（Taiheiyō）3(9)：1940　pp. 79-91

Title translation: An overview of the Portugese territory of Timor Island

齋藤　太郎（SAITŌ Tarō）

葡領チモールの経済資源と開発の現状（一）（Poryō Chimōru no keizai shigen to kaihatsu no genjō (1)）『南洋』（Nan'yō）27(3): 1941　pp. 2-14

Title translation: The current situation of economic resources and development of Portuguese Timor (1)

齋藤　太郎（SAITŌ Tarō）

葡萄牙領チモール植民地（Porutogaruryō Chimōru shokuminchi）『旅』（Tabi）18(1): 1941. 1　pp. 11-12

Title translation: The Portuguese colonial territory of Timor

斎藤　裕蔵（SAITŌ Yūzō）

葡領チモールを繞る外交戦（Poryō Chimōru o meguru gaikōsen）（上）、（下）『新亜細亜』（Shin Ajia）3(12)：1941　pp. 47-55，4(1): 1942　pp. 103-114

Title translation: The diplomatic war related to Portuguese Timor

〔同盟通信〕シンガラジャ支局（〔Dōmei Tsūshin〕Shingaraja shikyoku）

チモール島の報告　接敵第一線で米作り（Chimōrutō no hōkoku, setteki daiissen de komezukuri）『大東亜報』（Daitōahō）昭和19年11月15日号　pp. 22-24

Title translation: Timor report, producing rice at the front line facing the enemy

長谷川　直美（HASEGAWA Naomi）

チモール飛行（Chimōru hikō）『航空朝日』（Kōkū asahi）2(3): 1941. 3　pp. 24-25, 143-147

Title translation: Timor flight

早坂　一郎（HAYASAKA Ichirō）
　ポルトガル領ティモールの地質と鉱産（Porutogaruryō Timōru no chishitsu to kōsan）『南支南洋』（Nanshi nan'yō）（191）: 1941. 5　pp. 73-77
　Title translation: Geology and mining production of Portuguese Timor

L・ヘバイス（L. HEBAISU）
　チモール群島の自然と農業（Chimōru guntō no shizen to nōgyō）『南洋経済研究資料』（Nan'yō keizai kenkyū shiryō）3(3): 1940　pp. 46-54
　Title translation: Nature and agriculture in Timor archipelago

米田　実（MAIDA Minoru）
　大東亜戦争とチモール問題（Dai Tōa sensō to Chimōru mondai）『国際法外交雑誌』（Kokusaihō gaikō zasshi）41(2): 1942　pp. 38-56［(150)-(168)］
　Title translation: The Great East Asia War and the Timor problem

間宮　茂輔（MAMIYA Shigesuke）
　死都：デリーの十日間（Shito: derī no tōkakan）『日本評論』（Nihon hyōron）17 (9): 1942. 9　pp. 158-170
　Title translation: Dead city: ten days in Dili

松永　寿雄（MATSUNAGA Hisao）
　太平洋航空の現状と将来　チモール島に就て（Taiheiyō kōkū no genjō to shōrai, Chimōrutō ni tsuite）『旬刊講演集』（Junkan kōenshū）19(18): 1941.6　pp. 18-24
　Title translation: The current conditions and future of the Pacific flights, about Timor Island

松永　寿雄（MATSUNAGA Hisao）
　チモールに飛ぶ（Chimōru ni tobu）『文藝春秋』（Bungei shunjū）19(12): 1941　pp. 164-169
　Title translation: Flying to Timor

II. 雑誌論文 (Periodical Articles)

松原　晩香 (MATSUBARA Bankō)

　南方空路の拠点、チモール島はどんな所か (Nanpō kūro no kyoten, Chimōrutō wa donna tokoro ka) 『時局雑誌』(Jikyoku zasshi)　1(3): 1942　pp. 86-89

　Title translation: Base of the southern air-route, what kind of a place is Timor Island?

三吉　朋十 (MIYOSHI Tomokazu)

　南方メモ　チモール・クーパン (Nanpō memo, Chimōru, Kūpan) 『報道写真』(Hōdō shashin)　2(6): 1942. 6　p. 20

　Title translation: South area memorandum, Timor・Kupang

山辺生 (YAMABE)

　チモール島とその附近 (Chimōrutōto sonofukin) 『台湾時報』(Taiwan jihō)　23(12): 1941　pp. 93-96

　Title translation: Timor Island and its neighboring areas

横田　喜三郎 (YOKOTA Kisaburō)

　常設仲裁裁判所判例研究　14　ティモル島事件 (Jōsetsu chūsai saibansho hanrei kenkyū, 14, Timōrutō jiken) 『国際法外交雑誌』(Kokusaihō gaikō zasshi)　36(3): 1937　pp. 286-298

　Title translation: The study of legal precedents in permanent arbitration courts, 14, the case of Timor Island

英国の買収せんとする南太平洋チモール島 (Eikoku no baisyūsen to suru minami Taiheiyō Chimōrutō) 『有終』(Yūshū)　(246): 1934. 9　pp. 109-111

　Title translation: The South Pacific Timor Island which Britain is trying to purchase

感状　チモール攻略の神戸中隊、同配属部隊 (Kanjō Chimōru kōryaku no Kōbe Chūtai, dō haizoku butai) 『内外調査資料』(Naigai chōsa shiryō)　15(12): 1944. 1　pp. 764-765

　Title translation: A certificate of gratitude, The Timor conquering Kobe company, and attached units

第79回帝国議会資料（中編） 第2 軍務大臣の戦況報告 東条陸軍大臣 （3） チモール島方面（Dai-79-kai Teikoku Gikai shiryō（chūhen）dai-2 Gunmu Daijin no senkyō hōkoku TŌJŌ Rikugun Daijin（3）Chimōrutō hōmen）『内外調査資料』（Naigai chōsa shiryō） 14(3): 1942. 5 p. 10

    Title translation: The 79th Imperial Parliament materials (second volume), No. 2, Military situation report by the Minister of Military Affairs, Minister of Army TŌJŌ, (3) Timor island operation

チモール島買収説再燃（Chimōrutō baishūsetsu sainen）『有終』（Yūshū）（256）: 1935. 3 p. 88

    Title translation: Reviving the Timor Island purchase rumor

「チモール飛行」を語る〈座談会〉堂本内務部長他（'Chimōru hikō o kataru, "zadankai" Dōmoto naimu buchō hoka）『南洋群島』（Nan'yō gunto） 8(1): 1942 pp. 86-91

    Title translation: Discussion on "flying Timor",〈round table discussion〉the chief of the Department of Internal Affairs DŌMOTO, and others　　〔山口〕

チモルへの日本航空線（Chimoru e no Nihon kōkūsen）『南洋経済研究資料』（Nan'yō keizai kenkyū shiryō） 5(1): 1942 pp. 6-9

    Title translation: Japan Air Lines to Timor

南方共栄圏航空事情（Nanpō Kyōeiken kōkū jijō）『内外調査資料』（Naigai chōsa shiryō） 13(11): 1941. 12 253,29 p

    内容細目：チモール事情に就て（浅香良一述） pp. 224-248、附 日葡航空協定

    Title translation: Aviation conditions in the Southern Co-prosperity sphere

    Relevant section: About the condition of Timor (told by ASAKA Ryōichi), pp. 224-248, supplement, Japan-Portugal aviation agreement

包囲陣を截る（チモール航路開拓座談会）(Hōijin o kiru, Chimōru kōro kaitaku zadankai)『航空朝日』（Kōkū asahi） 3(1): 1942.1 pp. 154-161

    Title translation: Break the siege (round table discussion on Timor flight route pioneers)

葡領植民地チモールの為替基金規定（Poryō shokuminchi Chimōru no kawase kikin kitei）『外務省通商局日報』（Gaimushō tsūshōkyoku nippō）　第14号　昭和10年1月25日　1935　p. 86

　　Title translation: Regulations for the foreign exchange fund for the Portuguese colony of Timor

葡領チモール植民地事情（Poryō Chimōru shokuminchi jijō）『有終』（Yūshū）(273): 1936. 8　pp. 146-147

　　Title translation: Portuguese Timor colonial conditions

葡領チモール貿易年報（1933年）昭和10年5月18日附在葡帝国臨時代理公使隈部種樹報告（Poryō Chimōru bōeki nenpō, 1933 nen, Shōwa 10 nen 5 gatsu 18 nichi zuke zai Poteikoku Rinji Dairi Kōshi Kumabe Taneki hōkoku）『海外経済事情』（Kaigai keizai jijō）　1940年第14号　pp. 53-54

　　Title translation: The 1933 annual report on Portugese Timor trading, reported by KUMABE Taneki, chargé d'affairs to the Portuguese Empire, on May 18, 1935

葡領チモール植民地貿易年報（1934年）昭和11年12月3日附在葡帝国臨時代理公使大森元一郎報告（Poryō Chimōru shokuminchi bōeki nenpō, 1934 nen, Shōwa 11 nen 12 gatsu 3 nichi zuke zai Poteikoku Rinji Dairi Kōshi Ōmori Gen'ichirō hōkoku）『海外経済事情』（Kaigai keizai jijō）　1937年第7号　pp. 99-102

　　Title translation: The 1934 annual report on Portugese Timor colonial trading, reported by Ōmori Gen'ichirō, chargé d'affairs to the Portuguese Empire, on December 3, 1936.

葡国政府 Companhia Ultramarina de Petroleos 会社にチモール島石油試掘権許与（Pokoku seifu Companhia Ultramarina de Petroleos kaisha ni Chimōrutō sekiyu shikutsuken kyoyo）

　　『外務省通商局日報』（Gaimushō tsūshōkyoku nippō）　第251号　1939年11月1日　1939　p. 1390

　　Title translation: Receiving oil test drilling rights in Timor Island from the Portuguese Government for the Companhia Ultramarina de Petroleos

葡領チモール植民地貿易状況（1939年）（Poryō Chimōru shokuminchi bōeki jōkyō, 1939 nen）『外務省通商局日報』（Gaimushō tsūshōkyoku nippō）第198号　1940年8月27日　1940　pp. 1156-1157

　　Title translation: The trading situation of the Portuguese colony of Timor (1939)

蘭領チモール島事情（Ranryō Chimōrutō jijō）『参考記事摘要』（Sankō kiji tekiyō）20(6): 1942　pp. 309-360

　　Title translation: The situation of Dutch territory of Timor Island

Companhia Ultramarina de Petroleos 会社定款（Companhia Ultramarina de Petroleos kaisha teikan）

　　『外務省通商局日報』（Gaimushō tsūshōkyoku nippō）第251号　1939年11月1日　1939　p. 1390

　　Title translation: The Companhia Ultramarina de Petroleos articles of incorporation

戦後篇 [Postwar writings]

秋元　実（AKIMOTO Minoru）

餓兵戦記（Gahei senki）(9) – (18) 『静岡の教育』（Shizuoka no kyōiku） (45) – : 1984年2月　ページ数, (46) pp. 82-86, (47) pp. 80-86, (48) pp. 80-86, (49) pp. 80-86, (50) pp. 77-86, (51) pp. 81-88, (52) pp. 81-88, (53) pp. 81-88, (54) pp. 81-88
Title translation: Starving soldiers' war (9)-(18)

後藤　乾一（GOTŌ Ken'ichi）

戦時期「ティモール問題」の外交史的考察（Senjiki "Timōrut mondai" no gaikōshiteki kōsatsu）『社会科学討究』（Shakai kagaku tōkyū） 34(3): 1989　pp. 235-276
Title translation: Considerations on the wartime "Timor problem" from a diplomatic history perspective

後藤　乾一（GOTŌ Ken'ichi）

昭和期南進論と「ティモール島問題」（Shōwaki nanshinron to "Timōrutō mondai"）『社会科学討究』（Shakai kagaku tōkyū） 39(1): 1993　pp. 47-66
Title translation: Shōwa period south ward advance ideology and "the issue of Timor Island"

後藤　乾一（GOTŌ Ken'ichi）

東チモール独立とマカオ返還（Higashi Timōru dokuritsu to Makaohenkan）『世界』（Sekai） (672): 2000. 3　pp. 209-219
内容細目：第二次世界大戦とポルトガル植民地　pp. 214-217
Title translation: Independence of East Timor and reversion of Macao
Relevant section: Second World War Portuguese Colony

冨林　敏雄（TOMIBAYASHI Toshio）

チモール島の測地と逆無電（Chimōrutō no sokuchi to gyakumuden）『偕行』（Kaikō） (567): 1998. 3　pp. 21-22
Title translation: Land survey and deceptive radio operation in Timor Island

〔遊就館〕

野村　佳正（NOMURA Yosimasa）

軍事作戦と軍事占領政策：第２次世界大戦期東チモールの場合（Gunji sakusen to gunji senryō seisaku: Dainiji Sekai Taisenki Higashi Chimōru no baai）『戦史研究年報』（Senshi kenkyū nenpō）　7: 2004. 3　pp. 47-68

Title translation: Military operations and military occupation policy: the case of East Timor during the Second World War

古沢　希代子（FURUKAWA Kiyoko）

再会までの50年―手を結ぶ日豪旧軍人（Saikaimade no gojūnen―te o musubu nichigō kyūgunjin）『世界』（Sekai）（587）: 1993. 10　pp. 78-81

Title translation: The 50 years before the reunion: Japanese and Australian veterans' friendship

前田　透（MAEDA Tōru）

静かなる南海の戦記（Shizukanaru Nankainosenki）『文藝春秋』（Bungei shunju）38(2): 1970　pp. 204-233

Title translation: War memories in the calm South sea

前田　透（MAEDA Tōru）

神と共にとどまれ－チモールの友へ（Kami to tomoni todomare – Chimōru no tomo e）『中央公論』（Chūō kōron）91(1): 1976　pp. 204-209

Title translation: Stay with God: To Timorese friends

三浦　重介（MIURA Jūsuke）

チモール島の楠三成（Chimōrutō no Kusunoki Mitsushige）『文藝春秋』（Bungei shunju）39(9): 1961. 9　pp. 190-210

Title translation: Kusunoki Mitsushige on Timor Island

三宅　勝久（MIYAKE Katsuhisa）

老人たちが語る「日本軍の記憶」（Rōjin tachi ga kataru "Nihongun no kioku"）『週刊金曜日』（Shūkan kinyōbi）（406）: 2002. 4/5　pp. 20-21

Title translation: "Memories of Japanese Military" told by the elderly

山口　昌男（YAMAGUCHI Masao）

地揺れする辺境から―チモールからの手紙（Chiyuresuru henkyōkara: Chimōru karano tegami）『中央公論』（Chūō kōron）1975. 11　pp. 58-77

Title translation: From the land shaking marginal area: A letter from Timor

吉田　一（YOSHIDA Hajime）

落日のチモールの空に（Rakujitsu no Chimōru no sora ni）『特集丸』（Tokushū maru）3（3): 1959. 3　pp. 166-171

Title translation: To the setting-sun sky of Timor

Ⅲ. 地図類（Maps）

岡第一六〇一部隊（Oka Daiichi-roku-maru-ichi Butai）編
　（極秘）チモール島兵要地誌図　西部（Chimōrutō heiyō chishi zu, seibu）〔n.p.〕
　岡第一六〇一部隊　1944　1枚（78×110cm）　縮尺1：250,000
　Title translation:（Top secret）A military topography of Timor Island, western part

岡第一六〇一部隊（Oka Daiichi-roku-maru-ichi Butai）編
　（極秘）チモール島兵要地誌図　東部（Chimōrutō heiyō chishi zu, tōbu）〔n.p.〕
　岡第一六〇一部隊　1944　1枚（78×110cm）　縮尺1：250,000
　Title translation:（Top secret）A military topography of Timor Island, eastern part

海外鉱業協会（Kaigai Kōgyō Kyōkai）編
　葡萄牙領チモール島（Porutogaruryō Chimōrutō）　海外鉱業協会〔n.d.〕1枚（79×109cm）
　Title translation: Portuguese territory of Timor Island　　〔広大〕

海外鉱業協会（Kaigai Kōgyō Kyōkai）編
　葡萄牙領チモール島図（Porutogaruryō Chimōrutō zu）　海外鉱業協会　1937　1枚（108×77cm）
　scale　1: 1,000,000
　Title translation: Map of Portuguese Possessions on Timor Island　〔国学院〕

参謀本部（Sanbō Honbu）
　チモール島兵要地誌資料図（其ノ一）ポルトガル領チモール島全図（Chimōrutō heiyō chishi shiryō zu (sono ichi), Porutogaruryō Chimōrutō zenzu）　参謀本部　1943　1枚
　Title Translation: A military topography of Timor island, Part 1, Map of Portuguese Timor whole area　〔摂南〕

参謀本部（Sanbō Honbu）

　クーパン（Kūpan）　参謀本部　1943　1枚（48×64cm）（秘　チモール五十万分一図　壹貳南二五〇一　旧蘭領チモール州）　縮尺1：500,000

　Title translation: Kupang

　（Scale　1：500,000）

参謀本部（Sanbō Honbu）

　チモール島西部（Chimōrutō seibu）　参謀本部　1943　1枚（48×64cm）（秘　チモール五十万分一図　壹貳南ハ五〇二　旧蘭領チモール州　葡領チモール）　縮尺1：500,000

　Title translation: West part of Timor Island

　（Scale　1：500,000）

参謀本部（Sanbō Honbu）

　チモール島東部（Chimōrutō tōibu）　参謀本部　1943　1枚（48×64cm）（秘　チモール五十万分一図　壹壹南ハ五〇四　葡領チモール　旧蘭領チモール州）　縮尺1：500,000

　Title translation: East part of Timor Island

　（Scale　1：500,000）

芹沢　馨吾（SERIZAWA Keigo）編

　大東亜分布図10．ジャワ、小スンダ列島（Dai Tōa bunpuzu 10. Jawa, Shō-Sunda rettō）　統正社　1943　2枚　縮尺1：3,000,000

　Title translation: Cartography of Greater East Asia 10. Java, the Lesser Sunda archipelago（scale 1：3,000,000）

大日本帝国陸地測量部（Dainihon Teikoku Rikuchi Sokuryōbu）

　南方図　3号　ミンダナオ南部－セレベス・ティモール（Nanpō zu, 3-gō Mindanao nanbu, Serebesu, Timōru）　陸地測量部　1941　1枚（108×79cm）　縮尺1：2,000,000

　Title translation: Southern map no. 2, Southern part of Mindanao－Celebes-Timor

〔九大経〕

大日本帝国陸地測量部（Dainihon Teikoku Rikuchi Sokuryōbu）

太平洋周域与地図　13号　ボルネオ西部・ティモール（Taiheiyō shūiki yo chizu, 13-gō Boruneo seibu, Timōru）　陸地測量部　1942　1枚（80×109cm）　縮尺1：2,000,000

Title translation: Map of Occeania and its vicinity, no. 13, west part of Borneo-Timor

（scale 1: 2,000,000）　　　　　　　　　　　　　　　　　　〔九大経〕

陸地測量部・参謀本部（Rikuchi Sokuryōbu Sanbō Honbu）

ATAMBOEA　参謀本部　1942　1枚（61×53cm）（秘　十万分一図チモール島6号）　縮尺1：100,000

陸地測量部・参謀本部（Rikuchi Sokuryōbu Sanbō Honbu）

NOEAF MOETIS　参謀本部　1942　1枚（58×46cm）（秘　十万分一図チモール島10号）　縮尺1：100,000

陸地測量部・参謀本部（Rikuchi Sokuryōbu Sanbō Honbu）

KEFANNANOE　参謀本部　1942　1枚（57×43cm）（秘　十万分一図チモール島11号）　縮尺1：100,000

陸地測量部・参謀本部（Rikuchi Sokuryōbu Sanbō Honbu）

TOBAKI　参謀本部　1942　1枚（58×46cm）（秘　十万分一図チモール島12号）　縮尺1：100,000

陸地測量部・参謀本部（Rikuchi Sokuryōbu Sanbō Honbu）

NOIL BESIAM　参謀本部　1942　1枚（57×43cm）（秘　十万分一図チモール島15号）　縮尺1：100,000

陸地測量部・参謀本部（Rikuchi Sokuryōbu Sanbō Honbu）

SOË　参謀本部　1942　1枚（52×46cm）（秘　十万分一図チモール島16号）　縮尺1：100,000

Ⅲ．地図類（Maps）

陸地測量部・参謀本部（Rikuchi Sokuryōbu Sanbō Honbu）
　NOENKOLO　参謀本部　1942　1枚（54×56cm）（秘　十万分一図チモール島17-18号）　縮尺1：100,000

陸地測量部・参謀本部（Rikuchi Sokuryōbu Sanbō Honbu）編
　チモール概見図（秘）（Chimōru gaiken zu）　陸地測量部・参謀本部　1943　1枚（73×96cm）　縮尺1：250,000
　scale　1: 250,000
　Title translation: Timor survey map　　　　　　　　　　　　　　　　〔研究会〕

Ⅳ. 戦友会誌（Veteran's organization newsletters）

『南星』（Nansei）　第1−11号　台湾軍第四十八師団南星会機関誌

　　創刊号　　　昭和52年9月　　38 p
　　第2号　　　昭和53年9月　　63 p
　　第3号　　　昭和54年9月　　97 p
　　第4号　　　昭和56年4月　　75 p
　　第5号　　　昭和57年6月　　85 p
　　第6号　　　昭和58年4月　　93 p
　　第7号　　　昭和59年9月　　119 p
　　第8号　　　昭和61年3月　　133 p
　　第9号　　　昭和62年8月　　102 p
　　第10号　　　昭和63年12月　　153 p
　　第11号　　　平成元年11月　　76 p

『南星会報』（Nansei kaihō）　第1−5号　台湾軍第四十八師団南星会事務局

　　第1号　　　平成3年2月　　36 p
　　第2号　　　平成4年4月　　34 p
　　第3号　　　平成5年2月　　28 p
　　第4号　　　平成6月2月　　28 p
　　第5号　　　平成7年2月　　24 p

『榕樹東日本』（Yōju　higashinihon）

東日本台歩二会機関誌　第〔1〕−4号　三鷹市　東日本台歩二会

　　第1号　　　昭和49年7月　　34 p
　　第2号　　　昭和50年7月　　22 p
　　第3号　　　昭和51年11月　　48 p　「榕樹」第6号との合併号
　　第4号　　　昭和53年4月　　40 p　台湾特集号

『榕樹』（Yōju）

　　第1号　　　昭和45年5月27日
　　第2号　　　昭和46年5月27日
　　第3号　　　昭和47年5月27日
　　第4号　　　昭和48年5月27日
　　第5号　　　昭和49年5月27日

IV. 戦友会誌（Veteran's organization newsletters）

昭和52年7月1日号、昭和54年1月1日号、昭和54年8月1日号、昭和55年1月1日号、昭和55年8月30日号、昭和56年1月1日号、昭和56年9月15日号、昭和57年1月1日号、昭和57年8月15日号、昭和58年1月1日号、昭和58年8月15日号、昭和59年1月1日号、昭和59年8月15日号、昭和60年1月1日号、昭和60年8月1日号、昭和61年1月1日号、昭和61年8月1日号、昭和62年1月1日号、昭和62年8月1日号、昭和63年1月1日号、昭和63年8月1日号、昭和64年1月1日号、平成元年8月1日号、平成2年1月1日号、平成2年8月1日号、平成3年1月1日号、平成3年8月1日号、平成4年1月1日号、平成4年8月1日号、平成5年1月1日号、平成5年8月1日号、平成6年1月1日号、平成6年8月1日号、平成7年1月1日号、平成7年7月1日号、平成8年1月1日号、平成8年4月号

復員50周年記念：台湾軍・第四十八師団南星会戦没者慰霊祭（Fukuin gojūshūnen kinen: taiwangun・daiyonjūhachi shidan nanseikai senbotsusha ireisai） 1996　28p
Title translation: The 50th anniversary of demobilization remembrance: The Taiwanese army – The 48th division Southern Star Association (Nansei-kai) memorial service for the war dead

外国語文献

Foreign Language Publications

Akiu, a half-Chinese, half-Timorese boy who served as a creado for an Australian soldier. Photograph taken in Bobonaro in late 1945.
Australian War Memorial Negative Number 121422

I. English Language Publications

This list includes the more important publications related to the eastern part of Timor during the wartime years of 1941-1945. Due to the heavy involvement of Australia in Timor in 1941-1943, this means that most of these materials were published in Australia and can be most easily found there. The compilers have found that it is not feasible to provide references to every minor article ever published, nor is it advisable given that many are not particularly informative or duplicate information which is known to be incorrect. Rather some of the articles which are likely to be useful for researchers interested in Timor during this period have been listed (particularly academic works and interviews). In some cases a short annotation is included. Only a few items published before the war are listed, and these are included because of their special significance to the war period.

As it is not always easy to locate publications, an effort has been made to provide at least one public source for less-common publications, a tricky problem as what is common in one country in frequently rare or non-existent in another. A special effort has been made to provide Japanese sources as English language publications on Timor are generally rare in Japan. As in the rest of this bibliography, the rapidly growing body of electronic publications of the more informal sort have been excluded because of their ephemerality. References are made, however, to internet sources for some of the conventional publications listed.

Bibliographical and Archival Reference

Berlie, Jean A.
East Timor: A bibliography. Paris: Les Indes Savantes, 2001. 225p.

Metcalf, Karl.
Near Neighbors. Records on Australia's Relations with Indonesia. Research Guides, no. 16. Canberra: National Archives of Australia, 2001. [NAA-Dig]

Oliver, Pam.
Allies, Enemies and Trading Partners: Records on Australia and the Japanese. Research Guides, no. 20. Canberra: National Archives of Australia, 2004.

[NAA-Dig]

Rowland, Ian, comp.
Timor, Including the islands of Roti, and Ndao. Oxford: Clio Press, 1992.

Sherlock, Kevin, comp.
A Bibliography of Timor, Including East (formerly Portuguese) Timor, West (formerly Dutch) Timor and the island of Roti. RSPS, Aids to Research Series A/4. Canberra: ANU, 1980.

Sherlock, Kevin.
"Timor during World Wars I and II: Some Notes on Sources." 1985. 16 + 1p.
Notes: This was published in *Kabar Seberang*, no. 19-20 (1988) and includes the one page note entitled "Timor During World War II: Some Additional Notes on Sources."

Materials in Monographs

Area Study of Portuguese Timor. Brisbane: Allied Geographical Section, South West Pacific Area, 1943. 1 vol. varying pagination.
Notes: Around 70 pages of detailed description, followed by maps, areal photographs, drawings, and other illustrations. [NLA, AWM, PRO]

A Military Geography of the South-West Pacific Area, compiled from data in Collation Files. Queensland: L. of C. Area Sec. Aust. Inf. Corps., 1942. 48p.
Notes: Entry compiled from on-line catalog.

Documents on Australian Foreign Policy, vols. 1 (1937-38) to 10 (July-December 1946). Canberra: Department of Foreign Affairs and Trade.
Public Holdings: Most items seem to be available through the "Historical Documents Database" run by DFAT (http://www.dfat.gov.au/historical)

Units of the Royal Australian Air Force: A Concise History. Canberra: AGPS, 1995.
Notes: Especially "Volume 2, Fighter Units" and "Volume 3, Bomber Units."

Allied Mining Corporation and Asia Investment Company.
Exploration of Portuguese Timor: Report of the Allied Mining Corporation to Asia Investment Company, limited. Dilly: s.n., 1937. 137p. +2 pocket maps .
Notes: A standard work used during the war both for publications (e.g. Gutterres 1942) as well as for military purposes. [NLA]

Ayris, Cyril.
All the Bull's Men. Perth, WA: 2/2 Commando Association, 2006. 520p. [NLA]

Bennet, John.
Highest Traditions: The History of No. 2 Squadron, RAAF. Canberra: Australian Government Publishing Service, 1995. 431p.

Bowd, Reuben R. E.
A Basis for Victory: The Allied Geographical Section, 1942-1946. Canberra Papers on Strategy and Defence no. 157. Canberra: Strategic Defence Studies Centre, ANU, 2005.

Callinan, Bernard J.
Independent Company: The 2/2 and 2/4 Australian Independent Companies in Portuguese Timor, 1941-43. London/Melbourne/Sydney: William Heinemann, 1953. xxxiv, 236p.
Notes: Written by a former 2/2nd AIC/Sparrow Force commanding officer. Several editions have been issued in England and Australia (title varies).

Campbell, Archie.
The Double Reds of Timor. Swanbourne, WA: John Burridge Military Antiques, 1995. xii, 178p.
Notes: Written by a former officer of the 2/2nd AIC, and includes lists of the names of platoon members, the men killed-in-action, and the embarkation roll. AWM and ANU apparently have a different, possibly prepublication edition.

Coates, John. *An Atlas of Australia's Wars.* Second ed. Melbourne: Oxford University Press, 2006.
Notes: Pages 222-224 are directly related to the Timor invasion operations.

Courtney, Godfrey Basil.
Silent Feet: The History of 'Z' Special Operations, 1942-1945. McCrae: R.J. & S.P. Austin, 1993.
Notes: Discusses special operations in East Timor (e.g. Lizard) on pp. 2-6 and 193-236.
[OGU]

Doig, Colin D., compiler.
A Great Fraternity: The Story of the 2/2nd Commando Association, 1946-1992. N.p., 1993. 165, 7p. [AWM]

Doig, Colin D.
A History of the Second Independent Company [and 2/2 Commando Squadron]. Perth: published by author, 1986. viii + 270p.
Notes: Covers the history of this unit from its formation in Western Australia and training in Victoria to the actions in Dutch and Portuguese Timor. Subsequent actions are not included. Includes narratives by various individuals, but rounded out and sometimes rewritten by Doig. [AWM]

Evans, Peter, ed.
Fairmile Ships of the Royal Australian Navy. Loftus: Australian Military History Publications, 2002. 276p.

Farram, Steven.
Charles 'Moth' Eaton: Pioneer Aviator of the Northern Territory. Darwin: Charles Darwin University Press, 2007. 63p.

Farram, Steven. "From 'Timor-Koepang' to 'Timor NTT': A Political History of West Timor, 1901-1967," PhD Dissertation submitted to Charles Darwin University, 2004. 390p.

Francis, Ernest Dudley.
Recollections of My Military Service, 1936-1948. n.p.; n.d. xv + 104p.
Notes: Publication details unclear (probably published by the author). [AWM]

Frei, Henry P.
Japan's Southward Advance and Australia from the Sixteenth Century to World War II. Honolulu: University of Hawaii Press, 1991.

Gill, G. Herman.
Royal Australian Navy 1942-1945. Australia in the War of 1939-1945, Series II (Navy); v. 2. Canberra: Australian War Memorial, 1968.
Notes: Especially relevant to Timor are pp. 176-81, 213-224.   [OGU, AWM-Dig]

Gillison, Douglas.
Royal Australian Air Force 1939-1942. Australia in the War of 1939-1945, Series III (Air); v. 1. Canberra: Australian War Memorial, 1962.   [OGU, AWM-Dig]

Goto, Ken'ichi.
Tensions of Empire: Japan and Southeast Asia in the Colonial and Postcolonial World. Athens: Ohio University Press, 2003.
Notes: "Japan and Portuguese Timor," pp. 24-38.

Griffiths, Owen E.
Darwin Drama. Sydney: Bloxham and Chambers, [1947?]. 218p.
Notes: Chapter XV is entitled "Vale Voyager" and is most directly related to Timor.

Gunn, Geoffrey C.
Timor Loro Sae: 500 Years. Macao: Livros do Oriente, 1999.

Gunn, Geoffrey C.
"Wartime Portuguese Timor: The Azores Connection." Working Paper 50. Monash University Centre of Southeast Asian Studies, 1988.

Gutterres, M.H.
The Portuguese Colony of Timor. Shanghai: Shanghai Times, 1942. 84p.
Notes: Based almost entirely on the Allied Mining/Asia Investment publication of 1937, with the addition of announcements from the Japanese government related to the initial occupation of Timor.   [NLA]

Holland, Frank.
El Tigre: Frank Holland, M.B.E.-Commando, Coastwatcher. Wartime Rescue Operation in New Britain, 'Z' Special Unit Operation in Portuguese Timor, and Borneo. Edited by Peter Stone. Yarram, Victoria: Ocean Enterprises, 1999.

Horton, Dick.
Ring of Fire: Australian Guerrilla Operations against the Japanese in World War II. London: Secker & Warburg, 1983. x + 164p.
Notes: Of special interest is chapter 7 (pp.112-140), dealing exclusively with Timor.
[OGU]

Lambert, G.E.
Commando: From Tidal River to Tarakan. Melbourne: 2nd/4th Commando Association, 1997. xxvi, 510p.
Notes: Focuses on the No. 4 Australian Independent Company A.I.F., later called the 2/4 Australian Commando Squadron, A.I.F., 1941-1945. This narrative was assembled from both published and unpublished written accounts, unit diaries, and group interviews. Also includes numerous maps and photographs. [AWM, NLA]

Leggoe, John.
Trying to be Sailors. Perth: St. George Books, 1983.
Notes: Especially chapters 4-6 (pp. 35-65) on the "Timor ferry service," the Voyager and the Armidale. [OGU]

Lipman, Rex J.
Luck's been a Lady: The Autobiography of Rex J. Lipman. Adelaide, 2000. 288p.
Notes: An autobiography of a lieutenant in the 2/4th IC. Includes pictures taken with his own camera while in Timor. [NLA]

McCarthy, Dudley.
South-West Pacific Area-First Year: Kokoda to Wau. Australia in the War of 1939-1945, Series I (Army) v. 5. Canberra: Australian War Memorial, 1959.
Notes: Mentions ET in various places, but of particular interest is Appendix 2: Timor (pp. 598-624). [OGU, AWM-Dig]

McDonald, Neil.
Damien Parer's War. Rev. ed. South Melbourne: Thomas C. Lothian, 2004.
Notes: Originally published in 1994 as *War Cameraman: The Story of Damien Paper.* Chapter 18 on pp. 246-257 describes the politics behind Parer's trip to Timor and the story of his film. [NLA]

Military History Section, Army Forces Far East.
Ambon and Timor Invasion Operations. Japanese Monographs; v. 16. Tokyo: Office of the Chief of Military History, Department of the Army, [1953]. vii, 23p.
Notes: Rewritten based on a 1947 report written in Japanese by Lt. Col. Tozaka [Tozuka] Susumu. The description of the Timor invasion is problematic and sketchy, particularly with respect to Portuguese Timor operations. This is probably due to the fact that Maj. Susumu Tozaka was a staff officer with the West Timor detachment during the invasion of Timor. [NLA]

Military History Section, Army Forces Far East.
Naval Operations in the Invasion of the Netherlands East Indies, Dec. 1941-Mar. 1942. Japanese Monographs; v. 101. Tokyo: Office of the Chief of Military History, Department of the Army, n.d. 40p. [NLA]

Odgers, George.
Air War Against Japan 1943-1945. Australia in the War of 1939-1945, Series III (Air); v. 2. Canberra: Australian War Memorial, 1957.
Notes: East Timor mentioned in various places. Reprinted in 1968.
[OGU, AWM-Dig]

Powell, Alan.
The Shadow's Edge: Australia's Northern War. Carlton South, Vic.: Melbourne University Press; 1988.
Notes: Revised edition published by Charles Darwin University in 2007.
[OGU, NLA]

Powell, Alan.
War by Stealth: Australians and the Allied Intelligence Bureau, 1942-1945. Carlton South, Vic.: University of Melbourne Press, 1996.
Notes: Contains information related to Timor in various sections, most of which deal with special operations in Timor. Includes a map of entry and exit points of intelligence teams. [Keio, AWM, NLA]

Robertson, John and John McCarthy.
Australian War Strategy 1939-1945: A Documentary History. St. Lucia: University of Queensland Press, 1985.
Notes: Especially relevant are Chapter 9, "The Dutch Alliance and Portuguese Timor" (pp. 168-177) and Chapter 12, "Rabaul, Ambon, and Timor" (pp. 216-223).

Smailes, Jim.
The Independents. Perth: 2nd/2nd Commando Association, [1948]. 31p.
Notes: A poetic narrative of the experience of the 2/2 Independent Company in training and on Timor. Undated, but one of the appended poems is dated 1946. Another edition was published c. 1988. [NLA]

Thomas, W.J.
Yanks and Aussies in Battle: Official Photographs of Pacific War from Pearl Harbour to Timor. Sydney: N.S.W. Bookshop, 1945. 32p. [NLA]

Turner, Michele.
Telling: East Timor, Personal Testimonies 1942-1992. Kensington, NSW: N.S.W. University Press, 1992. xxii, 218p. [AWM, ANU]

Walker, Frank B.
HMAS Armidale: The Ship that Had to Die. Budgewoi, NSW: Kingfisher Press, 1990.
Notes: Includes various documents and appendices which detail mission, inquiry, losses, and survivors. Unfortunately details of the KNIL/NEFIS forces unclear as author was interested in documenting the navy experiences. [AWM]

Walkers, Alan S.
Middle East and the Far East. Australia in the War of 1939-1945, Series V (Medical); v. 2. Canberra: Australian War Memorial, 1953.
Notes: Parts of Chapter 22 are especially relevant to Timor. [OGU, AWM-Dig]

White, Ken.
Criado: A Story of East Timor. Indra, 2002. 175 pp.
Notes: A narrative based largely on interviews with Archie Campbell and his diaries.

Wigmore, Lionel.
The Japanese Thrust. Australia in the War of 1939-1945, Series I (Army); v. 4. Canberra: The Australian War Memorial, 1957. 718p.
Notes: Covers all of Southeast Asia and the Pacific. The situation on Timor up to March 15, 1942 is covered in Chapter 21 ("Resistance in Timor," pp. 466-95).
[OGU, AWM-Dig]

Wray, Christopher C.H.
Timor 1942: Australian Commandos at War with the Japanese. Hawthorne, Victoria: Hutchinson Australia, 1987. x, 190p. [OGU, AWM]

Veteran's Association Newsletters

2/2 Commando Courier. Perth: 2/2 Commando Association. 1946- [AWM]

The 2/4ther. Altona, Victoria: 2/4th Australian Commando Squadron Association. 1966- [NLA]

Periodical Articles

Bussemaker, Herman.
"Australian-Dutch Defence Cooperation, 1940-1941." *Journal of the Australian War Memorial* 29 (November 1996). [AWM-Dig]

Forsyth, W. D. "Timor II – The World of Dr. Evatt." *New Guinea and Australia, the Pacific and South-East Asia* 10,1 (May-June 1975): 31-37.

Frei, Henry.
"Japan's Reluctant Decision to Occupy Portuguese Timor, 1 January 1942-20 February 1942." *Australian Historical Studies* 27, 107 (1996): 281-302.

Hastings, Peter.
"The Timor Problem-II; Some Australian Attitudes, 1903-1941." *Australian Outlook* 29, 2 (August 1975): 180-196. [NLA]

Hastings, Peter.
"The Timor Problem-III; Some Australian Attitudes, 1941-1950." *Australian Outlook* 29, 3 (Dec 1975): 323-334. [NLA]

Horton, William Bradley.
"Ethnic Cleavage in Timorese Society – The Black Columns in Occupied Portuguese Timor (1942)." *Journal of International Development* 6, 2 (March 2007): 35-50.

Horton, William Bradley.
"Our Friends the Timorese: World War II in East Timor and Australian Memory Work." *Annual Journal of Cultural Anthropology* 3 (2006): 5-17.

Lee, Robert.
"Crisis in a Backwater: 1941 in Portuguese Timor." *Lusotopie* 2000: 175-189.

Levi, Werner.
"Portuguese Timor and the War." *Far Eastern Survey* XV, 14 (July 17, 1946): 221-223.

Manera, Brad.
"'H' Detachment Sparrow Force at Viqueque 1942." *Wartime: Official Magazine of the Australian War Memorial* 2002, 17 (Autumn): 56.

Morris, Cliff and Terry Lane.
"Australian WWII Commando Remembers," *Retrieval* 1977 (Apr-May 31): 12-18 + 19-21.
Notes: An ABC Radio interview with Cliff Morris, a former member of A Platoon of the 2/4th Company several months after he was caught trying to sail to East Timor with medical supplies. Some historical details are inaccurate, but general picture is of some value. Includes "Australia and East Timor, 1941-47.-Some Events." [NLA]

Robertson, Emma.
"Guerillas in Timor: Mates in the Hills." *Wartime: Official Magazine of the Australian War Memorial* 2000, 10 (Autumn 2000): 26-30.

Sowash, William.
"Colonial Rivalries in Timor." *Far Eastern Quarterly* VII, 3 (May 1948): 227-35.

Tarling, Nicholas.
"Britain, Portugal and East Timor in 1941." *Journal of Southeast Asian Studies* 27, 1 (March 1996): 132-8.

Williamson, Mitch.
"Moth Eaton: On a Wing and a Prayer 'Moth' Eaton over Timor." *Wartime: Official Magazine of the Australian War Memorial* 2000, 10 (Autumn 2000).

Wallis, B.K.
"Peace Comes to Dilli." *Walkabout* (February 1946).

Yanaghisawa, T.
"Timor and Macao." *Contemporary Japan* 10, 10 (October 1941): 1285-99.

Library Abbreviations

AWM	Australian War Memorial
AWM-Dig	Available in digital form from the AWM internet site
Keio	Keio University Library
NAA	National Archives of Australia (Canberra)
NAA-Dig	Available in digital form from the NAA internet site
NLA	National Library of Australia
OGU	Otemon Gakuin University
PRO	Public Records Office, National Archives, London

II. Portuguese Language Publications

Timor was one of Portugal's last remaining scattered colonial possessions and this is reflected in the Portuguese literature on Timor during World War II. Documents on foreign relations, especially related to efforts to liberate Timor from Allied or Japanese occupation, narratives by former officials and soldiers replete with criticisms of others, and biographical sketches of a few heroes and martyrs make up a significant portion of the publications in Portuguese. Mozambique as a staging point for both the effort to reinforce the tiny garrison in early 1942 and to "liberate" Timor in 1944~1945, as well as the various relations with Macao are frequently discussed.

The publications listed below include both official government publications and privately published materials. Many of the works found in periodicals were anonymously published, and thus these are listed at the beginning of each section of the bibliography alphabetically by title. We have followed the convention of skipping the particles "O," "Os," and "A" when alphabetizing, which we hope is not confusing.

Bibliographical Works

Frazão, António, Maria do Céu Barata Filipe, and Miguel de Barros Alves Caetano.
Arquivo Marcello Caetano: catálogo [The Marcello Caetano Archives: Catalogue].
Lisboa: Instituto dos Arquivos Nacionais/Torre do Tombo, 2005. 2 vol. xiv, 1119 p.

Garcia, Maria Madalena.
Arquivo Salazar: inventário e índices [Salazar Archives: Inventory and indexes].
Lisboa: Editorial Estampa, 1992. 684 p.

Gonçalves, Júlio.
Bibliografia do Ultramar Português existente na Sociedade de Geografia de Lisboa: Fascículo III Timor [A bibliography of materials on the Portuguese overseas in the Geographical Society of Lisbon: III Timor]. Lisboa: Sociedade de Geografia de Lisboa, 1961.

Materials in Monographs

O Caso de Timor: palavras de Salazar à Nação [The case of Timor: Words of Salazar to the nation]. Lisboa: Sindicatos Nacionais, 1941. 7 p.

Homenagem póstuma dos engenheiros geógrafos de Portugal no IX aniversário da morte do seu colega, em Timor: integrada nas cerimónias levadas a efeito em sua memória... [Posthumous homage of Geographical Engineers of Portugal on the 9th anniversary of the death of their friend in Timor: Joined in ceremonies putting into effect in his memory...]. [Lisboa]: Sindicato Nacional dos Engenheiros Geógrafos, [1954]. 16, [1] p.

In memoriam a Artur do Canto Resende, engenheiro geógrafo: herói e mártir da pátria em Timor [In memoriam to Artur do Canto Resende, a geographical engineer: Hero and martyr of the fatherland in Timor]. Lisboa: Sindicato Nacional dos Engenheiros Geógrafos, 1956. 149 p.

Almeida, Pedro Ramos de.
Salazar: biografia da ditadura [Salazar: biography of the dictator]. Lisboa: Edições "Avante!" 1999. 932 p.
Notes: Multiple index entries on Timor 1945-1946.

Álvarez, Eusébio Arnáiz.
Princesa mártir em Timor: Virgínia das Mercês Doutel Sarmento e Cardoso [Martyr princess in Timor: Virgínia das Mercês Doutel Sarmento e Cardoso]. 2.ª edição revista. Braga: Editorial A.O., 2003. 172 p.

Arbiru.
O problema de Timor [The problem of Timor]. Lisboa: Henry Gris, 1977. 16 p.

Arnáiz, Eusébio.
A Princesa mártir: missões ao vivo em Timor: obséquio filial à Virgem de Fátima [The Martyr princess: missions alive in Timor]. Macau: Tipografia Soi Sang Printing Press, 1951. 128 p.
Notes: Translated from the original Spanish by Manuel da Fonseca Moreira.

[Bastos, Aníbal Rebelo.]
À memória do engenheiro Artur do Canto Resende (um dos mártires da ocupação japonesa): alocução proferida na igreja da Motael, em 23-11-946, pelo Capelão do Quartel Geral das Forças Expedicionárias [In the memory of the engineer, Artur do Canto Resende (one of the martyrs of the Japanese occupation): A speech offered in the Motael church on 23 November, 1946, by the Chaplain of the Expeditionary Force Headquarters]. Lamego: [s.n.], 1946. 15 p.

Bessa, Carlos.
A libertação de Timor na II Guerra Mundial: importância dos Açores para os interesses dos Estados Unidos: subsídios históricos [The liberation of Timor in World War II: The importance of the Azores for the interests of the United States. Historical contributions]. Subsídios para a história portuguesa, v. 25. Lisboa: Academia Portuguesa da História, 1992. 175, [9] p.

Brandão, Carlos Cal.
Funo: guerra em Timor [Funo: war in Timor]. Porto: Edições "A.O.U.," 1946. 200 p.

Brandão, Carlos Cal.
Funo: guerra em Timor [Funo: war in Timor]. 5ª ed. [Porto: Tip. J.R. Gonçalves], 1953. 208 p.
Notes: Forward by Pina de Morais.

Brandão, Carlos Cal.
Funo: guerra em Timor [Funo: war in Timor]. 6ª ed. Lisboa: Edições Perspectivas e Realidades, 1987.
Notes: Preface by Mario Cal Brandão.

Bretes, Maria da Graça Marques Cardoso.
Timor Entre Invasores 1941-1945 [Timor between invaders 1941-1945]. Horizonte histórico 20. Lisboa: Livros Horizonte, 1989. 124, [4] p.

Brito, Francisco Garcia de.
Tata-mai-lau: Timor contra o Japão 1941-1945 [Tata-Mai-Lau: Timor against Japan 1941-1945]. Lisboa: Iniciativas Editoriais, 1977. 293, [2] p.

Caetano, Marcello.
Factos e Figuras do Ultramar [Facts and figures on overseas territories]. Figuras e feitos de além-mar 17. Lisboa: Agência-Geral do Ultramar, 1973. 162 p.
Notes: "Paixão e redenção de Timor [Passion and redemption of Timor]," pp. 123-162.
Also published in *Revista do Gabinete de Estudos Ultramarinos* 1(2): 3-21, Abril-Junho 1951.

Cardoso, António Monteiro.
Timor na 2ª Guerra Mundial: o diário do Tenente Pires [Timor in the Second World War: The diary of Lieutenant Pires]. Lisboa: Centro de Estudos de História Contemporânea Portuguesa, 2007. 271p.

Cardoso, Luís.
Requiem para o navegador solitário: romance [Requiem for the lonely navigator: A romance]. Lisboa: Publicações Dom Quixote, 2007. 223p.

Carvalho, José dos Santos.
Vida e morte em Timor durante a Segunda Guerra Mundial [Life and death in Timor during the Second World War]. Lisboa: Livraria Portugal, 1972. 208, [2] p.

Carvalho, Manuel de Abreu Ferreira de.
Relatório dos acontecimentos de Timor [Report of Timorese events]. Lisboa: Ministério das Colónias, 1947. 741p.

Carvalho, Manuel de Abreu Ferreira de.
Relatório dos acontecimentos de Timor (1942-45) [Report of Timorese events (1942-45)]. Lisboa: Edições Cosmos, 2003. 769p.
Notes: Introduction by former Macau Governor, Garcia Leandro.

Ferreira, José Rodrigo Dias.
Correio em Timor durante a ocupação japonesa: 1942-1945 [A post in Timor during the Japanese occupation: 1942-1945]. Lisboa: [União Gráfica], 1977. 7, [1] p. Sep. Bol. Clube Filatélico Portugal, 294.

Ferreira, Manuel.

Vida e morte de um bravo [Life and death of a courageous man]. Dili: Associação Académica de Timor, 1959. 28p.

Ferreira, Manuel.
Figuras portuguesas de Timor: homenagem a Celestino da Silva [Portuguese figure of Timor: Homage to Celestino da Silva]. Dili: Imprensa Nacional, 1961.
Notes: "Jeremias de Luca [Jeremias of Luca]," pp. 61-83.

Figueiredo, Fernando.
História dos portugueses no Extremo Oriente: Macau e Timor. No período republicano [History of the Portuguese in the Far East: Macau and Timor. In the republic period]. 4.° volume. Lisboa: Fundação Oriente, 2003.
Notes: "Timor (1910-1955)," pp. 519-584.

Goulart, Jaime Garcia.
Textos de D. Jaime Garcia Goulart [Texts of D. Jaime Garcia Goulart]. Macau: Fundação Macau, 1999. 370p.

Gunn, Geoffrey C.
Timor Loro Sae 500 anos [Timor Loro Sae 500 years]. Matosinhos, Porto: Tipografica Greca/Livros do Oriente, 1999.
Notes: "Capítulo 12: Timor em Tempo de Guerra, 1942-45 [Chapter 12: Timor in the time of war, 1942-45]," pp. 247-265.

Leitão, Humberto José dos Santos.
O régulo timorense D. Aleixo Corte-Real [The Timorese regulo D. Aleixo Corte-Real]. Lisboa: Edição do Grupo de Estudos de História Marítima, 1970. 27p.

Liberato, António de Oliveira.
O caso de Timor: invasões estrangeiras: revoltas indígenas [The case of Timor: Foreign invasions: indigenous revolts]. Lisboa: Portugália Editora, 1947. 241, [4] p.

Liberato, António de Oliveira.
Os japoneses estiveram em Timor [The Japanese were in Timor]. [Lisboa: Tip. da Emp. Nacional de Publicidade], 1951. 336, [1] p.

Liberato, Cacilda dos Santos Oliveira.
Quando Timor foi notícia [When Timor went news]. Braga: Pax, 1972. 205p.

Lima, Fernando.
Timor: da guerra do Pacífico à desanexação [Timor from the Pacific War until de-annexation]. Macau: Instituto Internacional de Macau, 2002. 368p.
Notes: "Capítulo 1: A Guerra do Pacífico [Chapter 1: The Pacific War]," pp. 31-62.

Magro, António Jacinto.
Tropa e aquartelamentos de Timor: subsídio para a história das unidades militares da colónia, Outubro de 1937 a Maio de 1940 [Troops and barracks of Timor: A contribution to the history of military units in the colony, October 1937 to May 1940]. Lisboa: Tip. da Liga dos Combatentes da Grande Guerra, 1947. 46p. Separata da *Revista Militar*.

Marques, A.H. de Oliveira.
História dos Portugueses no Extremo Oriente [History of the Portuguese in the Far East]. Vol. 4. [Lisboa]: Fundação Oriente, 2003.
Notes: "Timor (1910-1955)," pp. 519-582.

Martinho, José Simões.
Vida e morte do régulo timorense D. Aleixo [Life and death of the Timorese regulo D. Alexio]. Colecção pelo império, N.° 119. Lisboa: Divisão de Publicações e Biblioteca, Agência Geral das Colónias, 1947. 34p.

Martinho, José Simões.
D. Aleixo Corte-Real, português de Timor [D. Aleixo Corte-Real, Portuguese of Timor]. Figuras e feitos de além-mar 20. Lisboa: Agência-Geral do Ultramar, 1974. 41, [2] p.

Martins, Armando.
Portugal e o Japão: subsídios para a história diplomática [Portugal and Japan: contributions to diplomatic history]. Lisboa: Divisão de Publicações e Biblioteca, Agência Geral do Ultramar, 1955. 219p.

Ministério dos Negócios Estrangeiros [Ministry of Foreign Affairs].
Livro branco relativo à concessão de facilidades nos Açores, durante a guerra de

1939-1945 [White book related to the concession of facilities in the Azores during the war of 1939-1945]. Lisboa: Ministério dos Negócios Estrangeiros, 1946. 65p.
Notes: Cited in Revista Militar (8/9) (1946): 469.

Ministério dos Negócios Estrangeiros [Ministry of Foreign Affairs].
Dez anos de política externa (1936-1947): a nação portuguesa e a Segunda Guerra Mundial [Ten years of foreign policy (1936-1947): The Portuguese nation and the Second World War]. Lisboa: [Imprensa Nacional], 1961-1980. 11 volumes.

Miranda, Manuel Simões de.
1ᵒˢ jogos florais do Serviço de Reabilitação Profissional [First floral games of the Professional Rehabilitation Service]. Lisboa: Serviço de Reabilitação Profissional, 1969. 56p.
Notes: "A ocupação japonesa" [The Japanese occupation], pp. 29-33.

Mota, Carlos Teixeira da.
O caso de Timor na II Guerra Mundial: documentos britânicos [The case of Timor in the Second World War: British documents]. Estudos histórico-diplomáticos. Lisboa: Instituto Diplomático, Ministério dos Negócios Estrangeiros, 1997. 199, [3] p.

Oliveira, A.N. Ramires.
História do Exército Português: 1910-1945. [History of Portuguese Army: 1910-1945]. Vol. III. Lisboa: Estado-Maior do Exército, 1994. 638p.
Notes: "Quarta Parte: a Segunda Guerra Mundial, V: Timor" [Part Four: The Second World War, V: Timor], pp. 493-546.

Oliveira, Luna de.
Timor na história de Portugal do Século XVI ao Século XX, 1940 a 1946 [Timor in the history of Portugal from the 16th century to the 20th century, 1940 to 1946]. Vol. IV. Lisboa: Fundação Oriente, 2004. 332p.

Rocha, Carlos Vieira da.
Timor: ocupação japonesa durante a Segunda Guerra Mundial [Timor: The Japanese occupation during the Second World War]. 1ª ed. [Lisboa]: Sociedade Histórica da Independência de Portugal, 1994. 229p.

Rocha, Carlos Vieira da.
Timor: a ocupação japonesa durante a Segunda Guerra Mundial [Timor: The Japanese occupation during the Second World War]. 2ª ed., revised and expanded. [Lisboa]: Sociedade Histórica da Independência de Portugal, 1996. 309p.

[Salazar, António de Oliveira].
O caso de Timor: exposição do Presidente do Conselho à Assembleia Nacional em 19 de Dezembro de 1941 [The case of Timor: Explanation of the President of the Council to the National Assembly on 19 December 1941]. Lisboa: S.P.N., 1941. 15p.

Santa, José Duarte.
Australianos e japoneses em Timor na II Guerra Mundial, 1941-1945 [Australians and Japanese in Timor in the Second World War, 1941-1945]. Biblioteca de história 15. 1ª ed. Lisboa: Notícias, 1997. 302p.

Santos, António Policarpo de Sousa.
Duas palavras ao capitão Liberato a propósito de "O Caso de Timor" [A few words to Captain Liberato concerning The Case of Timor]. Lisboa: Excelsior, 1947. 148p., 1 map.

Santos, A. de Sousa.
Duas palavras ao Capitão Liberato a propósito de "O caso de Timor" [A few words to Captain Liberato concerning The Case of Timor]. 2a ed. Lourenço Marques: [s.n.] (Minerva Central), 1973. 142, [2] p., 1 map.

Santos, A. de Sousa.
Também quero depor sobre Timor: 1941-1946 [I too wish to testify on Timor]. Lourenço Marques: n.p., 1973. 82, [1] p.

Serrão, Joel, A. H. de Oliveira Marques, and Valentim Alexandre.
Nova história da expansão portuguesa: Volume X: o império africano, 1825-1890 [New history of Portuguese expansion. Volume X: African empire, 1825-1890]. Lisboa: Editorial Estampa, 1998. 864p.
Notes: Bretes, Maria da Graça Marques Cardoso. "Timor," pp. 767-803.

Sherlock, Kevin.

Índice alfabético de nomes de pessoas, de empresas, e de navios, encontrados no livro "Relatório dos acontecimentos de Timor pelo governador Manuel de Abreu Pereira de Carvalho ...": índice provisório extraído [Alphabetical index of names of persons, companies and ships, encountered in the book "Relatório dos acontecimentos de Timor by the governor Abreu Pereira de Carvalho...": provisionary extracted index.]. Darwin: self published manuscript. 1981. 14p.

Sousa, Fernando Louro de.
Moçambique na defesa de África e do ultramar português [Mozambique in the defense of Africa and the Portuguese overseas territories]. Lisboa: Revista Militar, 1952. 51p.

Teixeira, Nuno Severiano.
Portugal e a guerra: história das intervenções militares portuguesas nos grandes conflitos mundiais (sécs. XIX-XX) [Portugal and the war: A history of Portuguese military interventions in the great world conflicts (XIX-XX centuries)]. Lisboa: Edições Colibri, 1998.
Notes: Barata, Manuel Themudo. "Estado novo e política de defesa na II guerra mundial [The New State and the politics of defense in World War II]," pp. 127-143.
Telo, António José. "A neutralidade portuguesa na segunda guerra mundial [The Portuguese neutrality in the Second World War]," pp. 109-125.

Telo, António José.
Portugal na Segunda Guerra (1941-1945) [Portugal in the Second War (1941-1945)]. Colecção Documenta Historica. Lisboa: Vega, 1991. 2 volumes.
Notes: Vol I. pp. 43-65. Vol. II.

Vaz, J. Ferraro.
Moeda de Timor [Currency of Timor]. Lisboa: [Banco Nacional Ultramarino], 1964.

Journal Articles

"O 2.° aniversário da libertação de Timor" [The second anniversary of the liberation of Timor]. *Boletim Geral das Colónias* 23, 269 (Novembro, 1947): 102-103.

"4.° aniversário da libertação" [Fourth anniversary of the liberation]. *Revista Militar*

12 (1949): 733.

"Os acontecimentos de Timor durante a guerra no Pacífico" [The events of Timor during the Pacific War]. *Boletim Geral das Colónias* 21, 244 (Outubro, 1945): 3-14.

"Acordo aéreo de Timor entre o Japão e Portugal" [Timor air agreement between Japan and Portugal]. *Boletim Geral das Colónias* 17, 198 (1941): 93-94.

"Acto de posse do novo Governador de Timor" [Swearing-in ceremony of the new governor of Timor]. *Boletim Geral das Colónias* 22, 253 (Julho, 1946): 3-11.

"Aniversário da libertação" [Anniversary of the liberation]. *Revista Militar* 10 (1952): 734.

"A armada nacional: nos mares do Oriente" [The national navy: Our Oriental seas]. *Defesa Nacional* 143 (Março, 1946): 250-251.

"Crónica da viagem de novo em Moçambique: Jantar em honra da oficialidade do 《Bartolomeu Dias》 que partia para Timor; Partida das tropas para Timor" [Chronicle of the new voyage in Mozambique: Dinner in honor of the official "Bartolomeu Dias" departed for Timor; Departure of the troops for Timor]. *Boletim Geral das Colónias* 22, 248 (Fevereiro, 1946): 120-123; 200-205.

"Crónica do Ultramar: Timor" [The overseas chronicle: Timor]. *Revista Militar* 2 (Fevereiro, 1946): 109.

"D. Aleixo Corte Real." *Defesa Nacional* 152 (Dezembro, 1946): 225.

"Entrevista com o General Alcide de Oliveira" [Interviews with General Alcide de Oliveira]. *Independência: revista de cultura lusíada*. Nova Série 2 ([1992]): 9-11.

"Entrevistas sobre Timor" [Interviews about Timor]. *Boletim Eclesiástico da Diocese de Macau* XLVI, 527 (Março, 1948): 200-203.

"Entrevista sobre Timor concedida pelos Padres Januário Coelho da Silva e Manuel Silveira Luis sobre a ocupação Aliada (Australiana e Holandesa) e Japonesa"

[Interviews on Timor with Fathers Coelho da Silva and Manuel Silveira Luis on the Allied (Australian and Dutch) and Japanese occupation]. *Boletim Eclesiástico da Diocese de Macau* 527 (1948): 200.

"O fim da guerra no Oriente e a situação de Macau e Timor" [The end of the war in the Orient and the situation of Macau and Timor]. *Boletim Geral das Colónias* 244 (1945): 130-141.

"Governador de Timor" [Governor of Timor]. *Defesa Nacional* 148 (Agosto, 1946): 119.

"A história do timorense Nai-Sessu crismado de D. Aleixo Corte-Real" [The story of Timorese Nai-Sessu confirmation of D. Aleixo Corte-Real]. *História* XIV, 151 (1992): 49-51.

"Informações e notícias (secção portuguesa): A imprensa e as declarações do Chefe do Governo acerca do incidente de Timor" [Information and news (Portuguese section): The press and the declarations of the Chief of Government about the Timor incident]. *Boletim Geral das Colónias* 18, 200 (Fevereiro, 1942): 115-125.

"Informações e notícias (secção portuguesa): Portugueses residentes em Timor" [Information and news (Portuguese section): Portuguese residentes in Timor]. *Boletim Geral das Colónias* 20, 233 (Novembro, 1944): 97-101.

"Informações e notícias (secção portuguesa): O fim da guerra no Oriente e a libertação do território português de Timor" [Information and news (Portuguese section): The end of the war in the Orient and the liberation of Portuguese territory of Timor]. *Boletim Geral das Colónias* 21, 242-243 (Agosto-Setembro, 1945): 97-102.

"Informações e notícias (secção portuguesa): O fim da guerra no Oriente e a situação de Macau e Timor" [Information and news (Portuguese section): The end of the war in the Orient and the situation of Macau and Timor]. *Boletim Geral das Colónias* 21, 244 (Outubro, 1945): 130-141.

"Informações e notícias (secção portuguesa): A chegada dos repatriados de Timor" [Information and news (Portuguese section): The arrival of the repatriated from

Timor]. *Boletim Geral das Colónias* 22, 249 (Março, 1946): 161-163.

"Informações e notícias (secção portuguesa): Uma sugestão australiana para um acordo militar entre Portugal, a Holanda e a França" [Information and news (Portuguese section): An Australian suggestion for a military agreement between Portugal, the Netherlands and France]. *Boletim Geral das Colónias* 21, 244 (Outubro, 1945): 144.

"O inquérito a Timor" [The inquiry on Timor]. *Boletim Geral das Colónias* 20, 226 (Abril, 1944): 3.

"A libertação de Macau e de Timor" [The liberation of Macau and Timor]. *Defesa Nacional* 138 (Outubro, 1945): 125.

"A libertação de Timor. Uma mensagem telegráfica do Sr. Presidente do Conselho ao Governador da Colónia" [The liberation of Timor. A telegraphic message from the President of the Council to the Governor of the colony]. *Boletim Geral das Colónias* 21, 244 (Outubro, 1945): 15-16.

"A odisseia do actual Bispo de Dili ou a história da sua fuga com outros missionários para a Austrália durante a ocupação de Timor (De *A Voz*, Lisboa)" [The odyssey of the present Bishop of Dili or the story of his flight with other missionaries to Australia during the occupation of Timor (from *A Voz*, Lisboa)]. *Boletim Geral das Colónias* 22, 252 (Junho, 1946): 107-109.

"A questão de Timor" [The question of Timor]. *Boletim Geral das Colónias* 20, 226 (Abril, 1944): 99.

"Regresso dos Colonos de Timor" [Return of the settlers of Timor]. *Defesa Nacional* 143 (Março, 1946): 257.

"Restabelecimento das comunicações com Macau e a libertação de Timor" [Reestablishment of communications with Macau and the liberation of Timor]. *Revista Militar* XCVII 10 (Outubro, 1945): 537.

"O restabelecimento pleno da autoridade portuguesa de Timor" [The full reestablishment of Portuguese authority on Timor]. *Boletim Geral das Colónias* 22, 250 (Abril, 1946): 211-220.

"Revista da imprensa (secção portuguesa): A guerra no Extremo-Oriente e o sentido histórico português (artigo do sr. comandante Eduardo Lupi no jornal *A Voz*)" [The press review (Portuguese section): The war in the Far East and the Portuguese historical meaning (an article of Commander Eduardo Lupi in the *A Voz* newspaper)]. *Boletim Geral das Colónias* 18, 200 (Fevereiro, 1942): 155-160.

"Revista da imprensa (secção portuguesa): A questão de Timor (*Diário da Manhã*, editorial de 22 de Janeiro.)" [The press review (Portuguese section): The Timor question (*Diário da Manhã*, an editorial of 22 January)]. *Boletim Geral das Colónias* 20, 223 (Janeiro, 1944): 124-126.

"Telegramas, Lisboa, 25 Setembro 1942" [Telegrams, Lisbon, 25 September 1942]. *Boletim Oficial da Colónia de Macau*

"Terminou a guerra!..." [The war ended!...]. *Defesa Nacional* 137 (Setembro, 1945): 105.

"Timor." *Infantaria: revista técnica de cultura militar* 96 (Dezembro, 1941): 635.

"Timor." *Infantaria: revista técnica de cultura militar* 98 (Fevereiro, 1942): 126.

"Timor: o 4.° aniversário da libertação" [Timor: The fourth anniversary of the liberation]. *Boletim Geral das Colónias* 25, 294 (Dezembro, 1949): 133-137.

"Timor: entrevista com o sr. Governador; o 3.° aniversário da libertação" [Timor: Interview with Mr Governor; The third anniversary of liberation]." *Boletim Geral das Colónias* 24, 281 (1948): 143-145.

"Timor: notas da sua reconstrução" [Timor: Notes on its reconstruction]. *Boletim Geral das Colónias* 26, 304 (Outubro, 1950): 153-155.
"Timor e Macau" [Timor and Macau]. *Defesa Nacional* 139 (Novembro, 1945): 151.

"Todos, portugueses! (De *A Folha do Sul*, Montemor-o-Novo.)" [Everybody, Portuguese!

(from *A Folha do Sul,* Montemor-o-Novo.)]. *Boletim Geral das Colónias* 22, 252 (Junho, 1946): 121-122.

"Um régulo de Timor" [A regulo of Timor]. *Defesa Nacional* 141 (Janeiro, 1946): 212.

[Aguiar, João António.]
"Reconstrução de Timor" [Reconstruction of Timor]. *Boletim Geral das Colónias* 22, 257 (Novembro, 1946): 156-161.

A.P. [Armando Páschoa]
"Portugal e a Guerra" [Portugal and the war]. *Infantaria: revista técnica de cultura militar* XII, 134 (Setembro, 1945): 542.

Azevedo, Alves de.
"Como se firmou a soberania de Portugal em Timor" [How to confirm the sovereignty of Portugal in Timor]. *O Mundo Português.* 8, 90 (1941): 255-258.

Barata, Filipe Themudo.
"Timor: da ocupação japonesa à ocupação indonésia" [Timor: From Japanese occupation to Indonesian occupation]. *Revista Independência* 5 (Junho, 1987).

Borges, Vasco.
"Confiança e serenidade" [Confidence and serenity]. *Boletim Geral das Colónias* 18, 199 (Janeiro, 1942): 113-115.

Borges, Vasco.
"O caso de Timor" [The case of Timor]. *Boletim Geral das Colónias* 18, 200 (Fevereiro, 1942): 79-82.

Caléres Junior, João da Cruz.
"Os leais Moradores de Manatuto" [The loyal *Moradores* of Manatuto]. *Defesa Nacional* 193-4 (1950): 35.

[Caetano, Marcello.]
"O ressurgimento de Timor" [The resurgence of Timor]. *Boletim Geral das Colónias* 22, 248 (Fevereiro, 1946): 497-506.

[Caetano, Marcello.]
"Discurso de sua Ex.ª o Ministro das Colónias no acto de posse do novo Governador Geral de Moçambique" [Speech of His Excellency Minister of the Colonies in the swearing-in ceremony of the new Governor General of Mozambique]. *Boletim Geral das Colónias* 22, 258 (Dezembro, 1946): 3-11.

Coelho, Mário.
"Páginas timorenses: Mano Loi morreu, mas 《ressuscitou》 no fim da Guerra" [Timorese pages: Mano Loi died, but "revived" at the end of the war]. *Revista do Ultramar* 2ª série 2, 12 (Junho, 1949): 13-14.

Costa Lopes, Martinho.
"D. Aleixo de Corte-Real - Um Herói Lendário do Nosso Século" [Dom Aleixo de Corte-Real- A legendary hero of our century]. *Defesa Nacional* 193/4 (1950): 18.

Cunha, Luís.
"Timor a guerra esquecida" [Timor in the forgotten war]. *Macau* 2, 45 (Janeiro, 1996): 32-46.

Duarte Santana, José.
"Uma página da ocupação Japonesa" [A page in the Japanese occupation]. *Defesa Nacional* 193/4 (1950): 39.

Felgas, Hélio Esteves e.
"Timor e as convulsões politico-sociais do Oriente" [Timor and the political and social convulsions of the Orient]. *Revista Militar* 8/9 (1952): 583-591.

Felgas, Hélio Esteves e.
"Timor de há dez anos para cá" [Timor from ten years ago to now]. *Infantaria: revista técnica de cultura militar* 2.ª série 69/70 (Setembro/Outubro, 1952): 292-300; 71/72 (Novembro/Dezembro, 1952): 443-452.

Fernandes, Moisés Silva.
"Memorial de José Duarte Santa" [Memorial of José Duarte Santa]. *História* III série 33 (Fevereiro, 2001): 38-49; 34 (Março, 2001): 40-49.

Fontoura, Álvaro Neves da.
"II Congresso da União Nacional: Relações principais da Colónia de Timor com outros territórios" [Second Congress of the National Union: Principal relations of the colony of Timor with other territories]. *Boletim Geral das Colónias* 21, 237 (Março, 1945): 93-120.

Leal, Álvaro de Sousa.
"Reconstrução" [Reconstruction]. *Defesa Nacional* 193-194 (Maio-Junho, 1950): 22-25.

Liberato, António de Oliveira.
"O Capitão Freire da Costa" [Captain Freire da Costa]. *Revista Militar* 6 (Junho, 1946): 278-284.

Lopes, Martinho da Costa.
"D. Aleixo Corte Real, um herói já lendário do nosso século" [D. Aleixo Corte Real, an already legendary hero of our century]. *Defesa Nacional* 193-194 (Maio-Junho, 1950): 18-21.

Matos, João Pedro Correia de.
"Um legionário, herói e mártir da Pátria: Artur do Canto" [A legionary, hero and martyr of the homeland: Artur do Canto]. *Defesa Nacional* Ano XXI, 243-244 (Julho-Agosto, 1954): 42-43.

Magro, António Jacinto.
"Tropa e Aquartelamentos de Timor" [Troops and barracks of Timor]. *Revista Militar* XCIX, 2 (1947): 89-97; 3: 132-149; 4: 207-225.

Metelo, António.
"Crónica da vida colonial na metrópole: Dois polos, dois contrastes" [Chronicle of colonial life in the metropole: Two poles, two contrasts]. *Boletim Geral das Colónias* 21, 245 (Novembro, 1945): 38-41.

Metzner, Cabral.
""Gonçalves Zargo" regressou de Timor, Notas de viagem" [Gonçalves Zargo returns to Timor]. *Revista da Marinha* 272.

Pascoal, Ezequiel Ennes.
"As missões de Timor: 1556-1948" [The missions of Timor: 1556-1948]. *Defesa Nacional* 193-194 (Maio-Junho, 1950): 11-14.

Ramires, Filipe C.
"Timor durante a II Guerra Mundial" [Timor in World War II]. *História* 61 (Novembro, 2003): 68-70.

Ramires, Filipe.
"Objectivo: Timor: Portugal, Timor e a guerra no Pacífico (1941-1945)" [Objective: Timor: Portugal, Timor and the war in the Pacific (1941-1945)]. *Relações Internacionais* 11 (Setembro, 2006): 5-18.

Rodrigues, Luiz.
"Timor 1945." *Revista da Cavalaria* 8, 4 (Julho, 1947): 231-249.

Rodrigues, Sarmento.
"Timor foi a prova da unidade nacional" [Timor was proof of the national unity]. *Revista do Ultramar* 41 (1952): 15.

[Ruas, Óscar Freire de Vasconcelos.]
"Discurso do encarregado do Governo de Timor" [Speech of the acting Governor of Timor]. *Boletim Geral das Colónias* 22, 251 (Maio, 1946): 21-22.

Ruas, Óscar.
"Salvé Angola!: artigo escrito especialmente para a 《Revista do Ultramar》 pelo Governador de Timor." *Revista do Ultramar* Ano I, 7 (Setembro, 1948): 23.

Ruas, Óscar Freire de Vasconcellos.
"Aleluia!" *Defesa Nacional* 193-194 (Maio-Junho, 1950): 7-9.

[Salazar, António de Oliveira.]
"Exposição de S. Ex.ª o Sr. Presidente do Conselho acerca dos sucessos de Timor" [Statement of His Excellency the President of the Council concerning the successes of Timor]. *Boletim Geral das Colónias* 18, 199 (Janeiro, 1942): 3-12.
[Salazar, António de Oliveira.]

"Comunicação de S. Ex.ª o Presidente do Conselho à Assembleia Nacional acerca do ataque nipónico a Timor" [Communication of President of the Council of the National Assembly concerning the Japanese attack on Timor]. *Boletim Geral das Colónias*. 18, 200 (Fevereiro, 1942): 10-14.

[Salazar, António de Oliveira.]
"Comunicação do Sr. Presidente do Conselho à Assembleia Nacional" [Communication of the President of the Council to the National Assembly]. *Boletim Geral das Colónias* 19, 222 (Dezembro, 1943): 3-16.

Santa, José Duarte.
"Uma página da ocupação japonesa" [A page in the Japanese occupation]. *Defesa Nacional* 193-194 (Maio-Junho, 1950): 39-40.

Silva, Henrique Rola da.
"A invasão de Timor vista de Macau" [The invasion of Timor seen from Macau]. *Macau* 2nd series 1 (Maio, 1992): 87-89.

Silva, Rogério de Oliveira.
"Timor após a Guerra" [Timor after the war]. *Defesa Nacional* (193-194) (Maio-Junho, 1950): 26.

Soares, José de Freitas.
"Notas extraídas do meu diário, no decurso de uma expedição a Timor quando ali se encontravam as tropas japonesas" [Notes extracted from my diary, in the course of an expedition to Timor when the Japanese troops were there]. *Boletim do Arquivo Histórico Militar* 49 (1979): 57-152.

Sousa, Fernando Louro de.
"Moçambique na defesa de África e do Ultramar Português" [Mozambique in the defense of Africa and of the Portuguese Overseas]. *Revista Militar* II século, 3, 12 (Dezembro, 1951): 783-815.

V.C.
"Um episódio da reocupação de Timor" [An episode in the reoccupation of Timor]. *Defesa Nacional* 172 (Agosto, 1948): 94-95.

Masters Theses

Ramires, Filipe Costa.
"Portugal, Timor e a Guerra no Pacífico, (1941-1945) [Portugal, Timor and the war in the Pacific]." MA thesis. História das Relações Internacionais, Instituto Superior de Ciências do Trabalho e da Empresa, 2005. 165p.

Reis, Luís Manuel Moreira da Silva.
"Timor-Leste, 1953-1975: o desenvolvimento agrícola na última fase da colonização portuguesa [Timor-Leste, 1953-1975: Agricultural development in the final stage of colonization]." Instituto Superior de Agronomia, Universidade Técnica de Lisboa, 2000.
[Contains references to the destruction of agricultural systems stemming from the war]

Rocha, Carlos Ayala Vieira da.
"Moçambique na defesa do Ultramar português: Timor português ocupado pelos japoneses durante a Segunda Guerra Mundial [Mozambique in the Defense of Overseas Portugal: Portuguese Timor occupied by the Japanese during the Second World War]." MA thesis. Estudos Africanos, Instituto Superior de Ciências Sociais e Políiticas, Universidade Técnica de Lisboa, 1989. -2v.

Unpublished Manuscript

Laborinho, Álvaro Brilhante.
"Timor entre as Nações [Timor between the nations]." Setembro, 1950.
Notes: unpublished manuscript by former Portuguese Consul in Sydney.

Films

Jornal Português [Portuguese Journal] – 55 35mm-pb-284 mt- 9mn. [April 1946]
Director: António Lopes Ribeiro; Production: Sociedade Portuguesa de Actualidades Cinematográficas/SPAC.
Notes: Arriving in Lisbon the "long suffering" returnees from Timor endured years of anguish in the conflagration of war which engulfed the world.

Jornal Português [Portuguese Journal] – 57 35mm-pb-275 mt- 10mn. [May 1946]
Director: António Lopes Ribeiro; Production: Sociedade Portuguesa de Actualidades Cinematográficas/SPAC.

Notes: Arriving at the Alcantara Dock on the ship *Quanza* along with a contingent of Mid-East-Timor Expeditionary Forces; 1,200 men, two nephews of kinglet D. Francisco da Costa Aleixo, "victims of the Japanese invasion."

III. Dutch Language Publications

Publications in Dutch related to the war in the Indies rarely focus on Timor, but rather mention events there as part of the larger war. Short publications and short sections of monographs are thus of critical importance, and the short list we provide here may well be the tip of the iceberg. Shorter references which would be virtually impossible to locate outside of the Netherlands have been included here for the convenience of researchers.

For optimal clarity in this short list, items which were written anonymously have been listed alphabetically by title along with other items listed by author name. Items have been alphabetized by any word appearing in the name and title, thus particles like "de" are also subject to alphabetization.

Materials in Monographs

Bezemer, K.W.L.
Verdreven doch niet verslagen [Driven away but not beaten]. Hilversum, 1967.
Notes: Hoofdstuk IX [Chapter 9].

Bosscher, Ph. M.
De Koninklijke Marine in de Tweede Wereldoorlog, deel 2 [The Royal Dutch Navy during the Second World War, volume 2]. Franeker, 1986.
Notes: Especially p. 176.

Drooglever, P.J.
'Vreemd volk over de vloer. Interventies in de Indonesische archipel tussen 1941 en 1949' [Strange visitors. Interventions in the Indonesian archipelago between 1941 and 1949], in A.P. van Goudoever and J. Aalbers, eds. *Interventies in de internationale politiek*. Utrecht, 1990.
Notes: Especially pp. 199-200, 208.

Franks, H.G.
Oerwoudstrijders onder onze driekleur [Jungle warriors under our tri-colored flag].
Amsterdam, Brussels, London, and New York, 1946.

Helfrich, C.E.L.
Memoires I [Memoirs I]. Amsterdam, 1950.
Notes: Especially pp. 103, 206.

Hoogenband, C. van den and L. Schotborgh, eds.
Nederlands-Indië contra Japan, deel VI. De strijd op Ambon, Timor en Sumatra [The Netherlands East Indies versus Japan, volume VI. The fighting on Ambon, Timor and Sumatra]. The Hague, 1959.

Instituut voor Maritieme Historie.
De Koninklijke Marine in de Tweede Wereldoorlog. Deel IV, De Strijd in Nederlands-Oost-Indië [The Royal Dutch Navy during the Second World War. Part IV, The battle in the Netherlands East Indies]. Marinemonografieen. The Hague, 1961.
Notes: Hoofdstuk 12, "De Japanse opmars naar en in Nederlands-Indie en de acties op de maritieme steunpunten in de Buitengewesten" [Chapter 12, The Japanese advance to and in the Netherlands East Indies and the operations on the naval bases in the Outer Islands], especially pp. 26, 93-98.
Hoofdstuk 14, Het tijdvak 10 december 1941-8 maart 1942 [Chapter 14, The period from 10 December 1941 to 8 March 1942], especially pp. 25-27.

Jong, L. de.
Het Koninkrijk der Nederlanden in de Tweede Wereldoorlog, deel 11a (Netherlands-Indië I) [The Kingdom of the Netherlands during the Second World War, volume 11 a (Netherlands-Indies I)]. The Hague, 1984.

Jong, L. de.
Het Koninkrijk der Nederlanden in de Tweede Wereldoorlog, deel 11c (Netherlands-Indië III) [The Kingdom of the Netherlands during the Second World War, part 11 c (Netherlands-Indies III)]. Leiden, 1986.
Notes: Especially pp. 288-297.

Manning A.F. and A.E. Kersten.
Documenten betreffende de buitenlandse politiek van Nederland 1919-1945, periode c, 1940-1945 [Documents concerning the foreign politics of the Netherlands 1919-1945, period c, 1940-1945]. Rijksgeschiedkundige Publicatiën, Grote Serie. The Hague, 1984 and 1987.

Nortier, J.J.
De Japanse aanval op Nederlands-Indië [The Japanese attack on the Netherlands East Indies]. Rotterdam, 1988.

Nuboer, J.F.W.
De Japanse marine operaties tegen Nederlands-Indië (uit Japanse bron) [The Japanese naval operations against the Netherlands East Indies (from a Japanese source)]. The Hague, 1977.

Peet, A. van der and A. de Wit.
'*Schepen van geweld'. Acht keer Zeven Provinciën* ['Ships of violence.' Eight times Zeven Provinciën]. Franeker, 2002.
Notes: Especially pp. 79-80.

Periodical Articles

"Armidale, Nederlandse commando's uit Australie naar Timor" [Armidale, Dutch commandos from Australia to Timor]. *Terugblik '40-'45* 1991, 3: 94-96.

"De actie op Timor van december 1941-december 1942" [The action on Timor from December 1941-December 1942]. *Militaire Spectator* 117, 12 (1948): 703-714.

"De strijd op Timor" [The fighting on Timor]. *Stabelan* 7, 1 (31 augustus 1980).

"Hoe de 'Tjerk Hiddes' naar Timor sloop" [How the 'Tjerk Hiddes' crept to Timor]. *Onze Vloot* 42, 2 (februari 1953).

"Indische Engelandvaarders, een greep uit vele belevenissen" [Indies England-crossers, a group with many adventures]. *Legerkoerier* 27, 2 (februari 1977): 10.

"Landingen in bezet gebied" [Landings in occupied territory]. *Terugblik '40-'45* 1991, 2: 59.

Oranje (tijdschrift voor de Nederlandse en Nederlands-Indische gemeenschap in Australië) [Orange (magazine for the Dutch and Eurasian community in Australia)], 13 november 1943.

"Portugal, een lastige buur in Indië" [Portugal, a difficult neighbour in the Indies]. *Spiegel Historiael* 31, nr. 7-8 (1996).

"They had been given up as lost." *Voice of the Netherlands* 2, 32 (27 maart 1943).

Denu, J.B.
"De vergeten guerilla van het KNIL: Timor wapenfeiten van het KNIL op Timor tijdens Wereldoorlog II" [The forgotten guerillas of the KNIL: Timor feats of the KNIL on Timor during World War II]. *NRC Handelsblad*, 15 april 1985.

Hegener, M.
"Timor." *NRC Handelsblad*, 15 april 1985: 10.

Nortier, J.J.
"Guerilla op Timor" [Guerillas on Timor]. *De Legerkoerier* 26, 1 (januari 1976): 38.

Nortier, J.J.
"De guerilla op Timor (maart 1942 tot februari 1943)" [The guerillas on Timor (March 1942 to February 1943)]. *Mededelingen van de Sectie Krijgsgeschiedenis van de Koninklijke Landmacht* 1, 1 (1978): 24-74.

Nortier, J.J.
"Geallieerd initiatief in de eerste weken van de oorlog tegen Japan" [Allied initiative in the first weeks of the war against Japan]. *Ons Leger* 63 (sept 1979): 49.

Romijn, P.
"'Op Timor wordt nog gevochten.' De guerilla van het KNIL op Timor (1942) in het licht van het Nederlandse politieke en militaire beleid in de Pacific" ["They are still fighting on Timor." The guerillas of the KNIL on Timor (1942) in the light of the Dutch political and military policy in the Pacific], *Oorlogsdocumentatie '40-'45. Derde jaarboek van het Rijksinstituut voor Oorlogsdocumentatie* (1992): 45-74.

Vrijer, W.P.G. de.
"Guerilla Timor 1942 (deel I)" [Timor Guerillas 1942 (part I)]. *Stabelan* 11, 3 (15 december 1984): 26-32.

Vrijer, W.P.G. de.
"Guerilla Timor 1942 (deel II)" [Timor Guerillas 1942 (part II)]. *Stabelan* 11, nr. 4 (15 februari 1985): 34-47.

Vrijer, W.P.G. de.
"Guerilla Timor 1942 (deel III)" [Timor Guerillas 1942 (part III)]. *Stabelan* 11, nr. 5 (15 april 1985): 30-36.

Vrijer, W.P.G. de.
"Guerilla Timor 1942 (deel IV)" [Guerillas on Timor 1942 (part IV)]. *Stabelan* 11, nr. 6 (15 juni 1985).

IV. 中国語文献（台湾）

　東ティモールに関する中国語文献は、第2次世界大戦当時、台湾が日本植民地であったため台湾人が日本兵として東ティモールへ派遣された経緯から、本文献目録では台湾で出版された文献を収録した。内容は大別して、東ティモールへ派兵された元台湾人兵士の記録と中央研究院台湾史研究所の歴史研究者が編纂した台湾人日本兵のインタビュー記録からなっている。

In 1895, Taiwan became an official colony of Japan. During subsequent decades, Taiwanese were provided with training and in some cases even opportunities for higher education, and then recruited for various roles in the Empire. During World War II, Taiwanese were recruited as Japanese soldiers, and some of the units established in Taiwan were sent to East Timor. The Chinese language materials contained in this bibliography are all published in Taiwan. They are primarily memoirs of former Taiwanese soldiers who were dispatched to East Timor during the war, and collections of interviews edited by historians at the Institute of Taiwanese History, Academia Sinica.

陳　千武（CHEN Qian-wu）
獵女犯：台灣特別志願兵的回憶（Lieh nV fan: tai wan te bie zhi yuan bing di hui yi）熱点文化公司　1984　271p
Title translation: Hunting down female prisoners: memories of a Special Taiwan Volunteer Soldier.

陳　千武（CHEN Qian-wu）
活著回來：日治時期台灣特別志願兵的回憶（huo zhao hui lai: ri zhi shi qi tai wan te

bie zhi yuan bing di hui yi）晨星出版社　1999　394p

Title translation: Coming back alive: Memories of a Special Taiwanese Volunteer Soldier during Japanese rule

鄭　麗玲（ZHENG Li-ling）

台灣人日本兵的「戰爭經驗」（tai wan ren ri ben bing di "zhan zheng jing yan"）台北縣立文化中心　1995　254p

Title translation: "Experience of war" of Taiwanese soldiers in the Japanese Military

林　繼文（LIN Ji-wen）

日本據台末期（1930〜1945）戰爭動員體係之研究（ri ben ju tai mo qi（1930〜1945）zhan zheng dong yuan ti xi zhi yan jiu）稻鄉出版社　1996　268p

Title translation: Research on Japan's war mobilization system at the end of its occupation of Taiwan (1930-1945)

周　婉窈（ZHOU Wan-yao）

台籍日本兵座談會記録并相關資料（tai ji ri ben bing zuo tan hui ji lu bing xiang guan zi liao）中央研究院台灣史研究所（当時台湾史所籌備處）1997　324p

內容細目：鄭春河p. 299, 簡傳枝pp. 309-310

Title translation: A record of a round-table discussion with Taiwanese soldiers in the Japanese Military and related documents

Relevant section: ZHENG Chun-he p. 299; JIAN Chuan-zhi pp. 309-310

潘　國正（PAN Guo-zheng）

新竹人・日本兵・戰爭經驗（xin zhu ren・ri ben bing・zhan zheng jing yan）新竹市立文化中心　1997　203p

內容細目：「眼看著患難兄弟戰死沙場——黃逸庭的故事」pp. 104-115

Title translation: Hsinchu natives, Japanese soldiers and war experiences

Relevant section: Witnessing the death of brothers in the war: The story of Huang Yi-ting

陳　銘城 等（CHEN Ming-cheng deng）

台灣兵影像故事（tai wan bing ying xiang gu shi）前衛出版社　1997　223 p

Title translation: Stories of Taiwanese soldiers in pictures

蔡　慧玉（CAI Hui-yu）

走過両個時代的人：台籍日本兵（zou guo liang ge shi dai di ren: tai ji ri ben bing）
中央研究院台灣史研究所（当時台灣史所籌備處）1997　568p

Title translation: People across two ages: Taiwanese soldiers in the Japanese Military

湯熙勇・陳怡如（TANG Xi-yong and CHEN Yi-ru）

台北市台籍日兵査訪專輯（tai bei shi tai ji ri bing cha fang zhuan ji）台北市文獻委員會　2001　281p

内容細目：［表］2・3, pp. 258-260

Title translation: Special edition on research visits to Taiwanese soldiers in the Japanese Military in Taipei

Relevant section: "Chart" 2・3, pp. 258-260

賴采見・呉慧玲・游茹棻・Sheng-mei Ma（LAI Cai-er, WU Hui-ling and YOU Ru-fen）

沈默的傷痕：日軍慰安婦歷史影像書（chen mo di shang hen: ri jun wei an fu li shi ying xiang shu）商周出版　2005　196p

Title translation: Silent scars: A pictoral history of Japanese military comfort women

内容細目：日本軍「慰安所」分佈圖 pp. 36-39

Title translation: Distribution Map of the Japanese military "comfort stations" pp. 36-39

李　展平（LI Zhan-ping）

烽火歲月：台灣人的戰時經驗（feng huo sui yue—tai wan ren di zhan shi jing yan）

國史館台灣文獻館　2005　200p

內容細目：「辛酸・苦難・饑餓的日本軍記實－簡傳枝」pp. 123-136

Title translation: Years of warfare: War experiences of Taiwanese natives

Relevant section: A brief description of the reality of the Japanese military – bitter, painful, and starving, pp. 123-136

林　金田（LIN Jin-tian）

烽火歲月：戰時體制下的台灣史料特展　上・下（feng huo sui yue: zhan shi ti zhi xia di tai wan shi liao te zhan）國史館台灣文獻館　2003　468p

Title translation: Years of warfare: Special exhibition on historical materials related to Taiwan under the wartime system

彭　瑞金（PENG Rrui-jin）

瞄準台灣作家（miao zhun tai wan zuo jia）派色文化出版社　1992　332p

內容細目：「由詩人桓夫蛻變的小說家陳千武」pp. 117-131

Title translation: Outstanding writers in Taiwan

Relevant section: "CHEN Chien-wu, from poet to novelist" pp. 117-131

Journal Articles

周　婉窈（ZHOU Wan-yao）

歷史的記憶與遺忘：「台籍日本兵」之戰爭經驗的省思（li shi di ji yi yu yi wang: "tai ji ri ben bing" zhi zhan zheng jing yan di sheng si）『當代』（dang dai）　107期　1995　pp. 34-39

Title translation: Remembering and forgetting of history: A look back at the war experience of "Taiwanese soldiers in the Japanese Military" pp. 34-39

周　婉窈（ZHOU Wan-yao）

日本在台軍事動員與台灣人的海外參戰經驗1937～1945（ri ben zai tai jun shi dong yuan yu tai wan ren di hai wai can zhan jing yan 1937～1945）『臺灣史研究』（tai wan shi yan jiu）中央研究院台灣史研究所（当時台湾史所籌備處）第2巻第1期：1995　pp. 85-126

Title translation: Japan's military mobilization in Taiwan and Taiwanese overseas war experiences during 1937-1945" pp. 85-126

卓　麟聰（ZHUO Qi-cong）

二次世界大戰中台灣戰略地位及「台灣人日本兵」之研究（er ci shi jie da zhan zhong tai wan zhan lVe di wei ji "tai wan ren ri ben bing zhi yan jiu"『陸軍學術月刊』（lu jun xue shu yue kan）陸軍學術月刊社　35巻403期：1999　pp. 21-32

Title translation: Research on Taiwan's strategic status during the Second World War and "Taiwanese soldiers in the Japanese Military" pp. 21-32

公文書

Public Records

Col. Tatsuichi Kaida and Chief of Staff Maj. Shoji Minori at the signing of the intrument of surrender at Kupang (September 11, 1945).

Australian War Memorial Negative Number 019250

The Japanese delegation on its way to the H.M.A.S. Moresby for the signing of the instrument of surrender (September 11, 1945).
Courtesy of the Netherlands Institute for War Documentation

Ⅰ. 日本所蔵史料

Materials in Japanese Archives

解　　説

　東ティモールに関する日本語公文書に関しては、第2次世界大戦関連の公文書を多く所蔵する外務省外交史料館、防衛省防衛研究所戦史部、および国立公文書館の3公文書館所蔵の史料を調査収録した。各館所蔵の文書には、それぞれ特徴があり外務省外交史料館は、外交上重要となる条約文書類のほか、実質上日本軍占領下にあった東ティモールに植民地宗主国ポルトガルが視察員派遣を要求した文書、また派遣した視察員の動向に関する文書などがあり、東ティモールを巡り当時の日本とポルトガル両国の緊張感が読み取れる史料を所蔵している。防衛研究所には、防衛省という性格から軍事作戦および部隊の動向に関するものが多く所蔵されている。国立公文書館には、外務省外交史料館および防衛省防衛研究所戦史部所蔵の文書も重複して所蔵しているが、戦犯裁判資料が多数所蔵されている。

　Japanese archival documents related to East Timor are preserved in the major Japanese archival institutions related to World War II, the Diplomatic Records Office of the Ministry of Foreign Affairs, the Division of War History in the National Institute for Defense Studies of the Ministry of Defense, and the National Archives. Very briefly, the Diplomatic Records Office has treaties between Japan and Portugal related to East Timor, but also documents requesting permission to send Portuguese inspectors to East Timor. It also holds Japanese reports on these inspectors' activities in East Timor. These documents show clearly the tension between Japan and Portugal during the war. Documents in the Division of War History in the National Institute for Defense Studies of the Ministry of Defense relate to military campaigns and related activities. Quite a few of the documents in the National Archive are duplicates of documents in the Institute of Diplomatic History and the Defense Institute, however their holdings of documents in a variety of languages related to the war tribunals is unique.

2. 外務省外交
The Diplomatic Records Office

請求番号 File Number	日付 Date	資料名 Title
A.6.0.0.1-7	1933/8/25	葡国現下ノ政局ニ関スル件
A.6.0.0.1-7	1934/6/30	『ポルトガル』国一般情勢送付
A.6.0.0.1-7	1938/11/30	葡国議会開院式ニ於ケル大統領教書ニ関シ報告ノ件
A.7.0.0.9-36-1 第1巻	1942/10/14	「チモール」問題ノ件
A.7.0.0.9-36-1 第1巻	1944/3/1	「チモール」問題ニ関スル件
A.7.0.0.9-36-1 第1巻	1944/3/2	「チモール」視察員ニ関スル件
A.7.0.0.9-36-1 第1巻	1944/3/2	「チモール」視察員ニ関スル件
A.7.0.0.9-36-1 第1巻	1944/3/2	「チモール」視察員ニ関スル件
A.7.0.0.9-36-1 第1巻	1944/3/3	「チモール」視察員一行ニ対スル便宜供与方ノ件
A.7.0.0.9-36-1 第1巻	1944/3/3	視察員派遣ニ関スル件
A.7.0.0.9-36-1 第1巻	1944/3/4	「チモール」視察員立寄ニ関スル件
A.7.0.0.9-36-1 第1巻	1944/3/5	視察員派遣ニ関スル件
A.7.0.0.9-36-1 第1巻	1944/3/7	「チモール」視察員ニ関スル件
A.7.0.0.9-36-1 第1巻	1944/3/8	「チモール」視察員派遣ノ件
A.7.0.0.9-36-1 第1巻	1944/3/8	「チモール」視察員派遣ノ件
A.7.0.0.9-36-1 第1巻	1944/3/9	「チモール」視察員派遣ニ関スル件
A.7.0.0.9-36-1 第1巻	1944/3/9	「チモール」視察員「コスタ」一行着台ノ件
A.7.0.0.9-36-1 第1巻	1944/3/9	「チモール」視察員出発予定ノ件
A.7.0.0.9-36-1 第1巻	1944/3/10	「コスタ」大尉ノ人柄ニ関スル件
A.7.0.0.9-36-1 第1巻	1944/3/10	「チモール」視察員「コスタ」一行出発ノ件
A.7.0.0.9-36-1 第1巻	1944/3/12	「チモール」視察員派遣ニ関スル件
A.7.0.0.9-36-1 第1巻	1944/3/14	「チモール」視察員派遣ノ件
A.7.0.0.9-36-1 第1巻	1944/3/16	「チモール」問題ニ関スル件

史料館所蔵史料
of Ministry of Foreign Affairs

English Translation of Title	特記事項
Regarding current Portuguese political issues	在葡特命全権公使笠間杲雄発外相内田康哉
Shipment of information on the general situation in Portugal	在葡特命全権公使笠間杲雄発広田弘毅外相
Report regarding the annual presidential address at the opening of the Portuguese congress	在リスボン代理公使柳沢健発有田八郎
On the Timor Problem	リスボン千葉蓁一公使発谷正之大臣宛第763号
Regarding the Timor Problem	リスボン森島守人公使発重光葵大臣宛第74号
Regarding the Timor inspector	上村伸一政務局長発在台北・台湾総督府外事部長宛第1号
Regarding the Timor inspector	重光葵大臣発マニラ村田省蔵大使宛第21号
Regarding the Timor inspector	重光葵外相発リスボン森島守人公使宛第69号
On the means of providing assistance to the Timor inspector's party	上村伸一政務局長発台北・台湾総督府蜂谷外事部長宛第2号
On the dispatch of an inspector	青木一男大東亜大臣発ディリ淀川正樹総領事宛第8号
Regarding the stopover of the Timor inspector	青木一男大東亜大使発マニラ村田省蔵大使宛第114号
On the dispatch of an inspector	青木一男大東亜大臣発マカオ福井領事代理宛第12号
Regarding the Timor inspector	台北太田外事部長発重光葵外務大臣宛電信第11号
On the dispatch of a Timor inspector	ベルリン大島浩大使発重光葵外相宛第207号
On the dispatch of a Timor inspector	リスボン森島守人公使発重光葵外相宛第84号
Regarding the dispatch of a Timor inspector	リスボン森島守人公使発重光葵外相宛第83号
Regarding the arrival in Taiwan of Timor inspector Costa and his party	台北太田外事部長発重光葵外相宛第12号
On the scheduled departure of the Timor inspector	台北太田外事部長発重光葵外相宛第13号
Regarding the personality of Capt. Costa	リスボン森島守人公使発重光葵外相宛第88号
On the departure of the Timor inspector Costa party	台北太田外事部長発重光葵外相宛第14号
Regarding the dispatch of an inspector for Timor	マニラ村田省蔵大使発重光葵外相宛第26号
On the dispatch of an inspector for Timor	マニラ村田省蔵大使発重光葵外相宛第29号
Regarding the Timor problem	リスボン森島守人公使発重光葵外相宛第93号

請求番号 File Number	日付 Date	資料名 Title
A.7.0.0.9-36-1 第1巻	1944/3/22	「チモール」視察員動静ニ関スル件
A.7.0.0.9-36-1 第1巻	1944/3/27	「コスタ」大尉ニ関スル件
A.7.0.0.9-36-1 第1巻	1944/3/28	「コスタ」大尉ニ関スル件
A.7.0.0.9-36-1 第1巻	1944/3/28	「コスタ」「チモール」島滞在期間ニ関スル件
A.7.0.0.9-36-1 第1巻	1944/3/29	「チモール」視察員ニ関スル件
A.7.0.0.9-36-1 第1巻	1944/3/29	「コスタ」「チモール」島滞在期間ニ関スル件
A.7.0.0.9-36-1 第1巻	1944/3/30	「コスタ」大尉ニ関スル件
A.7.0.0.9-36-1 第1巻	1944/3/30	「チモール」視察員ニ関スル件
A.7.0.0.9-36-1 第1巻	1944/3/30	「コスタ」一行ニ関スル件
A.7.0.0.9-36-1 第1巻	1944/3/31	「チモール」視察員ニ関スル件
A.7.0.0.9-36-1 第1巻	1944/3/31	「コスタ」一行動静ニ関スル件
A.7.0.0.9-36-1 第1巻	1944/4/1	「コスタ」一行出発延期ノ件
A.7.0.0.9-36-1 第1巻	1944/4/2	「コスタ」一行出発ニ関スル件
A.7.0.0.9-36-1 第1巻	1944/4/3	「チモール」視察員ニ関スル件
A.7.0.0.9-36-1 第1巻	1944/4/4	「コスタ」一行ニ関スル件
A.7.0.0.9-36-1 第1巻	1944/4/5	「チモール」視察員ニ関スル件
A.7.0.0.9-36-1 第1巻	1944/4/5	「チモール」視察員ニ関スル件
A.7.0.0.9-36-1 第1巻	1944/4/5	「チモール」島旅行記
A.7.0.0.9-36-1 第1巻	1944/4/7	「チモール」視察員ニ関スル件
A.7.0.0.9-36-1 第1巻	1944/4/7	「チモール」視察員ニ関スル件
A.7.0.0.9-36-1 第1巻	1944/4/7	「チモール」視察員ニ関スル件
A.7.0.0.9-36-1 第1巻	1944/4/7	「チモール」嶋ニ於ケル葡国政府派遣視察員「コスタ」大尉ノ動静ニ関シ報告ノ件
A.7.0.0.9-36-1 第1巻	1944/4/7	葡国政府派遣「チモール」嶋視察員ニ交附セル説明資料ニ関スル件
A.7.0.0.9-36-1 第1巻	1944/4/8	「チモール」視察ニ関スル件
A.7.0.0.9-36-1 第1巻	1944/4/8	「チモール」視察ニ関スル件(「コスタ」報告書)
A.7.0.0.9-36-1 第1巻	1944/4/10	「コスタ」及福井領事到着ノ件
A.7.0.0.9-36-1 第1巻	1944/4/11	「チモール」視察員ニ関スル件

English Translation of Title	特記事項
Regarding the activities of the Timor inspector	重光葵外相発リスボン森島守人公使宛第85号
Regarding Capt. Costa	重光葵外相発マニラ村田省蔵大使宛第30号、副件名は「曾禰書記官ヘ古内ヨリ」
Regarding Capt. Costa	マニラ村田省蔵大使発重光葵外相宛第32号
Regarding the duration of Costa's visit to Timor island	重光葵外相発リスボン森島守人公使宛第91号
Regarding the Timor inspector	マニラ村田省蔵大使発重光葵外相宛第34号
Regarding the duration of Costa's visit to Timor island	重光葵外相発リスボン森島守人公使宛第92号
Regarding Capt. Costa	マニラ村田省蔵大使発重光葵外相宛第36号、副件名は「古内課長ヘ曾禰ヨリ」
Regarding the Timor inspector	マニラ村田省蔵大使発重光葵外相宛第39号
Regarding the Costa party	台北太田外事部長発重光葵外相宛第21号
Regarding the Timor inspector	台北太田外事部長発重光葵外相宛第22号
Regarding the activities of the Costa party	台北太田外事部長発重光葵外相宛第23号、副件名は「古内課長ヘ曾禰ヨリ」
On the delayed departure of the Costa party	台北太田外事部長代理発重光葵外相宛第25号
Regarding the departure of the Costa party	台北太田外事部長代理発重光葵外相宛第25号、上とは別史料
Regarding the Timor inspector	台北太田外事部長発重光葵外相宛第27号
Regarding the Costa party	台北太田外事部長発重光葵外相宛第28号
Regarding the Timor inspector	重光葵外相発リスボン森島守人公使宛第96号
Regarding the Timor inspector	重光葵外相発リスボン森島守人公使宛第97号（別電）
Timor Island Travelogue	曾禰益政務二課長の報告書
Regarding the Timor inspector	重光葵外相発ダバオ加藤総領事宛第1号
Regarding the Timor inspector	重光葵外相発チモール細川総領事代理宛
Regarding the Timor inspector	重光葵外相発マニラ村田省蔵大使宛、上村伸一政務局長発台湾総督府外事部長宛、合182号
Report on the Portuguese government dispatched inspector Capt. Costa's activities in Timor	「コスタ」一行の動静に関する報告書、ディリ淀川正樹総領事作成
Regarding explanatory materials submitted to the Portuguese government dispatched inspector for Timor Island	コスタに本説明書のポルトガル訳文を提出した経緯を記したもの、ディリ淀川正樹総領事作成
Regarding the Timor inspector	重光葵外相発リスボン森島守人公使宛第99号
Regarding the Timor inspector （The Costa Report）	重光葵外相発リスボン森島守人公使宛第100号（別電）
On the arrival of Costa and Consul Fukui	台北太田外事部長発重光葵外相宛第29号
Regarding the Timor inspector	台北蜂谷外事部長発重光葵外相宛第30号

請求番号 File Number	日付 Date	資料名 Title
A.7.0.0.9-36-1 第1巻	1944/4/12	「葡萄牙人「コスタ」大尉ヘノ便宜供与ニ対シ謝意表明ノ件」
A.7.0.0.9-36-1 第1巻	1944/4/14	「チモール」状況改善実情電報方ノ件
A.7.0.0.9-36-1 第1巻	1944/4/15	「コスタ」大尉謝意表明ノ件
A.7.0.0.9-36-1 第1巻	1944/4/15	「チモール」視察員謝意伝達方ノ件
A.7.0.0.9-36-1 第1巻	1944/4/15	「チモール」視察員着任ニ関スル件
A.7.0.0.9-36-1 第1巻	1944/4/17	「チモール」島事情改善ノ件
A.7.0.0.9-36-1 第1巻	1944/4/19	「チモール」島事情改善ノ件
A.7.0.0.9-36-1 第1巻	1944/4/19	「チモール」視察員ニ関スル件
A.7.0.0.9-36-1 第1巻	1944/4/20	「コスタ」大尉「チモール」視察ニ関スル件
A.7.0.0.9-36-1 第1巻	1944/4/23	「コスタ」一行諸経費ノ件
A.7.0.0.9-36-1 第1巻	1944/4/27	「コスタ」一行諸経費電送ノ件
A.7.0.0.9-36-1 第1巻	1944/5/6	「コスタ」一行諸経費電送ノ件
A.7.0.0.9-36-1 第1巻	1944/5/8	「チモール」島視察員ニ関スル件
A.7.0.0.9-36-1 第1巻	1944/5/16	「チモール」島課税実施ニ関スル件
A.7.0.0.9-36-1 第1巻	1944/5/20	「チモール」島ニ於ケル通貨等ニ関スル件
A.7.0.0.9-36-1 第1巻	1944/5/23	「チモール」問題伊紙論説
A.7.0.0.9-36-1 第1巻	1944/5/25	「チモール」問題ニ関スル伊紙論説ノ件
A.7.0.0.9-36-1 第1巻	1944/6/6	葡萄牙視察員ノ「チモール」視察ニ関スル件
A.7.0.0.9-36-1 第1巻	1944/6/13	「チモール」問題ニ関スル澳門政庁「コスタ」大尉報告ノ件
A.7.0.0.9-36-1 第1巻	1944/6/13	「チモール」問題ニ関スル澳門政庁「コスタ」大尉報告ノ件
A.7.0.0.9-36-1 第1巻	1944/6/17	再電ノ件
A.7.0.0.9-36-1 第1巻	1944/6/27	「コスタ」大尉「チモール」視察ニ関スル件
A.7.0.0.9-36-1 第1巻	1944/6/29	「チモール」問題ニ関スル件
A.7.0.0.9-36-1 第1巻	1944/7/1	転電ノ件
A.7.0.0.9-36-1 第1巻	1944/7/7	「チモール」撤兵提言ニ関スル件
A.7.0.0.9-36-1 第1巻	1944/7/8	「チモール」問題等ニ関シ米大使申入レニ関スル件

English Translation of Title	特記事項
On appreciation for assistance to Portuguese Capt Costa	上村伸一政務局長発雪澤京都府知事・吉田福岡県知事・薄田警視総監・町田内務省警保局長宛、古内課長発加賀山鉄道総局第二輸送課長宛
On the means of telegramming about improvement of the Timor situation	リスボン森島守人公使発重光葵外相宛第136号
On appreciation from Capt. Costa	マカオ福井領事代理発重光葵外相・青木一男大東亜相宛第2号
On the way of passing on appreciation from the Timor Inspector	マカオ福井領事代理発重光葵外相宛第3号
Regarding the arrival of the Timor Inspector	重光葵外相発リスボン森島守人公使宛第110号
On improvement of conditions on Timor island	重光葵外相発リスボン森島守人公使宛第111号
On improvement of conditions on Timor island	重光葵外相発リスボン森島守人公使宛第113号
Regarding the Timor inspector	重光葵外相発リスボン森島守人公使宛第115号
Regarding Capt. Costa's Timor inspection	リスボン森島守人公使発重光葵外相宛第145号
On overhead expences for the Costa party	台北太田外事部長代理発重光葵外相宛第33号
On wiring overhead expences of the Costa party	重光葵外相発台北太田外事部長代理宛第8号
On wiring overhead expences of the Costa party	台北大田外事部長発重光葵外相宛第36号
Regarding the Timor Island inspector	重光葵外相発リスボン森島守人公使宛第128号
Regarding taxation on Timor Island	リスボン森島守人公使発重光葵外相宛第168号
Regarding local currency on Timor Island	重光葵外相発リスボン森島守人公使宛第139号
Editorial on the Timor problem in an Italian newspaper	ヴァチカン原田健公使発重光葵外相宛第129号
On an editorial regarding the Timor problem in an Italian newspaper	ヴァチカン原田健公使発重光葵外相宛第130号
Regarding inspection of Timor by the Portuguese Inspector	リスボン森島守人公使発重光葵外相宛合大4号
On the report regarding the Timor problem by Macao governor's office Capt. Costa	重光葵外相発リスボン森島守人公使宛第160号
On the report regarding the Timor problem by Capt. Costa of the Macao Governor's Office	重光葵外相発リスボン森島守人公使宛第161号（別電）
On resending	重光葵外相発リスボン森島守人公使宛第167号
Regarding inspections of Timor by Capt. Costa	リスボン森島守人公使発重光葵外相宛第212号
Regarding the Timor problem	リスボン森島守人公使発重光葵外相宛第213号、訂正報あり
On forwarding a telegram	リスボン森島守人公使発重光葵外相宛第219号
Regarding the forwarding by telegram of the proposal for military withdrawal from Timor	リスボン森島守人公使発重光葵外相宛第226号
Regading requests from the American Ambassador on the Timor problem	リスボン森島守人公使発重光葵外相宛第231号

請求番号 File Number	日付 Date	資料名 Title
A.7.0.0.9-36-1 第1巻	1944/7/10	米ノ対葡申入ニ関スル件
A.7.0.0.9-36-1 第1巻	1944/7/22	「チモール」問題ト葡国ノ動向ニ関スル件
A.7.0.0.9-36-1 第1巻	1944/7/28	「チモール」問題ト葡国ノ動向ニ関スル件
A.7.0.0.9-36-1 第1巻	1944/8/3	日葡関係ニ関スル件
A.7.0.0.9-36-1 第1巻	1944/8/7	日葡関係ニ関スル件
A.7.0.0.9-36-1 第1巻	1944/8/8	「チモール」撤兵要求確定情報ノ件
A.7.0.0.9-36-1 第1巻	1944/8/8	「サ」首相トノ会見ニ関スル件
A.7.0.0.9-36-1 第1巻	1944/8/8	「サ」首相トノ会見ニ関スル件
A.7.0.0.9-36-1 第1巻	1944/8/10	「チモール」問題ニ関スル件
A.7.0.0.9-36-1 第1巻	1944/8/10	八月十一日葡来電大二五八号ノ一（総一二〇四六）ノ続
A.7.0.0.9-36-1 第1巻	1944/8/11	「サ」首相森島公使会談ノ件
A.7.0.0.9-36-1 第1巻	1944/8/23	「チモール」問題ニ関スル件
A.7.0.0.9-36-1 第1巻	1944/8/25	「チモール」問題ニ関スル件
A.7.0.0.9-36-1 第1巻	1944/8/29	「チモール」問題ニ関スル件
A.7.0.0.9-36-1 第1巻	1944/9/8	日葡関係ニ関スル件
A.7.0.0.9-36-1 第1巻	1944/9/8	日葡関係ニ関スル件
A.7.0.0.9-36-1 第1巻	1944/9/10	「サ」首相ノ陸相就任式ニ於ケル陳述ノ件
A.7.0.0.9-36-1 第1巻	1944/9/12	「チモール」政庁宛借款供与方ノ件
A.7.0.0.9-36-1 第1巻	1944/9/18	葡内閣改造ニ関スル件
A.7.0.0.9-36-1 第1巻	1944/9/23	日葡関係ニ関スル同盟電報ノ件
A.7.0.0.9-36-1 第1巻	1944/9/29	葡国ノ「チモール」出兵ト日葡国交ニ関スル件
A.7.0.0.9-36-1 第1巻	1944/10/5	西葡対日断交問題
A.7.0.0.9-36-1 第1巻	1944/10/6	「チモール」問題情報ノ件

English Translation of Title	特記事項
Regarding U.S. requests to the Portuguese Government	リスボン森島守人公使発重光葵外相宛第232号
Regarding the Timor problem and the situation of Portugal	リスボン森島守人公使発重光葵外相宛第243号
Regarding the Timor problem and the situation of Portugal	リスボン森島守人公使発重光葵外相宛第247号
Regarding Japan-Portuguese Relations	リスボン森島守人公使発重光葵外相宛第249号
Regarding Japan-Portuguese Relations	重光葵外相発モスクワ佐藤尚武大使・満州山田乙三大使宛合440号
On the information about confirmation of the request for military withdrawal from Timor	リスボン森島守人公使発重光葵外相宛第254号
Regarding meeting with P.M. Salazar	リスボン森島守人公使発重光葵外相宛第255号
Regarding meeting with P.M. Salazar	リスボン森島守人公使発重光葵外相宛第256号
Regarding the Timor problem	リスボン森島守人公使発重光葵外相宛第258号の1
Continuation of Telegram No. Dai 258-1 (So 12046) from Portugal on August 11	リスボン森島守人公使発重光葵外相宛第258号の2
Conversation between P.M. Salazar and Minister Morishima	リスボン森島守人公使発重光葵外相宛第260号
Regarding the Timor problem	リスボン森島守人公使発重光葵外相宛第270号
Regarding the Timor problem	リスボン森島守人公使発重光葵外相宛第276号
Regarding the Timor problem	リスボン森島守人公使発重光葵外相宛第287号
Regarding Japan-Portuguese Relations	マドリード須磨弥吉郎公使発重光葵外相宛第953号
Regarding Japan-Portuguese Relations	マドリード須磨弥吉郎公使発重光葵外相宛第954号
On the speech of P.M. Salazar at the inauguration of the Minister of the Army	リスボン森島守人公使発重光葵外相宛第310号
On providing a load to the Timorese government	重光葵外相発リスボン森島守人公使宛第227号
Regarding the reformation of the Portuguese government	重光葵外相発モスクワ佐藤尚武大使・満州山田乙三大使宛合555号
On a Domei press telegram regarding Japan-Portuguese relations	リスボン森島守人公使発重光葵外相宛第323号
Regarding the dispatch of a Portuguese Timor convoy and Japan-Portugal relations	リスボン森島守人公使発重光葵外相宛第332号
The problem Spain's cutting relations with Japan	マドリード須磨弥吉郎大使発重光葵外相宛第1072号・マドリード須磨弥吉郎公使発リスボン・森島公使宛第13号
On Timor problem information	マドリード須磨弥吉郎大使発重光葵外相宛第1080号、マドリード須磨弥吉郎公使発リスボン森島守人公使宛第14号

請求番号 File Number	日付 Date	資料名 Title
A.7.0.0.9-36-1 第1巻	1944/10/7	「チモール」問題ニ関スル件
A.7.0.0.9-36-1 第1巻	1944/10/7	葡国諮問会議、葡大統領宛米大統領書、米国映画ニ関スル件
A.7.0.0.9-36-1 第1巻	1944/10/16	「チモール」ヨリ日本軍撤収ト題スル「デリー」紙報道ノ件
A.7.0.0.9-36-1 第1巻	1944/10/18	「チモール」撤兵ニ関スル日葡間協定ニ関スル件
A.7.0.0.9-36-1 第1巻	1944/10/22	「チモール」問題ニ関スル件
A.7.0.0.9-36-1 第1巻	1944/10/27	「チモール」政庁ニ借款供与方ノ件
A.7.0.0.9-36-1 第1巻	1944/11/20	「チモール」派兵説ニ関スル件
A.7.0.0.9-36-1 第1巻	1944/11/26	敵機来襲ト館員並ニ収容葡萄牙人ノ生命保護ニ関スル件
A.7.0.0.9-36-1 第1巻	1944/11/27	中立国外相会議「チモール」派兵等ニ関スル聞込
A.7.0.0.9-36-1 第1巻	1944/12/1	「チモール」問題ニ関スル件
A.7.0.0.9-36-1 第1巻	1944/12/2	敵機来襲ニ関スル件
A.7.0.0.9-36-1 第1巻	1944/12/2	敵機来襲ト館員並ニ収容葡萄牙人ノ生命保護ニ関スル件
A.7.0.0.9-36-1 第1巻	1944/12/7	「チモール」問題ニ関シ「サラザール」首相トノ会談ノ件
A.7.0.0.9-36-1 第1巻	1944/12/7	敵機来襲ト在留葡萄牙人ノ生命保護ニ関スル件
A.7.0.0.9-36-1 第1巻	1944/12/21	「チモール」問題ニ関スル件
A.7.0.0.9-36-1 第1巻	1945/5/21	「サ」首相トノ会見ニ関スル件
A.7.0.0.9-36-1 第1巻	1945/5/23	淀川総領事発令問題
A.7.0.0.9-36-1 第1巻	1945/5/26	「チモール」問題ニ関スル件
A.7.0.0.9-36-1 第1巻	1945/5/31	「チモール」撤兵ニ関スル件
A.7.0.0.9-36-1 第1巻	1945/6/4	「チモール」撤兵ニ関する件
A.7.0.0.9-36-1 第1巻	1945/6/4	「チモール」問題
A.7.0.0.9-36-1 第1巻	1945/6/8	「電報」
A.7.0.0.9-36-1 第1巻	1945/7/11	「チモール」問題等ニ関スル件
A.7.0.0.9-36-1 第1巻	1945/7/16	「チモール」問題其ノ他
A.7.0.0.9-36-1 第1巻	1945/8/9	「チモール」問題ニ関スル件
A.7.0.0.9-36-1 第1巻	1945/8/15	在「チモール」我軍武装解除ノ件

English Translation of Title	特記事項
Regarding the Timor problem	マドリード須磨弥吉郎公使発重光葵外相宛第1084号
Regarding the Portuguese Advisory Conference, a letter of the US president to the Portuguese president, US movies	リスボン森島守人公使発重光葵外相宛第337号、リスボン森島守人公使発マドリード須磨弥吉郎公使宛第145号
Regarding a Dili newspaper report entitled Japan's Retreat from Timor	リスボン森島守人公使発重光葵外相宛第349号
Regarding a Portugal-Japan agreement on the retreat of Japanese troops from Timor	重光葵外相発リスボン森島守人公使・マドリード須磨弥吉郎公使宛合第660号
Regarding the Timor problem	リスボン森島守人公使発重光葵外相宛第357号
On the provision of loans for the Timor government	重光葵外相発リスボン森島守人公使宛第259号
Regarding rumours of the dispatch of troops to Timor	リスボン森島守人公使発重光葵外相宛第385号
Regarding the attacks of enemy bombers and the protection of Portuguese internees lives	ディリ細川総領事代理発重光葵外相宛第104号・第105号、細川は
Regarding a conference of neutral coutries' foreign ministers and the dispatch of troops to Timor	重光葵外相発モスクワ佐藤尚武大使宛第1714号
Regarding the Timor problem	リスボン森島守人公使発重光葵外相宛第393号
Regarding attacks by enemy bombers	重光葵外相発リスボン森島守人公使宛第278号
Regarding the attacks of enemy bombers and the protection of Portuguese internees lives	重光葵外相発リスボン森島守人公使宛第279号
On a conversation with P.M. Salazar about the Timor problem	リスボン森島守人公使発重光葵外相宛第396号
Regarding enemy bombing and the protection of Portuguese residents' lives	リスボン森島守人公使発重光葵外相宛第398号
Regarding the Timor problem	リスボン森島守人公使発重光葵外相宛第416号
Regarding a conversation with P.M. Salazar	リスボン森島守人公使発東郷茂徳外相宛第186号
The issue of Consul-general Yodogawa's order	東郷茂徳外相発リスボン森島守人公使宛第111号
Regarding the Timor problem	リスボン森島守人公使発東郷茂徳外相宛第201号
Regarding the military withdrawal from Timor	リスボン森島守人公使発東郷茂徳外相宛第204号
Regarding the military withdrawal from Timor	東郷茂徳外相発リスボン森島守人公使宛第117号
The Timor problem	東郷茂徳外相発リスボン森島守人公使宛第118号。この後ろに、発電されなかった電信案あり
Telegram	「澳門政庁ノ動向ニ関スル件　五月六日「リスボン」ヨリ澳門総督宛電報要旨左ノ如シ」との記述あり。波集団参謀長作成
Regarding Timor and other problems	リスボン森島守人公使発東郷茂徳外相宛第238号
Timor and other problems	東郷茂徳外相発リスボン森島守人公使宛第137号
Regarding the Timor problem	東郷茂徳外相発リスボン森島守人公使宛第153号
On disarmament of our military in Timor	リスボン森島守人公使発東郷茂徳外相宛第276号

請求番号 File Number	日付 Date	資料名 Title
A.7.0.0.9-36-1 第1巻	1945/8/15	在「チモール」我軍武装解除ノ件
A.7.0.0.9-36-1 第1巻	1945/8/15	「チモール」問題ニ関スル件
A.7.0.0.9-36-1 第1巻	1945/8/15	在「チモール」我軍武装解除ノ件
A.7.0.0.9-36-1 第1巻	1945/8/20	「チモール」問題ニ関スル件
A.7.0.0.9-36-1 第1巻	1945/8/29	「チモール」問題ニ関スル件
A.7.0.0.9-36-1 第1巻	1945/8/31	「チモール」問題ニ関スル件
A.7.0.0.9-36-1 第1巻	1945/9/1	「チモール」問題
A.7.0.0.9-36-1 第1巻	1945/9/3	「チモール」問題ニ関スル件
A.7.0.0.9-36-1 第1巻	1945/9/5	「チモール」問題ニ関スル件
A.7.0.0.9-36-1 第1巻	1945/9/6	「チモール」問題ニ関スル件
A.7.0.0.9-36-1 第1巻	1945/9/6	「チモール」問題ニ関スル件
A.7.0.0.9-36-1 第1巻	1945/9/7	「チモール」澳門間無線連絡ノ件
A.7.0.0.9-36-1 第1巻	1945/9/7	「チモール」問題ニ関スル件
A.7.0.0.9-36-1 第1巻	1945/9/8	「チモール」問題ニ関スル件
A.7.0.0.9-36-1 第1巻	1945/9/10	
A.7.0.0.9-36-1 第1巻	1945/9/11	「チモール」問題ニ関スル件
A.7.0.0.9-36-1 第1巻	1945/9/11	「チモール」問題ニ関スル件
A.7.0.0.9-36-1 第1巻	1945/9/13	「チモール」総督府行政権接収ノ件
A.7.0.0.9-36-1 第1巻	1945/9/13	「チモール」問題ニ関スル件
A.7.0.0.9-36-1 第1巻	1945/9/14	「チモール」問題ニ関スル件
A.7.0.0.9-36-1 第1巻	1945/9/15	「チモール」ト葡本国間ニ直接無電再開ニ関スル件
A.7.0.0.9-36-1 第1巻	1945/9/22	本邦澳門間通信ニ関スル件
A.7.0.0.9-36-1 第1巻	1945/9/28	「チモール」問題ニ関スル件
A.7.0.0.9-36-1 第1巻	1945/9/28	「チモール」問題ニ関スル件
A.7.0.0.9-36-1 第1巻	1945/10/8	「チモール」問題経緯公表
A.7.0.0.9-36-1 第1巻	1945/10/13	
A.7.0.0.9-36-1 第1巻	1945/10/23	「チモール」問題ニ関スル件
A.7.0.0.9-36-1 第1巻	1945/10/23	「チモール」問題ニ関スル件

English Translation of Title	特記事項
On disarmament of our military in Timor	リスボン森島守人公使発東郷茂徳外相宛第276号、上と同文書に手書きの修正記入
Regarding the Timor problem	東郷茂徳大臣発リスボン森島守人公使宛第156号
On disarmament of our military in Timor	リスボン森島守人公使発東郷茂徳大臣宛第276号、先の文書と同。記入者不明のサインあり
Regarding the Timor problem	重光葵外相発リスボン森島守人公使宛第162号
Regarding the Timor problem	リスボン森島守人公使発重光葵外相宛第309号
Regarding the Timor problem	リスボン森島守人公使発重光葵外相宛第311号
The Timor problem	重光葵外相発リスボン森島守人公使宛第169号
Regarding the Timor problem	リスボン森島守人公使発重光葵外相宛第316号
Regarding the Timor problem	重光葵外相発リスボン森島守人公使宛第172号
Regarding the Timor problem	リスボン森島守人公使発重光葵外相宛第324号
Regarding the Timor problem	重光葵外相発リスボン森島守人公使宛第174号
On wireless communication between Macao and Timor	リスボン森島守人公使発重光葵外相宛第327号
Regarding the Timor problem	重光葵外相発リスボン森島守人公使宛第175号
Regarding the Timor problem	リスボン森島守人公使発重光葵外相宛第333号
	クーパン派遣隊長発軍務局長宛
Regarding the Timor problem	リスボン森島守人公使発重光葵外相宛第345号
Regarding the Timor problem	リスボン森島守人公使発重光葵外相宛第345号、上と同文書。
On the requisition of administrative rights of the Timor Governor's office	リスボン森島守人公使発重光葵外相宛第351号
Regarding the Timor problem	重光葵外相発リスボン森島守人公使宛第177号
Regarding the Timor problem	リスボン森島守人公使発重光葵外相宛第355号
Regarding resumption of direct communication between Timor and metropolitan Portugal	リスボン森島守人公使発重光葵外相宛第358号
Regarding communication beween Japan and Macao	吉田外相発リスボン森島守人公使宛第182号
Regarding the Timor problem	リスボン森島守人公使発吉田外相宛第376号
Regarding the Timor problem	リスボン森島守人公使発吉田外相宛第378号
Public announcement of the circumstance of the Timor problem	リスボン森島守人公使発吉田外相宛第397号「チモール問題の経緯」というメモ添付。
	海部隊参謀長（チモール）発吉田外相宛海司電第88号
Regarding the Timor problem	吉田外相発リスボン森島守人公使宛第192号
Regarding the Timor problem	吉田外相発リスボン森島守人公使宛第193号、内容は（別紙）にあり

請求番号 File Number	日付 Date	資料名 Title
A.7.0.0.9-36-1 第1巻		（資料一）　チモール嶋土民蜂起経緯並ニポルトガル人保護ニ関スル彼我現地官憲交渉顛末（昭和十七年十月二十五日附　在ディリー帝国領事ヨリ外務大臣宛報告写）
A.7.0.0.9-36-1 第1巻		葡領「チモール」視察員ニ対スル応酬資料
A.7.0.0.9-36-1 第1巻		「ポルトガル」森島公使来電238号
A.7.0.0.9-36-1 第1巻		
A.7.0.0.9-36-1 第1巻		
A.7.0.0.9-36-1 第1巻	1945/9/12	Formal Surrender of Timor Signed
A.7.0.0.9-36-1 第1巻	1945/9/6 （受）	
A.7.0.0.9-36-1 第1巻		（資料二）葡人「リキサ」「マウバラ」収容保護経緯（現地軍ノ記録ニ依ル）
A.7.0.0.9-36-1 第1巻		（資料三）「チモール」土民蜂起ノ情況（当時日本軍関係部隊ノ調査ニ依ル）
A.7.0.0.9-36-1 第1巻		（資料四）葡側ノ中立違反及利敵通敵行為ノ実例
A.7.0.0.9-36-1 第1巻		（資料五）葡人収容ニ関スル総督ノ布告

English Translation of Title	特記事項
(document 1) The progress of Timor natives uprising and the results of our local officials' negotiations for the protection of Portuguese (a copy of a report from the local consulate at Dili to the Minister of Foreign Affairs on October 25, 1942)	上記添付文書。1942年10月24日付　マヌエル・デ・アブレウ・フェレイラ・デ・カルバリヨより在「ディリー」帝国領事宛書簡添付
Preparatery documents for the inspector for Portuguese "Timor"	「調書(1)葡領「チモール」ノ主権及行政権ニ関スル件」、「調書(2)英国軍侵入当時ノ現地葡側ノ態度ニ関スル応酬振リ」、「調書(3)「チモール」嶋葡国人ノ犯セル中立違反及通敵行為ノ実例（詳細ノ資料ハ現地軍ニ於テ入手スルヲ要ス）」、「調書(4)土民蜂起ヨリ現地協定締結ニ至ル経緯」、「調書(5)（一）「チモール」島ニ濠蘭軍侵入迄ノ経緯　（二）「チモール」島ニ葡国兵派遣　（三）「チモール」島ヘノ皇軍進駐　（四）日本軍ノ葡領「チモール」進駐ニ際シ葡側ヘ与ヘタル反撃　（五）皇軍進駐後ノ現地葡側官憲ノ態度　（六）無電台押収事件　（七）総督更迭問題　（八）「チモール」問題ニ関スル我方要求ト之ニ対スル葡側態度　（九）土人蜂起ト葡人保護問題（現地協定）　（十）本件交渉中絶ヨリ葡側視察員派遣ニ至ル経緯」、「調書(6)「チモール」島在留葡人関係状況（昭和一九、大東亜省南方事務局政務課）」
Telegram no. 238 from Minister Morishima in Portugal	リスボン森島守人公使発東郷茂徳外相宛第238号についての海軍の意見
	クーパン派遣隊長発軍務局長宛、軍務021611番電関連。軍務021611番電も添付
	二南遣艦隊長官発軍務局長宛
	六警クーパン派遣隊発軍務局長宛第051915番電
(document 2) Circumstances of internment for the protection of Portuguese at Liquicia and Maubara (based on local military records)	上記説明文書
(document 3) Situation of the native Timorese uprising (based on the investigation of the Japanese military unit related to the incident at that time)	上記説明文書
(document 4) Examples of Portuguese violations of neutrality and their behavior which is beneficial and communicative to the enemy	上記説明文書
(document 5) The Governor-general's announcement of Portuguese internment	上記説明文書

請求番号 File Number	日付 Date	資料名 Title
A.7.0.0.9-36-1 第1巻		（資料六）「リキサ、マウバラ」収容地域ニ於ケル日本軍ノ葡人取扱ニ関スル葡側ノ感謝文
A.7.0.0.9-36-1 第1巻		（資料七）葡国視察員ニ交附セル身分証明書寫
A.7.0.0.9-36-1 第2巻	1944/1/17	「ホルダナ」外相ノ時局ニ関スル内話
A.7.0.0.9-36-1 第2巻	1944/1/22	電報
A.7.0.0.9-36-1 第2巻	1944/1/24	葡萄牙人対策ニ関スル件
A.7.0.0.9-36-1 第2巻	1944/1/28	葡萄牙人対策ニ関スル件
A.7.0.0.9-36-1 第2巻	1944/1/26	「チモール」島問題ニ関スル件
A.7.0.0.9-36-1 第2巻	1944/1/26	「チモール」問題ニ関スル件
A.7.0.0.9-36-1 第2巻	1944/1/26	「チモール」問題ニ関スル件
A.7.0.0.9-36-1 第2巻	1944/2/4	「チモール」視察員派遣ニ関スル件
A.7.0.0.9-36-1 第2巻	1944/2/4	「チモール」視察員派遣ニ関スル件
A.7.0.0.9-36-1 第2巻	1944/2/4	淀川総領事帰任ニ関スル件
A.7.0.0.9-36-1 第2巻	1944/3/4	視察員派遣ニ関スル件
A.7.0.0.9-36-1 第2巻	1944/3/4	視察員派遣ニ関スル件
A.7.0.0.9-36-1 第2巻	1944/2/9	「チモール」問題ノ件
A.7.0.0.9-36-1 第2巻	1944/2/10	「チモール」視察員派遣ニ関スル件
A.7.0.0.9-36-1 第2巻	1944/2/10	「チモール」視察員派遣ニ関スル件
A.7.0.0.9-36-1 第2巻	1944/2/11	「チモール」視察員派遣ニ関スル件
A.7.0.0.9-36-1 第2巻	1944/2/16	「チモール」問題ニ関スル件
A.7.0.0.9-36-1 第2巻	1944/2/12	「チモール」問題ニ関スル件
A.7.0.0.9-36-1 第2巻	1944/2/16	「チモール」問題ニ関スル件
A.7.0.0.9-36-1 第2巻	1944/2/16	「チモール」視察員派遣ニ関スル件
A.7.0.0.9-36-1 第2巻	1944/2/16	「チモール」問題ニ関スル件
A.7.0.0.9-36-1 第2巻	1944/2/16	「チモール」視察員派遣ニ関スル件
A.7.0.0.9-36-1 第2巻	1944/2/17	「チモール」視察員派遣ニ関スル件
A.7.0.0.9-36-1 第2巻	1944/2/18	福井副領事一時帰朝方ノ件

English Translation of Title	特記事項
(document 6) Portuguese letter of appreciation related to the Japanese military's treatment of Portuguese in the Liquicia and Maubara internment camps	上記関連資料（訳文）
(document 7) Copies for the issuance of identification cards to Portuguese inspectors	上記関連資料（葡文・訳文）
Unofficial Comment on the current situation by Minister of Foreign Affairs Fordana	マドリード須磨弥吉郎公使発重光葵外相宛第43号
Telegram	軍参謀長発軍務局長宛
Regarding the way to deal with the Portuguese	ディリ富永総領事代理発青木一男大東亜相宛第8号
Regarding the way to deal with the Portuguese	青木一男大東亜相発ディリー富永総領事代理宛大4号
Regarding the Timor island problem	リスボン森島守人公使発重光葵外相宛第27号
Regarding the Timor problem	リスボン森島守人公使発重光葵外相宛第28号
Regarding the Timor problem	リスボン森島守人公使発重光葵外相宛第28号、上と同文書
Regarding the dispatch of the Timor inspector	リスボン森島守人公使発重光葵外相宛第42号
Regarding the dispatch of the Timor inspector	リスボン森島守人公使発重光葵外相宛第40号
Regarding the return of Consul-general Yodogawa	ディリ富永総領事代理発青木一男大東亜相宛第9号
Regarding the dispatch of an inspector	ディリ淀川正樹総領事発青木一男大東亜相宛第16号
Regarding the dispatch of an inspector	ディリ淀川正樹総領事発青木一男大東亜相宛第17号、上16号の続き
On the Timor problem	マカオ福井領事代理発青木一男大東亜相宛第8号
Regarding the dispatch of the Timor inspector	リスボン森島守人公使発重光葵外相宛第49号
Regarding the dispatch of the Timor inspector	リスボン森島守人公使発重光葵外相宛第49号、上と同文書
Regarding the dispatch of the Timor inspector	リスボン森島守人公使発重光葵外相宛第50号
Regarding the Timor problem	重光葵外相発リスボン森島守人公使宛第50号
Regarding the Timor problem	重光葵外相発リスボン森島守人公使宛第45号
Regarding the Timor problem	マカオ福井領事代理発重光葵外相宛第1号
Regarding the dispatch of the Timor inspector	リスボン森島守人公使発重光葵外相宛第53号
Regarding the Timor problem	マカオ福井領事代理発重光葵外相宛第1号、既出文書と同じもの
Regarding the dispatch of the Timor inspector	リスボン森島守人公使発重光葵外相宛第53号、既出文書と同じもの
Regarding the dispatch of the Timor inspector	リスボン森島守人公使発重光葵外相宛第54号、「絶対『極秘』ニ付取扱御注意相成度」の印
On the temporary return of Deputy Consul Fukui	マカオ福井領事代理発青木一男大東亜相宛第10号

I. 日本所蔵史料 (Materials in Japanese Archives)

請求番号 File Number	日付 Date	資料名 Title
A.7.0.0.9-36-1 第2巻	1944/2/18	澳門ニ於ケル日本船舶爆沈ニ関スル件
A.7.0.0.9-36-1 第2巻	1944/2/19	「チモール」問題ニ関スル件
A.7.0.0.9-36-1 第2巻	1944/2/17	「チモール」問題ニ関スル件
A.7.0.0.9-36-1 第2巻	1944/2/17	「チモール」視察員派遣ニ関スル件
A.7.0.0.9-36-1 第2巻	1944/2/17	「チモール」視察員派遣ニ関スル件
A.7.0.0.9-36-1 第2巻	1944/2/21	視察員派遣ニ関スル件
A.7.0.0.9-36-1 第2巻	1944/2/21	「チモール」問題ニ関スル件
A.7.0.0.9-36-1 第2巻	1944/2/26	「チモール」視察員派遣ニ関スル件
A.7.0.0.9-36-1 第2巻		「チモール」島視察員「コスタ」大尉経歴及傾向（在澳門福井領事代理報告）
A.7.0.0.9-36-1 第2巻		
A.7.0.0.9-36-1 第2巻		
A.7.0.0.9-36-1 第2巻	1944/2/23	視察員派遣ニ関スル件
A.7.0.0.9-36-1 第2巻	1944/2/19	電報
A.7.0.0.9-36-1 第2巻	1944/2/23	視察員派遣ニ関スル件
A.7.0.0.9-36-1 第2巻	1944/2/27	電報
A.7.0.0.9-36-1 第2巻	1944/2/26	「チモール」視察員派遣ニ関スル件
A.7.0.0.9-36-1 第2巻	1944/2/26	「チモール」視察員派遣ニ関スル件
A.7.0.0.9-36-1 第2巻	1944/2/29	「チモール」視察員派遣ニ関スル件
A.7.0.0.9-36-1 第2巻		加藤中佐ヨリ
A.7.0.0.9-36-1 第2巻	1944/2/29	「チモール」視察員ニ関スル件
A.7.0.0.9-36-1 第2巻	1944/3/2	「チモール」派遣葡側視察員行動予定
A.7.0.0.9-36-1 第2巻	1944/3/3	澳門ニ於ケル日本船舶爆沈ニ関スル件
A.7.0.0.9-36-1 第2巻	1944/3/3	澳門ニ於ケル我外交機関強化ノ件
A.7.0.0.9-36-1 第2巻	1944/3/1	「チモール」視察員派遣ニ関スル件
A.7.0.0.9-36-1 第2巻		淀川総領事宛大東亜省電信案

2．外務省外交史料館所蔵史料
The Diplomatic Records Office of Ministry of Foreign Affairs

English Translation of Title	特記事項
Regarding the explosion of a Japanese ship in Macao	重光葵外相発リスボン森島守人公使宛第53号
Regarding the Timor problem	重光葵外相発リスボン森島守人公使宛第55号
Regarding the Timor problem	マカオ福井領事代理発重光葵外相宛第2号
Regarding the dispatch of the Timor inspector	リスボン森島守人公使発重光葵外相宛第54号、既出文書と同じもの
Regarding the dispatch of the Timor inspector	リスボン森島守人公使発重光葵外相宛第54号、既出文書と同じもの
Regarding the dispatch of an inspector	青木一男大東亜相発ディリ淀川正樹総領事宛第6号
Regarding the Timor problem	リスボン森島守人公使発重光葵外相宛第59号
Regarding the dispatch of the Timor inspector	リスボン森島守人公使発重光葵外相宛第69号
The Career and Character of Capt. Costa, Timor inspector (Report from the substitute of Consul Fukui in Macao)	マカオ福井領事代理作成の報告書
	広東武官作成、「海軍」の罫紙
	広東武官作成、「海軍」の罫紙
Regarding the dispatch of an inspector	青木一男大東亜相発ディリ淀川正樹総領事宛第6号
Telegram	葡国公使館附武官発次長宛第654号、「軍機極秘親展」
Regarding the dispatch of an inspector	ディリ淀川正樹総領事発青木一男大東亜相宛第12号
Telegram	葡国公使館附武官発次長宛第658号、「軍機極秘親展」
Regarding the dispatch of the Timor inspector	リスボン森島守人公使発重光葵外相宛第69号、既出文書と同じもの
Regarding the dispatch of the Timor inspector	リスボン森島守人公使発重光葵外相宛第69号、既出文書と同じもの
Regarding the dispatch of the Timor inspector	青木一男大東亜相発マカオ福井領事代理宛第9号、転電ディリ淀川正樹総領事第7号
From Lt. Col. Kato	輝集團参謀長発軍務局長宛、陸軍の罫紙
Regarding the Timor inspector	リスボン森島守人公使発重光葵外相宛第73号
Schedule of inspections sent by Portugal	軍務課作成の政策文書
Regarding the explosion of a Japanese ship in Macao	マドリード須磨弥吉郎公使発重光葵外相宛第80号
On Japan's strengthening of diplomatic organization in Macao	リスボン森島守人公使発重光葵外相宛第81号
Regarding the dispatch of the Timor inspector	青木一男大東亜相発マカオ福井領事代理宛第10号
Draft of a telegram from the Ministry of Great Asia to Consul-general Yodogawa	外務省の罫紙

I. 日本所蔵史料（Materials in Japanese Archives）

請求番号 File Number	日付 Date	資料名 Title
A.7.0.0.9-36-1 第2巻	1944/3/2	視察員派遣ニ関スル件
A.7.0.0.9-36-1 第2巻	1944/3/3	視察員派遣ニ関スル件
A.7.0.0.9-36-1 第2巻	1944/3/2	葡側視察員ニ関スル件
A.7.0.0.9-36-1 第2巻	1944/3/2	葡側視察員ノ行動ニ関スル件
A.7.0.0.9-36-1 第2巻	1944/3/2	葡側視察員ノ行動ニ関スル件
A.7.0.0.9-36-1 第2巻	1944/3/2	葡側視察員行動予定ノ件
A.7.0.0.9-36-1 第2巻	1944/3/4	「チモール」視察員立寄ニ関スル件
A.7.0.0.9-36-1 第2巻	1944/3/4	視察員派遣ニ関スル件
A.7.0.0.9-36-1 第2巻	1944/3/6	視察員派遣ニ関スル件
A.7.0.0.9-36-1 第2巻	1944/3/4	視察員派遣ニ関スル件
A.7.0.0.9-36-1 第2巻	1944/3/7	視察員派遣ニ関スル件
A.7.0.0.9-36-1 第2巻	1944/3/7	視察員派遣ニ関スル件
A.7.0.0.9-36-1 第2巻	1944/3/6	葡側視察員「コスター」ニ関連シ阿片供給問題ニ関スル件
A.7.0.0.9-36-1 第2巻		
A.7.0.0.9-36-1 第2巻	1944/3/7	「チモール」問題ニ関スル件
A.7.0.0.9-36-1 第2巻	1944/3/9	「チモール」派遣葡側視察員行動予定
A.7.0.0.9-36-1 第2巻	1944/3/9	電報訳
A.7.0.0.9-36-1 第2巻		
A.7.0.0.9-36-1 第2巻	1944/3/7	葡萄牙国旗送付ニ関スル件
A.7.0.0.9-36-1 第2巻	1944/3/8	視察員派遣ニ関スル件
A.7.0.0.9-36-1 第2巻	1944/3/10	視察員派遣ニ関スル件
A.7.0.0.9-36-1 第2巻	1944/3/10	「チモール」視察員「コスタ」一行出発ノ件

2．外務省外交史料館所蔵史料　　　　　　　　　　　　　　　　　　　　　　　　　　　　*161*
The Diplomatic Records Office of Ministry of Foreign Affairs

English Translation of Title	特記事項
Regarding the dispatch of an inspector	青木一男大東亜相発マカオ福井総領事宛第11号
Regarding the dispatch of an inspector	青木一男大東亜大臣発ディリ淀川正樹総領事宛第8号
Regarding the Portuguese inspector	陸軍省軍務局長発輝・堅部隊参謀長宛軍務電第211号、陸軍の罫紙
Regarding the behavior of the Portuguese inspector	陸軍省軍務局長発台湾軍参謀長宛軍務電第212号、陸軍の罫紙
Regarding the behavior of the Portuguese inspector	陸軍省軍務局長発渡集團参謀長宛軍務電第213号、陸軍の罫紙
On the inspection schedule of the Portuguese inspector	陸軍省軍務局長発輝・堅部隊参謀長宛軍務電第210号、陸軍の罫紙
Regarding the stop-over of the Timor inspector	青木一男大東亜相発マニラ村田省蔵大使宛第114号
Regarding the dispatch of an inspector	青木一男大東亜相発マカオ福井領事代理宛第12号、転電ディリ淀川正樹総領事第9号
Regarding the dispatch of an inspector	青木一男大東亜相発マカオ福井領事代理宛第13号
Regarding the dispatch of an inspector	ディリ淀川正樹総領事発青木一男大東亜相宛第18号、後半電文不明
Regarding the dispatch of an inspector	マカオ朝比奈事務代理青木一男大東亜相宛第15号
Regarding the dispatch of an inspector	朝比奈事務代理発青木一男大東亜相宛第15号、上と同文書
Regarding the opium supply problem in connection to Portuguese Inspector Costa	軍務課作成の政策文書、陸軍の罫紙
	陸軍の罫紙、同文書既出、広東武官作成
Regarding the Timor problem	大東亜省の罫紙、起案者名なし。陸軍省からの文書（昭和19年3月6日付、「堅部隊参謀ヨリ」）の供覧
Plan of inspections sent by Portugal	陸軍の罫紙、軍務課作成の政策文書
Telegram translation	台湾軍参謀長発軍務局長宛・台依頼電146号
	香港総督部参謀長発軍務局長宛・香総参電第909号、陸軍の罫紙
Regarding sending the Portuguese national flag	ディリ淀川正樹総領事発青木一男大東亜省宛第19号
Regarding the dispatch of an inspector	青木一男大東亜相発ディリー淀川正樹総領事宛第13・14号、リスボン森島守人公使発重光葵外相宛第74号の内容の伝える
Regarding the dispatch of an inspector	ディリ淀川正樹総領事発青木一男大東亜相宛第20号
On the departure of Timor Inspector Costa's party	台北太田外事部長発重光葵外相宛第14号、同文書既出

請求番号 File Number	日付 Date	資料名 Title
A.7.0.0.9-36-1 第2巻	1944/3/9	「チモール」視察員派遣ニ関スル件
A.7.0.0.9-36-1 第2巻	1944/3/10	「チモール」視察員立寄ニ関スル件
A.7.0.0.9-36-1 第2巻	1944/3/14	「チモール」視察員派遣ノ件
A.7.0.0.9-36-1 第2巻	1944/3/12	「チモール」視察員派遣ニ関スル件
A.7.0.0.9-36-1 第2巻	1944/3/13	曾禰課長及石井事務官出張ノ件
A.7.0.0.9-36-1 第2巻	1944/3/11	視察員派遣ニ関スル件
A.7.0.0.9-36-1 第2巻	1944/3/8	視察員派遣ニ関スル件
A.7.0.0.9-36-1 第2巻	1944/3/15	「コスタ」大尉比島向出発ノ件
A.7.0.0.9-36-1 第2巻	1944/3/16	「チモール」視察員立寄ニ関スル件
A.7.0.0.9-36-1 第2巻	1944/3/15	「コスタ」大尉一行動静ノ件
A.7.0.0.9-36-1 第2巻	1944/3/18	「コスタ」大尉比島向出発ノ件
A.7.0.0.9-36-1 第2巻	1944/3/18	「コスタ」大尉比島向出発ノ件
A.7.0.0.9-36-1 第2巻	1944/3/20	「コスタ」大尉一行到着ノ件
A.7.0.0.9-36-1 第2巻	1944/3/21	「コスタ」大尉到着ニ関スル件
A.7.0.0.9-36-1 第2巻	1944/3/23	「チモール」問題ニ関スル件
A.7.0.0.9-36-1 第2巻	1944/3/23	「コスタ」大尉ノ人柄ニ関スル件
A.7.0.0.9-36-1 第2巻		大東亜省東光課長ヘ　石井事務官ヨリ
A.7.0.0.9-36-1 第2巻		大東亜省東光課長ヘ　石井事務官ヨリ
A.7.0.0.9-36-1 第2巻	1944/3/26	淀川総領事及「コスタ」一行出発ノ件
A.7.0.0.9-36-1 第2巻	1944/3/26	「コスタ」依頼電ノ件

English Translation of Title	特記事項
Regarding the Timor inspector	リスボン森島守人公使発重光葵外相宛第83号、同文書既出
Regarding the stop-over of the Timor inspector	青木一男大東亜相発マニラ村田省蔵大使宛第121号
On the dispatch of the Timor inspector	マニラ村田省蔵大使発重光葵外相宛第29号、同文書既出
Regarding the dispatch of the Timor inspector	マニラ村田省蔵大使発重光葵外相宛第26号、同文書既出
On the dispatch of departmental chief Sone and admnistrative officer Ishii	台北太田外事部長発重光葵外相宛第16号
Regarding the dispatch of an inspector	青木一男大東亜相発マカオ朝比奈領事代理宛第15号
Regarding the dispatch of an inspector	マカオ朝比奈領事代理発青木一男大東亜相宛第16号
On the departure of Capt. Costa to the Philippines	マニラ村田省蔵大使発青木一男大東亜相宛第139号
Regarding the stop over of the Timor inspector	青木一男大東亜相発台湾総督府蜂谷外事部長宛第18号
On the activities of Capt. Costa's party	ダバオ加藤総領事発青木一男大東亜相宛第47号
On the departure of Capt. Costa for the Philippines	マカオ朝比奈事務代理発青木一男大東亜相宛（本官発比大宛電報第1号）
On the departure of Capt. Costa for the Philippines	マカオ朝比奈事務代理発青木一男大東亜相宛（本官発比大宛電報第1号）、上と同文書
On the arrival of Capt. Costa's party	ディリ淀川正樹総領事発青木一男大東亜相宛第23号
Regarding the arrival of Capt. Costa	青木一男大東亜相発マカオ朝比奈事務代理宛第17号
Regarding the Timor problem	青木一男大東亜相発ディリー淀川正樹総領事宛第20・21・22号、リスボン森島守人公使発重光葵外相宛第93号の内容伝える
Regarding the personality of Captain Costa	青木一男大東亜相発ディリー淀川正樹総領事宛第23号、リスボン森島守人公使発重光葵外相宛第88号の内容伝える
Administrative officer Ishii to Department Chief T?mitsu in the Ministry of Great East Asia	陸軍の罫紙、大東亜省東光武三宛
Administrative officer Ishii to Department Chief T?mitsu in the Ministry of Great East Asia	陸軍の罫紙、上と同文書
On the departure of Consul-general Yodogawa and the Captain Costa party	ディリ富永総領事代理発青木一男大東亜相宛第33号
On Costa's request to send a telegram	ディリ富永総領事代理発青木一男大東亜相宛第34号

I．日本所蔵史料（Materials in Japanese Archives）

請求番号 File Number	日付 Date	資料名 Title
A.7.0.0.9-36-1 第2巻	1944/3/26	「コスタ」依頼電
A.7.0.0.9-36-1 第2巻	1944/3/29	「コスタ」大尉依頼電ニ関スル件
A.7.0.0.9-36-1 第2巻	1944/3/26	富永副領事「デイリー」帰還ノ件
A.7.0.0.9-36-1 第2巻	1944/3/28	「コスタ」一行ノ行動ニ関スル件
A.7.0.0.9-36-1 第2巻	1944/3/27	「コスタ」大尉ニ関スル件
A.7.0.0.9-36-1 第2巻	1944/3/27	「コスタ」大尉ノ談話ノ件
A.7.0.0.9-36-1 第2巻	1944/3/27	「コスタ」大尉到着ニ関スル件
A.7.0.0.9-36-1 第2巻	1944/3/27	「チモール」視察員ニ関スル件
A.7.0.0.9-36-1 第2巻	1944/3/29	「コスタ」ニ関スル件
A.7.0.0.9-36-1 第2巻	1944/3/21	「コスタ」滞島期間ニ関スル件
A.7.0.0.9-36-1 第2巻	1944/3/21	「コスタ」滞島期間ニ関スル件
A.7.0.0.9-36-1 第2巻	1944/3/19	淀川総領事更迭ニ関スル件
A.7.0.0.9-36-1 第2巻	1944/3/29	「コスタ」大尉一行動静ニ関スル件
A.7.0.0.9-36-1 第2巻	1944/3/30	「コスタ」大尉ニ関スル件
A.7.0.0.9-36-1 第2巻	1944/3/31	「チモール」視察員ニ関スル件
A.7.0.0.9-36-1 第2巻		葡領「チモール」島視察ニ関スル件
A.7.0.0.9-36-1 第2巻		「コ」行動ニ関シ
A.7.0.0.9-36-1 第2巻		「コ」行動ニ関シ
A.7.0.0.9-36-1 第2巻	1944/4/5	「コスタ」大尉一行ニ関スル件
A.7.0.0.9-36-1 第2巻	1944/4/5	「コスタ」大尉一行ニ関スル件
A.7.0.0.9-36-1 第2巻	1944/4/6	「コスタ」大尉便宜供与ノ件

English Translation of Title	特記事項
The telegram of Costa's request	ディリ富永総領事代理発青木一男大東亜相宛第35号
Regarding Capt. Costa's request to send a telegram	青木一男大東亜相発マカオ朝比奈領事代理宛第19号
On the return of Deputy Consul Tominaga to Dili	ディリ富永総領事代理発青木一男大東亜相宛第36号
Regarding the behavior of the Costa party	ダバオ加藤総領事発青木一男大東亜相宛（本官発比大宛電報第58号）
Regarding Capt. Costa	ディリ細川総領事代理発青木大東亜大臣宛第38号
On a conversation with Captain Costa	ディリ細川総領事代理発青木大東亜大臣宛第39号（別電）
Regarding the arrival of Capt. Costa	マカオ朝比奈事務代理発青木一男大東亜相宛第19号
Regarding the Timor inspector	青木一男大東亜相発マニラ村田省蔵大使宛、電信番号なし
Regarding Costa	青木一男大東亜相発マカオ朝比奈領事代理宛第20号、青木一男大東亜相発ディリ淀川正樹総領事宛第29号の内容伝える
Regarding the period of Costa's stay on the island	ディリ淀川正樹総領事発青木一男大東亜相宛第26号
Regarding the period of Costa's stay on the island	ディリ淀川正樹総領事発青木一男大東亜相宛第27号、上26号の続き
Regarding the demotion of Consul-general Yodogawa	ディリ淀川正樹総領事発青木一男大東亜相宛第25号、「曽根ヨリ」との副題あり
Regarding the activities of Captain Costa's party	ダバオ加藤総領事発青木一男大東亜相宛、（本官発比大宛電報第59号）
Regarding Capt. Costa	マニラ村田省蔵大使発重光葵外相宛第36号、副件名は「古内課長へ曽根ヨリ」、同文書既出
Regarding the Timor inspector	台北太田外事部長発重光葵外相宛第22号、同文書既出
Regarding inspection of Portuguese Timor island	1（軍務局長宛「加藤中佐ヨリ」及び軍務局長宛「堅集参電第226号」）、2（「チモール」派遣員ニ関スル件）の供覧
Regarding behavior of Costa	軍務局長宛、陸軍の罫紙
Regarding behavior of Costa	軍務局長宛、陸軍の罫紙、上と同文書
Regarding Capt. Costa's party	青木一男大東亜相発マカオ朝比奈領事代理宛第21号
Regarding Capt. Costa's party	青木一男大東亜相発ディリ細川総領事代理宛第28号
On the provision of conveniences for Captain Costa	青木一男大東亜相発広東中野参事官宛第105号

請求番号 File Number	日付 Date	資料名 Title
A.7.0.0.9-36-1 第2巻	1944/4/6	福井帰任ノ件
A.7.0.0.9-36-1 第2巻	1944/4/7	「コスタ」大尉ニ関スル件
A.7.0.0.9-36-1 第2巻	1944/4/8	「チモール」視察員ニ関スル件
A.7.0.0.9-36-1 第2巻	1944/4/13	「チモール」視察ニ関スル件
A.7.0.0.9-36-1 第2巻	1944/4/8	「チモール」視察ニ関スル件（「コスタ」報告書）
A.7.0.0.9-36-1 第2巻	1944/4/8	「チモール」視察ニ関スル件
A.7.0.0.9-36-1 第2巻		「コスタ」大尉「マカオ」帰還旅程
A.7.0.0.9-36-1 第2巻	1944/4/13	「コスタ」大尉帰任ノ件
A.7.0.0.9-36-1 第2巻	1944/4/14	「チモール」状況改善実情電報方ノ件
A.7.0.0.9-36-1 第2巻	1944/4/15	「チモール」視察員謝意伝達方ノ件
A.7.0.0.9-36-1 第2巻	1944/4/15	「コスタ」大尉謝意表明ノ件
A.7.0.0.9-36-1 第2巻	1944/4/15	「コスタ」大尉ト新聞記者団会見ノ件
A.7.0.0.9-36-1 第2巻	1944/4/15	「チモール」視察員報告ニ関スル件
A.7.0.0.9-36-1 第2巻	1944/4/16	「コスタ」大尉旅行ニ対スル謝意伝達ノ件
A.7.0.0.9-36-1 第2巻	1944/4/17	「コスタ」大尉旅行ニ対スル謝意伝達ノ件
A.7.0.0.9-36-1 第2巻	1944/4/17	「チモール」島事情改善ノ件
A.7.0.0.9-36-1 第2巻	1944/4/17	「コスタ」大尉ノ「チモール」島視察ニ関スル件
A.7.0.0.9-36-1 第2巻	1944/4/18	「コスタ」大尉道中談要旨ノ件
A.7.0.0.9-36-1 第2巻	1944/4/18	「コスタ」大尉帰任後政庁模様ノ件
A.7.0.0.9-36-1 第2巻	1944/3/4	領収書
A.7.0.0.9-36-1 第2巻	1944/4/11	「チモール」視察員ニ関スル件
A.7.0.0.9-36-1 第2巻		「チモール」派遣葡側視察員取扱ニ関スル件
A.7.0.0.9-36-1 第2巻	1943/3/28	葡領「チモール」問題ノ経緯
A.7.0.0.9-36-1 第2巻	1944/2/10	「チモール」派遣葡側視察員取扱ニ関スル打合ニ関スル件

English Translation of Title	特記事項
On the return of Fukui	青木一男大東亜相発マカオ朝比奈事務代理宛第22号
Regarding Captain Costa	青木一男大東亜相発台北蜂谷外事部長宛第24号
Regarding inspectors for Timor	青木一男大東亜相発マカオ朝比奈領事代理宛第23号
Regarding the inspection of Timor	青木一男大東亜相発ディリ細川総領事代理宛第31号
Regarding the inspection of Timor (the Costa Report)	重光葵外相発リスボン森島守人公使宛第100号（別電）、同文書既出
Regarding the Timor inspection	重光葵外相発リスボン森島守人公使宛第99号、同文書既出
The return schedule of Capt. Costa to Macao	
On the return of Capt. Costa	マカオ福井総領事発青木一男大東亜相宛第27号
Telegram on the improvement of the current Timor situation	リスボン森島守人公使発重光葵外相宛第136号、同文書既出
Passing information on appreciation from the Timor inspector	マカオ福井領事代理発重光葵外相宛第3号、同文書既出
On the announcement of appreciation by Captain Costa	マカオ福井領事代理発重光葵外相・青木一男大東亜相宛第2号、同文書既出
Press conference with Captain Costa	マカオ福井総領事発青木一男大東亜相宛第29号
Regarding the Timor Inspector's report	マカオ福井総領事発青木一男大東亜相宛第30号
On Captain Costa's sending appreciation regaring the trip	マカオ福井総領事発青木一男大東亜相宛第28号
On Captain Costa's sending appreciation regarding the trip	青木一男大東亜相発マニラ森重代理大使宛第215号
On improvement of the Timor situation	重光葵外相発リスボン森島守人公使宛第111号、同文書既出
Regarding Captain Costa's inspection of Timor island	青木一男大東亜相発ディリ細川総領事代理宛第32号
Summary of Capt. Costa's talk during the inspection trip	マカオ福井領事代理発重光葵外相・青木一男大東亜相宛第3号
On the governmental situation after Costa's return	マカオ福井領事代理発重光葵外相・青木一男大東亜相宛第4号
Receipt	コスタ接待に関する領収書、大東亜省南方事務局政務課長東光武三作成
Regarding the Timor inspector	台北蜂谷外事部長発重光葵外相宛第30号、同文書既出
Regarding treatment of the Portuguese inspector dispatched to Timor	外務省の罫紙
Details of the Portuguese Timor problem	南政（大東亜省南洋政）作成
On the meeting about treatment of the Portuguese inspector	大東亜省の罫紙、起案者名なし、供覧文書

請求番号 File Number	日付 Date	資料名 Title
A.7.0.0.9-36-1 第2巻		（チモール関係参考資料）
A.7.0.0.9-36-1 第2巻	1944/2/2	「チモール」派遣葡側視察員取扱ニ関スル件
A.7.0.0.9-36-1 第2巻		葡領「チモール」島派遣葡側視察員取扱ニ関スル件
A.7.0.0.9-36-1 第2巻		「帝国カ作戦上許シ得ル限リ葡国主権及行政実施ヲ尊重セントスル誠意ヲ示ス為必要トナル措置」
A.7.0.0.9-36-1 第2巻		「チモール」派遣葡側視察員取扱ニ関スル打合ニ関スル件
A.7.0.0.9-36-1 第2巻	1944/1/21	チモール派遣葡側視察員取扱ニ関スル打合ニ関スル件
A.7.0.（大東亜戦争関係一件／交戦国間敵国人及俘虜取扱振関係／在敵国本邦人関係 第一巻	1942/1/9	（無題）
大東亜戦争関係一件／館長符号扱来電綴??第四巻	1942/2/2	「チモール」島問題ニ関スル件

English Translation of Title	特記事項
Reference materials on Timor	上の供覧文書に添えられたもの。①「葡領「チモール」ニ対スル葡国主権及行政実施ノ制限ニ関スル応酬要領」、②「土民蜂起問題ニ関スル応酬要領（土民蜂起ヨリ現地協定締結ニ至ル経緯参照）」、③「英蘭軍進入当時ノ現地葡側ノ態度ニ関スル応酬振リ」、④「「チモール」嶋葡国人ノ犯セル中立違反及通敵行為ノ実例（詳細ノ資料ハ現地軍ニ於テ入手スルヲ要ス）」、⑤「土民蜂起ヨリ現地協定締結ニ至ル経緯」、⑥（「豪蘭軍侵入」から「葡国視察員派遣」至る経緯を記したもの）、⑦「「チモール」島在留葡人関係状況（大東亜省調）　一、葡人ノ保護収容ニ関スル件　二、無電通信ニ関スル件　三、帝国政府ノ「チモール」総督ニ対スル融資ニ関スル件」、外務省作成
Regarding treatment of the Portuguese inspector for Timor	「葡領「チモール」島派遣葡側視察員取扱ニ関スル件（昭和十九年二月五日　大本営政府連絡会議ニ報告）」及び、その参考「帝国カ作戦上許シ得ル限リ葡国主権及行政実施ヲ尊重セントスル誠意ヲ示ス為必要トナル措置」の供覧
Regarding treatment of the Portuguese inspector for Portuguese Timor	外務省が作成した、上の供覧文書の原案
Necessary measures for showing the utmost sincere respect for the sovereignty and administration of Portugal in the context of the Imperial operation	外務省が作成した、上の供覧文書の原案
Regarding meeting about treatment of the Portuguese inspector	大東亜省の罫紙、起案者名および日付なし。1944年1月下旬に作成か。外務省作成の文書（①「葡領「チモール」ノ主権及行政権ニ関スル件」、②「「チモール」嶋葡国人ノ犯セル中立違反及通敵行為ノ実例（詳細ノ資料ハ現地軍ニ於テ入手スルヲ要ス）」、③「英蘭軍進入当時ノ現地葡側ノ態度ニ関スル応酬振リ」、④政四「「チモール」派遣葡側視察員取扱ニ関スル件」（昭和19年1月21日））を別添として供覧か
Regarding meeting about treatment of the Portuguese inspector	外務省作成文書（「チモール」派遣葡側視察員取扱ニ関スル件）及び陸軍作成文書（軍務課「「チモール」派遣葡側視察員取扱ニ関スル件（案）」昭和19年1月18日）を別添として供覧か
no title	リスボン千葉公使発東郷外相宛第14号
Regarding the Timor island problem	リスボン千葉公使発東郷外相宛第104号

請求番号 File Number	日付 Date	資料名 Title
大東亜戦争関係一件／館長符号扱来電綴??第四巻	1942/2/20	「チモール」作戦ニ関スル件
大東亜戦争関係一件／館長符号扱来電綴??第四巻	1942/2/20	「チモール」作戦に関スル申入ノ件
大東亜戦争関係一件／館長符号扱来電綴??第四巻	1942/2/20	「チモール」作戦に関スル申入ノ件
大東亜戦争関係一件／館長符号扱来電綴??第四巻	1942/2/20	「チモール」島作戦ニ関スル件
大東亜戦争関係一件／館長符号扱来電綴??第四巻	1942/2/18	葡領「チモール」問題ニ付葡側ヘノ申入ニ関スル件
E 108	1933/7/5	葡領ティモール島ニ関シ調査依頼ノ件
E 1208	1933/8/1	『ティモール』資源開発ニ関シ新総督ト会見ノ件
E 2-2-1-3-9	1939/1/6	弊社外南洋事業ニ関スル件
E 2-2-1-3-9	1941/4/16	最近ノ情勢ニ付キ
I 4-3-10	1909/2/4	蘭葡間竝ニ蘭伯間国境画定条約本文送付ノ件
I 4-3-10	1911/6/28	チモール島葡蘭両国国境ニ於ケル紛争
I 4-3-10	1912/2/6	『チモール』島問題ニ関シ取調方訓令ノ件
I 4-3-10	1913/3/10	『チモール』島問題ニ関シ報告ノ件
I 4-3-10	1917/1/29	蘭葡チモール境界限定ニ関スル件
I 4-3-15	1912/2/20	葡領チモール島土民反乱ノ件
I 4-3-15	1912/2/20	葡領チモール島土民反乱ノ件続報
	1944/2/16	『チモール』問題ニ関スル件
	1944/1/25	『チモール』島在留葡人関係概況

English Translation of Title	特記事項
Regarding the Timor operation	リスボン千葉公使発東郷外相宛第147号
On the request concerning the Timor operation	リスボン千葉公使発東郷外相宛第148号ノ1
On the request concerning the Timor operation	リスボン千葉公使発東郷外相宛第148号ノ2
Regarding the Timor island operation	リスボン千葉公使発東郷外相宛第149号
Regarding a request to Portugal on the Portuguese Timor problem	ベルリン大島大使発東郷外相宛第241号
On the request to survey Portuguese Timor island	坂本通商局第二課長発在葡隈部書記官
On the meeting with the new Governor-general regarding development of natural resources in Timor	在葡笠間公使発内田外相
Regarding our company's project in the outer South Sea	南洋興発社長松江春次発欧亜局長井上庚二郎
On the current situation	南洋興発チモール事務所発社長
On sending documents related to border-treaties between the Netherlands and Portugal as well as the Netherlands and Belgium	在蘭特命全権公使佐藤愛麿発外相小村寿太郎
Dispute on the border between the Dutch and Portuguese in Timor	在バタビア領事染谷成章発外相小村寿太郎
On an order to investigate the Timor issue	加藤高明外相発在蘭信夫淳平臨時代理公使・在葡荒川公使
On a report concerning the Timor problem	在蘭臨時代理公使信夫淳平発外相牧野伸顕
Regarding the determination of the Portuguese-Dutch Timor border	在バタビア領事松本幹之亮発外相本野一郎
On the native uprising in Portuguese Timor	在バタビア領事染谷成章発外相内田康哉
On the native uprising in Portuguese Timor, continuation	在バタビア領事染谷成章発外相内田康哉
Regarding the Timor problem	駐マカオ福井領事代理発重光葵外相
Survey of Portuguese residents on Timor island	

3. 防衛省防衛
The National Institute for Defense

請求番号 Call Number	日付 date	資料名 title	Title	著者 author
濠北－全般 1	1946/7	濠北作戦記録	The North-Australia area campaign records	第一復員局
濠北－全般 10	－	チモール島クーパン港より撤退して復員まで	Retreat from Kupang Bay, Timor Island to demobilization	第48師団衛生隊 諸橋敏夫
濠北－全般 21	1947/6	東方支隊アンボン、チモール攻略作戦	The Eastern Detachment Ambon Timor Invasion Operations	復員局
濠北－全般 42	－	蘭印・濠北・比島の船舶作戦史料	Vessel operations in the Dutch Indies, North-Australia and the Philippine Islands	松木秀満
濠北－全般 75	－	濠北作戦記録の参考　第19軍の誕生より第2方面軍の濠北進出迄	Reference to North Australia Campaign, Birth of 19th Army to North Australia invasion of 2nd Area Army	第19軍参謀 北森信男中佐
濠北－全般 90	1942/3	給養兵額調書綴		クーパン野戦倉庫
陸空－濠北方面 38	1943年	「チモール」周辺地区航空撃滅戦戦闘詳報　昭和18年2月1日～昭和18年4月30日	Battle report of air combat in Timor area (February 1, 1943 - April 30, 1943)	第4野戦飛行場設定隊

研究所所蔵史料
Studies of the Ministry of Defense

Author	特記事項 remarks	Remarks
First Demobilization Bureau		
48th Division Health Unit, MOROHASHI Toshio		
Demobilization Bureau		Monograph No.16 (Army) Ambon and Timor Invasion Operations. Prepared by First Demobilization Bureau. First Mimeographing Jun 47. Second Mimeographing Oct 49. (Both issues are identical except for pagination).
MATSUKI Hidemitsu	昭和30〜51.3収集	Collected in 1950 - March 1971.
19th Army, Staff, Lt. Col. KITAMORI Nobuo	91ページ、手書き	91 pages, hand written.
Kupang Field Warehouse	沼8933部隊、1943年3月15日Seized documents at Buellebo[?]	Numa 8933 unit, March 15, 1943. Seized documents at Buellebo [?].
4th Field Airbase Construction Unit	90ページ。作戦、警備治安、飛行場、行動経過、展開配置並に戦力の現況、衛生経理、総合成果、詳報付録表、受領作命などの項目について記述（主にディリ）	90 pages. On operations, guard and security, airfields, activities, deployment and strength, health and administration, results, details tables, orders received. (Mainly in Dili).

I. 日本所蔵史料 (Materials in Japanese Archives)

請求番号 Call Number		日付 date	資料名 title	Title	著者 author
④－戦闘詳報戦時日誌	327	1942－1944	第二十四特別根拠地隊戦時日誌　昭和17年2月～昭和19年7月	Unit diary of 24th Naval Special Base Unit (February 1942 - July 1944)	第24特別根拠地隊
④－戦闘詳報戦時日誌	326	－	第二十三特別根拠地隊戦時日誌　昭和17年3月～昭和19年12月	Unit diary of 24th Naval Special Base Unit (March 1942 - December 1944)	第23特別根拠地隊
④－陸上部隊	12	1977/12	チモール島クーパン飛行場攻略作戦記録　昭和17年2月20日～昭和17年2月22日	Operation invading Kupang Airfiled, Timor Island (Februrary 20, 1942 - February 22, 1942)	横須賀鎮守府第3特別陸戦隊副官湯原博
④－陸上部隊	19	－	横三特功績者概見表	Yokosuka 3rd Special Landing Unit commendation list	横須賀鎮守府第3特別陸戦隊副官湯原博
豪北－19A	3	－	第四十八師団（ジャワ・豪北）史料1/2　昭和31年～昭和51年収集	48th Division (Java and North Australia) materials, collected in 1951 - 1971)	松木秀満
南西－マレー・ジャワ	328	－	第四十八師団終戦処理状況報告　昭和21年3月12日～昭和21年7月5日	48th Division situation report at the end of war (March 12, 1946 - July 5, 1946)	－
豪北－19A	1	－	第19軍聴取史料	19th Army interview materials	松木秀満
沖台－台湾	61	－	台湾人方面別（部隊別）人員統計表　昭和28年8月1日	Taiwanese mobilization statistics by area and by unit (August 1, 1953). Table.	留守業務部
豪北－日誌回想	33	－	第三十八師団蘭印豪北作戦史料　昭和32年収集	38th Division Dutch Indies and North Australia campaign materials (collected in 1957)	松木秀満

Author	特記事項 remarks	Remarks
24th Naval Special Base Unit	各月毎の経過、人員の現状、主要令達報告、作戦経過概要、艦船の行動（表）などの項目について記述。各月20ページ前後	Monthly report of activities, personnel, orders received, operations overview, fleet movements (table). Each month runs about 20 pages.
23rd Naval Special Base Unit	各月毎の経過、人員の現状、主要令達報告、作戦経過概要、艦船の行動（表）などの項目について記述。各月20ページ前後	Monthly report of activities, personnel, orders received, operations overview, fleet movements (table). Each month runs about 20 pages.
Yokosuka 3rd Special Naval Landing Force Vice Commander YUHARA Hiroshi	16ページ。編成の概要、戦死・戦傷者名簿、作戦概要、手書き地図あり	16 pages. Organization overview, list of war deaths and casualties, operation overview, hand written map attached.
Yokosuka 3rd Special Naval Landing Force Vice Commander YUHARA Hiroshi	28ページ。大東亜戦役功績者概見表（クーパン攻略作戦）、「チモール」島各地戡定作戦竝ニ討伐掃蕩戦 昭和17年2月24日－5月27日	28 pages. List of Great East Asian War commendations (Kupang invasion campaign), Timor Island pacification and subjugation operations (February 24 - May 27, 1942).
MATSUKI Hidemitsu		Miscellaneous documents.
－		
MATSUKI Hidemitsu	第19軍司令官・参謀から聴取	Interviews with 19th Army Commander and Staff.
	台湾人軍人・軍属の人員調査統計表	Taiwanese military personnel and civilian employees statistics table.
MATSUKI Hidemitsu	第38師団司令官・参謀の陳述	Interviews with 38th Division Commander and Staff.

I．日本所蔵史料（Materials in Japanese Archives）

請求番号 Call Number		日付 date	資料名 title	Title	著者 author
濠北−日誌回想	46	−	歩四七蘭印チモール島戡定作戦　昭和17年3月5日〜昭和18年2月18日	47th Infantry Regiment Dutch Timor Island pacification campaign (March 5, 1942 - February 18, 1943)	大分合同新聞社　平松鷹史
南西−マレー・ジャワ	305	1945/7/31	第七方面軍戦力概況表・兵力配置要図	7th Area Army Force allocation map	第7方面軍司令部
南西−マレー・ジャワ	384	1945/5	第七方面軍兵力配備要図	7th Area Army units allocation map	−
陸空−濠北方面	3	1956/6	第三飛行団濠北方面作戦経過の概要　昭和16年11月15日〜昭和20年8月15日	3rd Air Division North Australia Area campaign overview (November 15, 1941 - August 15, 1945)	元第3飛行団長塚田理喜智中将
⑧参考−写真	98	1962/2	錦隊（元鳳隊）の思いで	Memories of Nishiki Unit (former Otori Unit)	ビンタンチモール会
①中央−日誌回想	51	1962/10/22	錦隊（元鳳隊）回想録	Memoir of Nishiki Unit (former Otori Unit)	元海軍奏任嘱託　石川尚市
陸空−濠北方面	4	−	第七飛行師団関係史料	7th Air Division materials	第7飛行師団須藤栄之助
文庫−依託	188	−	第十九軍の濠北作戦　昭和18年1月15日〜昭和20年4月	19th Army North Australia campaign (January 15, 1943 - April 1945)	第19軍参謀弘中辰夫大佐
中央−部隊歴史師団	70	1946/7/5	第四十八師団戦史資料並に終戦状況	48th Division war documents and situation report at the end of war	第48師団長山田国太郎中将
④−戦闘詳報戦時日誌	54	−	第十六戦隊　戦時日誌・戦闘詳報　昭和17年3月〜昭和17年5月	16th Squadron war diaries and battle reports (March 1942 - May 1942)	−

Author	特記事項 remarks	Remarks
Oita Godo Shinbunsha HIRAMATSU Takashi		
7th Area Army command		
-		
Former 3rd Air Division Commander Lt. Gen. TSUKADA Rikichi	手書き回想	Hand-written memoir.
Bintang Timor Kai	アルバム（写真51葉）、インドネシア地図（隊行動地域全図）	Photo album (51 pictures), map of Indonesia with the unit activities.
Former Imperial Navy appointed civilian employee ISHIKAWA Hisaichi	30ページ、手書き。奏任嘱託証明書（昭和20年11月30日付）、給与通牒、ビンタンチモール会名簿	30 pages, hand-written. Imperial Navy appointed civilian employee certificate (November 30, 1945), salary payment record, member list of Bintang Timor Kai.
7th Air Division SUDO Einosuke	19ページ、手書き。濠北方面7FDの戦況ほか	19 pages, hand-written. 7FD battle reports in North Australia Area.
19th Army, Staff, Col. HIRONAKA Tatsuo	21ページ、手書き	21 pages, hand-written.
48th Division Commander Lt. Gen. YAMADA Kunitaro		
-		

請求番号 Call Number	日付 date	資料名 title	Title	著者 author
④－戦闘詳報戦時日誌 55	－	第十六戦隊　戦時日誌・戦闘詳報　昭和17年8月～昭和17年11月	16th Squadron war diaries and battle reports (August 1942 - November 1942)	－
④－戦闘詳報戦時日誌 56	－	第十六戦隊　戦時日誌・戦闘詳報　昭和17年12月～昭和18年2月	16th Squadron war diaries and battle reports (December 1942 - February 1943)	－
④－戦闘詳報戦時日誌 19	－	第四南遣艦隊　戦時日誌　昭和18年11月～昭和19年7月	4th Southern Expeditionary Fleet war diaries (November 1943 - July 1944)	第4南遣艦隊司令部
⑤－戦闘詳報戦時日誌 80	－	第二十三航空戦隊司令官撮要綴　昭和16年～昭和17年	The files of the 23rd Air Unit commander (1941 - 1942)	－

Author	特記事項 remarks	Remarks
-		
-		
4th Southern Expeditionary Fleet Command		
-	クーパンほか基地における爆撃などによる戦死者名簿ほか	List of persons killed by air raids in Kupang and other bases.

4. 国立公文書
The National

請求番号 Call Number	日付 Date	件名 Title	Translated or Original English Title
本館・2A-012-00・類02411100	1941/7/30	葡領「チモール」「ディリー」に領事館新設	The establishment of Consulate at Dili, Portuguese Timor
本館・2A-015-00・纂02640100	1941/10/7	「ポルトガル」国所領「チモール」島「ディリー」駐在領事黒木時太郎ヘ御委任状御下付ノ件	Official imperial appointment letter sent to Consul Kuroki Tokita at Dili in Portuguess Timor
本館・2A-015-06・枢A00120100	1941/9/17	「パラオ」「ディリー」間航空業務ノ設定ニ関スル日本国政府「ポルトガル」国政府間協定締結ノ件	Regarding the concluding the agreement between the Japanese Government and the Portuguese Government on the establishment of an air service between Palau and Dili
本館・2A-015-10・枢D00872100	1941/10/1	枢密院会議筆記　「パラオ」「ディリー」間航空業務ノ設定ニ関スル日本国政府「ポルトガル」国政府間協定締結ノ件（昭和16年10月1日）	The Privy Council minutes: on concluding the agreement between the Japanese Government and the Portuguese Government on the establishment of an air service between Palau and Dili (1 October, 1941)
本館・2A-016-01・枢F01077100	1941/10/1	枢密院決議　「パラオ」「ディリー」間航空業務ノ設定ニ関スル日本国政府「ポルトガル」国政府間協定締結ノ件　昭和16年10月1日決議	The Privy Council resolution: on concluding the agreement between the Japanese Government and the Portuguese Government on the establishment of an air service between Palau and Dili (1 October, 1941)
本館・2A-016-01・枢F01077100	1941/10/1	「パラオ」「ディリー」間航空業務設定ニ関スル日本国政府「ポルトガル」国政府間協定説明書（外務省条約局、昭和16年9月）	Explanatory note on the agreement between the Japanese Government and the Portuguese Government on the establishment of an air service between Palau and Dili (Bureau of Treaties, Ministry of Foreign Affairs, September 1941)

館所蔵史料
Archives

注記 Remarks	Remarks	リール Reel	コマ Location on Reel	作成部局 Archival Institution	
在外公館職員増設説明書（1941年6月）	Explanatory note on increasing staff members at diplomatic establishments abroad (June, 1941)	058900	1451	内閣	Cabinet
		070300	1261-1266	内閣	Cabinet
				内閣	Cabinet
		Digital		内閣	Cabinet
		Digital		内閣	Cabinet
上記添付書類　極秘参照　全6ページ	Attached documents to the above, Most Secret, Reference, 6pages	Digital		内閣	Cabinet

I. 日本所蔵史料 (Materials in Japanese Archives)

請求番号 Call Number	日付 Date	件名 Title	Translated or Original English Title
本館・2A-016-01・枢F01077100	1941/10/1	ポルトガル領チモール事情（外務省欧亜局）	The situation of Portuguese Timor (Bureau of European and Asian Affairs, Ministry of Foreign Affairs)
本館・2A-016-01・枢F01077100	1941/10/1	「ポルトガル」領「チモール」ニ於ケル日「ポルトガル」合弁開発事業ニ関スル経緯（外務省南洋局）	Details of Japan-Portugal joint development project in Portuguese Timor (Bureau of South Sea, Ministry of Foreign Affairs)
本館・2A-016-01・枢F01077100	1941/10/1	日本「チモール」定期航空路開設ニ関スル資料	Documents on the establishment of regular flight route between Japan and Timor
本館・2A-016-01・枢F01077100	1941/10/1	国際航空路の現状（航空局、昭和16年9月）	Current situation of international flight routes (Bureau of Air Service, September, 1941)
本館・2A-016-01・枢F01077100	1941/10/1	地図	Maps
本館・2A-016-01・枢F01077100	1941/10/1	「パラオ」「ディリー」間航空業務ノ設定ニ関スル日本国政府「ポルトガル」国政府間協定締結ノ件審査報告（昭和16年9月26日）	Report on the examination on the agreement between the Japanese Government and the Portuguese Government on the establishment of an air service between Palau and Dili (26 September, 1941)
本館・2A-012-00・類02494100	1941/10/4	「パラオ」「ディリー」間航空業務ノ設定ニ関スル日本国政府「ポルトガル」国政府間協定締結ノ件ヲ決定ス	Descion on concluding the agreement between the Japanese Government and the Portuguese Government on the establishment of an air service between Palau and Dili
本館・2A-012-00・類02494100	1941/10/4	「パラオ」「ディリー」間定期航空業務ニ依ル航空郵便物ノ交換開始ニ関シ関係郵政庁間ニ協議スベキ事項	Discussion points for concerned post agencies on the commencement of exchanging air mail by the regular air service between Palau and Dili

4．国立公文書館所蔵史料　　The National Archives

注記 Remarks	Remarks	リール Reel	コマ Location on Real	作成部局 Archival Institution	
上記添付書類　参照　全12ページ	Attached documents to the above, Reference, 12pages	Digital		内閣	Cabinet
上記添付書類　極秘　全5ページ	Attached documents to the above, Most Secret, 5pages	Digital		内閣	Cabinet
上記添付書類　秘　参照　全8ページ	Attached documents to the above, Secret, Reference, 8pages	Digital		内閣	Cabinet
上記添付書類　参照　全7ページ	Attached documents to the above, Reference, 7pages	Digital		内閣	Cabinet
上記添付書類　域内各国の航空路線図	Attached documents to the above, Various flight routes in the Asia Pacific area	Digital		内閣	Cabinet
上記添付資料　秘　全10ページ	Attached documents to the above, Secret, 10pages	Digital		内閣	Cabinet
		061000	278-314?	内閣	Cabinet
上記添付書類	Attached documents to the above	061000	320-322	内閣	Cabinet

184　　I．日本所蔵史料（Materials in Japanese Archives）

請求番号 Call Number	日付 Date	件名 Title	Translated or Original English Title
本館・2A-012-00・類02494100	1941/10/4	「オーストラリア」ト「ポルトガル」領「ティモール」トノ間ニ航空業務ヲ開設スルコトニ関スル「オーストラリア」政府「ポルトガル」国政府間交換公文	Exchange of notes between the Australian Government and the Portuguese Government regarding the establishment of an air service between Australia and Portuguese Timor
分館・KS-000-00・御25766100	1941年	「パラオ」「ディリー」間航空業務ノ設定ニ関スル日本国政府「ポルトガル」国政府間協定・御署名原本・昭和十六年・条約一五号	
本館・2A-012-00・類02494100	1941/10/25	「パラオ」「ディリー」間航空業務設定ニ関スル日本国政府「ポルトガル」国政府間協定ヲ公布ス	Promulgating the agreement between the Japanese Government and the Portuguese Government on the establishment of an air service between Palau and Dili
	[1935年]	葡領「チモール」植民地調査報告書	Report of research on the Portuguese colony of Timor
	1937年10月	瀬川技師葡国出張報告書並S・A・P・T・他二社定款邦訳	Engineer Segawa report on an official trip to Portugal and translations of the articles of incorporation of SAPT and two others companies
	1939/4/10	チモール合弁事業ニ関スル件	Regarding the joint Timor project
	1939/12/1	SAPTLda改組方式変更ニ関スル件	Regarding the change on proceeding of reorganizaion of SAPT Lda
	1937/8/9	南洋興発株式会社ノ葡領チモールニ於ケル日葡合弁事業経営ノ件	Regarding the Japan-Portugal joint project management in Portuguese Timor by the Southsea Development Company

注記 Remarks	Remarks	リール Reel	コマ Location on Real	作成部局 Archival Institution	
上記添付書類 Exchange of notes between the Australian Government and the Portuguese Government regarding the establishment of an air service between Australia and Portuguese Timor, December 11, 1940	Attached documents, Exchange of notes between the Australian Government and the Portuguese Government regarding the establishment of an air service between Australia and Portuguese Timor, December 11, 1940	061000	327-335	内閣	Cabinet
		Digital		内閣	Cabinet
条約第15条起案書・条約文（日・仏語）	Draft of the article 15 of the treaty, and the texts of the treaty (in Japanese and French)	061000	493-504	内閣	Cabinet
		Digital	0139-0179	熱帯文化協会 Nettai Bunka Kyokai	
		Digital	0184-0237	南洋興発株式会社 Nan'yo Kohatsu KK	
		Digital	0394-0397	南洋興発株式会社 Nan'yo Kohatsu KK	
		Digital	0284-0290	南洋興発株式会社 Nan'yo Kohatsu KK	
		Digital	0076-0084	拓務省 Ministry of Overseas Development	

請求番号 Call Number	日付 Date	件名 Title	Translated or Original English Title
	1937年6月	葡領チモールニ於ケル日葡合弁事業ニ関スル件	Regarding the Japan-Portugal joint project in Portuguese Timor
	1937年5月	葡領チモール事業計画	Portuguese Timor project plan
本館-4A-018-00・平11法務01929100	1946/12/27	NETHERLANDS INDIES. TIMOR and LESSER SUNDA ISLANDS. Synopsis. Netherlands Division I.P.S. December 1946. Lt.Col. J.S. Sinninghe Damste R.N.I.A., Assistant Prosecutor	
本館-4A-018-00・平11法務01929100	1946/12/27	Affidavit of the Australian Private R. B. Crow: Killing of prisoners of war at Usapa Besar, Dutch Timor, February 1942	
本館-4A-018-00・平11法務01929100	1946/12/27	Interrogation report of the Australian Army Chaplain Th. W. Binderman: Killing of an Australian Medical corporal at Babau, Dutch Timor, February 1942	
本館-4A-018-00・平11法務01929100	1946/12/27	Statement of the Australian Lt. Col. W. W. Leggatt: Killing of prisoners of war at Babau, February 1942	
本館-4A-018-00・平11法務01929100	1946/12/27	Excerpts. Summary of examination of Sebastiao Graca: Killing of Australian soldiers at Fatu Meta, February and March 1942.	
本館-4A-018-00・平11法務01929100	1946/12/27	Statement of Melkianus Augustun, an interpreter: Beheading of a Dutch officer at Suai, August 1942	
本館-4A-018-00・平11法務01929100	1946/12/27	Affidavit of Sergeant C. H. van der Sloot, R.N.I.A.: Illtreatment and killing at prisoner of war camp Kupang	

注記 Remarks	Remarks	リール Reel	コマ Location on Real	作成部局 Archival Institution
		Digital	0086-0097	南洋興発株式会社 Nan'yo Kohatsu KK
棉作事業、サイザル繊維事業、蒟蒻事業、繰綿工場経営、沿岸航路各計画書	Plans of Cotton plantation project, Konnyaku project, Sisal fibers project, Cotton factory management, Coastal shipment service	Digital	0098-0125	南洋興発株式会社 Nan'yo Kohatsu KK
東京裁判検察側証拠書類番号5682、証拠書類番号1779	Tokyo Tribunal Prosecutor Evidence Document 5682, Evidence Document 1779	0010	597-603	法務省大臣官房司法法制調査部
東京裁判検察側証拠書類番号5571、証拠書類番号1780	Tokyo Tribunal Prosecutor Evidence Document 5571, Evidence Document 1780	0010	604-605	法務省大臣官房司法法制調査部
東京裁判検察側証拠書類番号5573、証拠書類番号1781	Tokyo Tribunal Prosecutor Evidence Document 5573, Evidence Document 1781	0010	606-609	法務省大臣官房司法法制調査部
東京裁判検察側証拠書類番号5579、証拠書類番号1782	Tokyo Tribunal Prosecutor Evidence Document 5579, Evidence Document 1782	0010		法務省大臣官房司法法制調査部
東京裁判検察側証拠書類番号5802、証拠書類番号1783	Tokyo Tribunal Prosecutor Evidence Document 5802, Evidence Document 1783	0010	614-617	法務省大臣官房司法法制調査部
東京裁判検察側証拠書類番号5585、証拠書類番号1784	Tokyo Tribunal Prosecutor Evidence Document 5585, Evidence Document 1784	0010	617-619	法務省大臣官房司法法制調査部
東京裁判検察側証拠書類番号5597、証拠書類番号1787	Tokyo Tribunal Prosecutor Evidence Document 5597, Evidence Document 1787	0010	644-646	法務省大臣官房司法法制調査部

I. 日本所蔵史料 (Materials in Japanese Archives)

請求番号 Call Number	日付 Date	件名 Title	Translated or Original English Title
本館・4A-018-00・ 平11法務01929100	1946/12/27	Affidavit of Carlos Jose Sequeira: Conditions of Liquica camp	
本館・4A-018-00・ 平11法務01929100	1946/12/27	Summary of examination of Ernesto Simoes: Killing of Portuguese troops at Aileu, September 1942	
本館・4A-018-00・ 平11法務01929100	1946/12/27	Affidavit of William Anderson Beattie: Killing of Catholic priests at Ainaro, October 1942 and natives near Atsabe, December 1942	
本館・4A-018-00・ 平11法務01929100	1946/12/27	Summary of examination of Lois Antonio Nunes Rodreigues: Tortures and killing of natives at Ossu, attacks on villages, and forced prostitutions	
本館・4A-018-00・ 平11法務01929100	1946/12/27	Statement of Maj. Gen. Tanaka Yuki, Commander of 2nd Formosan Infantry Regiment: Incidents at Lautem	
本館・4A-018-00・ 平11法務01929100	1946/12/27	Statement of Lt. Ohara Seidai, 2nd Formosan Infantry Regiment: Forced prostitution at Lautem	
本館・4A-018-00・ 平11法務01929100	1946/12/27	Summary of examination of Chung Hai Cheng: Names of Kenpei-tai officers and illtreatment in Dili jail	
本館・4A-018-00・ 平11法務01929100	1946/12/27	J.S.シニング・ダムステ蘭印王国軍陸軍中佐・検事補：チモール及び小スンダ諸島における残虐行為証拠要約	NETHERLANDS INDIES. TIMOR and LESSER SUNDA ISLANDS. Synopsis. Netherlands Division I.P.S. December 1946. Lt.Col. J.S. Sinninghe Damste R.N.I.A., Assistant Prosecutor
本館・4A-018-00・ 平11法務01929100	1946/12/27	R.B.クロー（豪軍兵卒）宣誓供述書：ウサパ・ブサール（蘭領チモール）における射殺（1942年2月）	Affidavit of the Australian Private R. B. Crow: Killing of prisoners of war at Usapa Besar, Dutch Timor, February 1942

注記 Remarks	Remarks	リール Reel	コマ Location on Real	作成部局 Archival Institution
東京裁判検察側証拠書類番号5803、証拠書類番号1789	Tokyo Tribunal Prosecutor Evidence Document 5803, Evidence Document 1789	0010	649-651	法務省大臣官房司法法制調査部
東京裁判検察側証拠書類番号5804、証拠書類番号1790	Tokyo Tribunal Prosecutor Evidence Document 5804, Evidence Document 1790	0010	652-653	法務省大臣官房司法法制調査部
東京裁判検察側証拠書類番号5805、証拠書類番号1791	Tokyo Tribunal Prosecutor Evidence Document 5805, Evidence Document 1791	0010	654-655	法務省大臣官房司法法制調査部
東京裁判検察側証拠書類番号5806、証拠書類番号1792	Tokyo Tribunal Prosecutor Evidence Document 5806, Evidence Document 1792	0010	656-657	法務省大臣官房司法法制調査部
東京裁判検察側証拠書類番号5594、証拠書類番号1793	Tokyo Tribunal Prosecutor Evidence Document 5594, Evidence Document 1793	0010	658-662	法務省大臣官房司法法制調査部
東京裁判検察側証拠書類番号5591、証拠書類番号1794	Tokyo Tribunal Prosecutor Evidence Document 5591, Evidence Document 1794	0010	663-666	法務省大臣官房司法法制調査部
東京裁判検察側証拠書類番号5807、証拠書類番号1795	Tokyo Tribunal Prosecutor Evidence Document 5807, Evidence Document 1795	0010	667-669	法務省大臣官房司法法制調査部
東京裁判検察側証拠書類番号5682、証拠書類番号1779(和文)	Tokyo Tribunal Prosecutor Evidence Document 5682, Evidence Document 1779 (Japanese translation)	0052	760-775	法務省大臣官房司法法制調査部
東京裁判検察側証拠書類番号5571、証拠書類番号1780(和文)	Tokyo Tribunal Prosecutor Evidence Document 5571, Evidence Document 1780 (Japanese translation)	0052	776-778	法務省大臣官房司法法制調査部

I. 日本所蔵史料 (Materials in Japanese Archives)

請求番号 Call Number	日付 Date	件名 Title	Translated or Original English Title
本館-4A-018-00・ 平11法務01929100	1946/12/27	T.W.ビンデマン（豪軍従軍司祭）尋問調書：ババウ（蘭領チモール）における豪軍兵の殺害（1942年2月）	Interrogation report of the Australian Army Chaplain Th. W. Binderman: Killing of an Australian Medical corporal at Babau, Dutch Timor, February 1942
本館-4A-018-00・ 平11法務01929100	1946/12/27	W.W.レガット中佐陳述：ババウにおける豪軍兵の殺害（1942年2月）	Statement of the Australian Lt. Col. W. W. Leggatt: Killing of prisoners of war at Babau, February 1942
本館-4A-018-00・ 平11法務01929100	1946/12/27	S.グラサ宣誓供述書：ファトゥ・メタにおける俘虜の刺殺（1942年2月・3月）	Excerpts. Summary of examination of Sebastiao Graca: Killing of Australian soldiers at Fatu Meta, February and March 1942.
本館-4A-018-00・ 平11法務01929100	1946/12/27	M.アウグストゥン（通訳）の報告：スアイにおける和蘭軍人の斬首（1942年8月）	Statement of Melkianus Augustun, an interpreter: Beheading of a Dutch officer at Suai, August 1942
本館-4A-018-00・ 平11法務01929100	1946/12/27	C.ファン・デル・スルート（蘭印軍曹）宣誓供述書：クーパン収容所における俘虜の虐待処刑	Affidavit of Sergeant C. H. van der Sloot, R.N.I.A.: Illtreatment and killing at prisoner of war camp Kupang
本館-4A-018-00・ 平11法務01929100	1946/12/27	C.J.セケイラ宣誓供述書：リキサ収容所における虐待	Affidavit of Carlos Jose Sequeira: Conditions of Liquica camp
本館-4A-018-00・ 平11法務01929100	1946/12/27	E.シモイス宣誓供述書：アイレウにおけるポルトガル護衛兵の射殺（1942年9月）	Summary of examination of Ernesto Simoes: Killing of Portuguese troops at Aileu, September 1942
本館-4A-018-00・ 平11法務01929100	1946/12/27	W.Aビアティ（豪空軍中尉）陳述：アイナロおよびアトサベにおいて神父・住民を射殺（1942年12月）	Affidavit of William Anderson Beattie: Killing of Catholic priests at Ainaro, October 1942 and natives near Atsabe, December 1942
本館-4A-018-00・ 平11法務01929100	1946/12/27	L..A.N.ロドリゲス宣誓供述書：ケリカイ、ナハレカ村における無差別機銃掃射と略奪	Summary of examination of Lois Antonio Nunes Rodreigues: Tortures and killing of natives at Ossu, attacks on villages, and forced prostitutions

注記 Remarks	Remarks	リール Reel	コマ Location on Reel	作成部局 Archival Institution
東京裁判検察側証拠書類番号5573、証拠書類番号1781（和文）	Tokyo Tribunal Prosecutor Evidence Document 5573, Evidence Document 1781 (Japanese translation)	0052	779-783	法務省大臣官房司法法制調査部
東京裁判検察側証拠書類番号5579、証拠書類番号1782（和文）	Tokyo Tribunal Prosecutor Evidence Document 5579, Evidence Document 1782 (Japanese translation)	0052	784-788	法務省大臣官房司法法制調査部
東京裁判検察側証拠書類番号5802、証拠書類番号1783（和文）	Tokyo Tribunal Prosecutor Evidence Document 5802, Evidence Document 1783 (Japanese translation)	0052	789-794	法務省大臣官房司法法制調査部
東京裁判検察側証拠書類番号5585、証拠書類番号1784（和文）	Tokyo Tribunal Prosecutor Evidence Document 5585, Evidence Document 1784 (Japanese translation)	0052	795-799	法務省大臣官房司法法制調査部
東京裁判検察側証拠書類番号5597、証拠書類番号1787（和文）	Tokyo Tribunal Prosecutor Evidence Document 5597, Evidence Document 1787 (Japanese translation)	0052	829-835	法務省大臣官房司法法制調査部
東京裁判検察側証拠書類番号5803、証拠書類番号1789（和文）	Tokyo Tribunal Prosecutor Evidence Document 5803, Evidence Document 1789 (Japanese translation)	0052	842-845	法務省大臣官房司法法制調査部
東京裁判検察側証拠書類番号55　、証拠書類番号1790（和文）	Tokyo Tribunal Prosecutor Evidence Document 5804, Evidence Document 1790 (Japanese translation)	0052	846-849	法務省大臣官房司法法制調査部
東京裁判検察側証拠書類番号5805、証拠書類番号1791（和文）	Tokyo Tribunal Prosecutor Evidence Document 5805, Evidence Document 1791 (Japanese translation)	0052	850-852	法務省大臣官房司法法制調査部
東京裁判検察側証拠書類番号5806、証拠書類番号1792（和文）	Tokyo Tribunal Prosecutor Evidence Document 5806, Evidence Document 1792 (Japanese translation)	0052	853-855	法務省大臣官房司法法制調査部

I. 日本所蔵史料 (Materials in Japanese Archives)

請求番号 Call Number	日付 Date	件名 Title	Translated or Original English Title
本館・4A-018-00・平11法務01929100	1946/12/27	田中透（台湾歩兵第二連隊長）少将宣誓供述書：ルアン地方ラジャの処刑および犯行者の殺害（1944年9月）	Statement of Maj. Gen. Tanaka Yuki [Toru], Commander of 2nd Formosan Infantry Regiment: Incidents at Lautem
本館・4A-018-00・平11法務01929100	1946/12/27	オハラセイダイ（台湾歩兵第二連隊）宣誓供述書：モア島における住民殺戮およびラウテンにおける強制売淫	Statement of Lt. Ohara Seidai, 2nd Formosan Infantry Regiment: Forced prostitution at Lautem
本館・4A-018-00・平11法務01929100	1946/12/27	チュン・ハイ・チェン宣誓供述書：ディリ監獄における俘虜の虐待およびマナトゥトゥにおけるポルトガル行政官の殺害	Summary of examination of Chung Hai Cheng: Names of Kenpei-tai officers and illtreatment in Dili jail
本館・4A-018-00・平11法務02652100		チモール問題の経緯	Details of the Timor problem
本館-4A-020-00・平11法務04795100		BC級（オーストラリア裁判関係）ポート・ダーウィン裁判・第1号事件（9名）	BC class war crime trial (Australian trials), Port Darwin, Case No. 1 (9 individuals)
本館-4A-020-00・平11法務04796100		BC級（オーストラリア裁判関係）ポート・ダーウィン裁判・第2号事件（3名）	BC class war crime trial (Australian trials), Port Darwin, Case No. 2 (3 individuals)
本館-4A-020-00・平11法務04797100		BC級（オーストラリア裁判関係）ポート・ダーウィン裁判・第3号事件（10名）	BC class war crime trial (Australian trials), Port Darwin, Case No. 3 (10 individuals)
本館・4A-020-00・平11法務05112100		BC級（オランダ裁判関係）クーパン裁判・第1号事件（1名）	BC class war crime trial (N.E.I trials), Kupang, Case No. 1 (1 individual)
本館・4A-020-00・平11法務05119100		BC級（オランダ裁判関係）クーパン裁判・第20号事件（1名）	BC class war crime trial (N.E.I trials), Kupang, Case No. 20 (1 individual)
本館・4A-020-00・平11法務05120100		BC級（オランダ裁判関係）クーパン裁判・第21号事件（2名）	BC class war crime trial (N.E.I trials), Kupang, Case No. 21 (2 individuals)
本館-4A-020-00・平11法務05140100		BC級（オランダ裁判関係）アンボン裁判・第23号事件（1名）	BC class war crime trial (N.E.I trials), Ambon, Case No. 23 (1 individual)

4．国立公文書館所蔵史料
The National Archives

193

注記 Remarks	Remarks	リール Reel	コマ Location on Real	作成部局 Archival Institution
東京裁判検察側証拠書類番号5594、証拠書類番号1793（和文）	Tokyo Tribunal Prosecutor Evidence Document 5594, Evidence Document 1793 (Japanese translation)	0052	856-861	法務省大臣官房司法法制調査部
東京裁判検察側証拠書類番号5591、証拠書類番号1794（和文）	Tokyo Tribunal Prosecutor Evidence Document 5591, Evidence Document 1794 (Japanese translation)	0052	862-867	法務省大臣官房司法法制調査部
東京裁判検察側証拠書類番号5807、証拠書類番号1795（和文）	Tokyo Tribunal Prosecutor Evidence Document 5807, Evidence Document 1795 (Japanese translation)	0052	868-871	法務省大臣官房司法法制調査部
東京裁判弁護関係資料、森島守人記（1946年5月20日）7ページ	Tokyo Tribunal Defence Council Document, written by MORISHIMA Morito (20 May, 1946), 7pages			法務省大臣官房司法法制調査部
				法務省大臣官房司法法制調査部
				法務省大臣官房司法法制調査部
				法務省大臣官房司法法制調査部
公判記録	Records of trial			法務省大臣官房司法法制調査部
面接調書5ページ、判決に対する蘭印副総督の確認書の抜粋コピー（蘭文1枚）	Records of interview, 5pages, copy of excerpts of N.E.I. Vice Governor's confirmation on the judgement (Dutch text, 1page)			法務省大臣官房司法法制調査部
附託礼状（和文）、公判記録概要	Letter of appreciation (Japanese text), summary of records of trial			法務省大臣官房司法法制調査部
				法務省大臣官房司法法制調査部

I．日本所蔵史料 (Materials in Japanese Archives)

請求番号 Call Number	日付 Date	件名 Title	Translated or Original English Title
A03022301900		ポパム元帥、英極東軍準備を声明　大美晩報電台（UP電）10月17日	
A03024781600		日葡航空協定の目的は蘭印石油獲得　重慶電台（中華通訊）11月7日	
A03024782400	1941/11/13	蘭印、チモール島向石油を完全禁輸　桑港電台　11月5日	
A03024807400	1942/2/26	ポルトガル兵、チモール島に急行　リスボン電台（アバス電）　2月22日	
A03024818900	1942/4/1	ポルトガル兵印度に待機　サンフランシスコ電台　3月27日	
A03025143700	1943/8/4	米通信員、チモール、ジャワニ於ケル日本軍基地強化ト報ズ　サクラメント　8月3日	
A03025266400		日葡関係益々悪化セリト　ソートレーキ　10月9日	
A03025335300		日本軍の南太平洋戦略　米誌「タイムス」4月26日号所報	

注記 Remarks	Remarks	リール Reel	コマ Location on Real	作成部局 Archival Institution
各種情報資料・外国宣伝情報		Digital		内閣
各種情報資料・外国宣伝情報		Digital		
各種情報資料・外国宣伝情報		Digital		内閣
各種情報資料・外国宣伝情報		Digital		内閣
各種情報資料・外国宣伝情報		Digital		内閣
各種情報資料・米国内放送傍受情報		Digital		内閣
各種情報資料・米国内放送傍受情報		Digital		内閣
各種情報資料・海外特殊情報		Digital		内閣

II. ポルトガル所蔵史料

Materials in Portuguese Archives

1. Libraries and Archives in Portugal and Macau

This introduction briefly describes the most important libraries and archives which hold materials relevant to Timor in general and wartime Timor in particular, although there may be also numerous private or small archival collections awaiting discovery. We also have included one institution in Macau, a former colony of Portugal with close ties to Timor. While not discussed here, archives in Mozambique such as the Arquivo Histórico de Moçambique (Historical Archive of Mozambique) may hold relevant materials. We hope that this set of descriptions will guide researchers to an appropriate major archive of Portuguese materials at which to start work, and that they will then be able to progress to other sources.

Biblioteca Nacional de Portugal (The National Library of Portugal)

The National Library of Portugal in Lisbon is the major locus of printed works on Timor in Portuguese. Besides publications, unpublished Portuguese language theses and dissertations on Timor are also held in the library and can be located through the electronic catalog.

The National Library newspaper and journal reading room also holds extensive runs of the key journals carrying articles on Timor, as well as metropolitan newspapers (eg. *Diário do Notícias*). Notably, the National Library holds a complete run of the single pre-war newspaper in Timor, *Timor. Publicação eventual de carácter literário e científico* (1938-39). Unfortunately, there is no special article index, merely a card catalog listing of the journals.

Sociedade de Geografia de Lisboa (Geographical Society of Lisbon)

The Geographical Society of Lisbon is a colonial-era institution dating back to 1886 which collected print materials relating to the colonies with the goal of improving scholarship, but it also undoubtedly served as an instrument of colonial expansion. The Geographical Society now offers a treasure trove of books, articles, charts, and graphics on Portugal's former colonies. Working from a printed catalog (1961) we can identify 30 journal articles under the heading "Ocupação Japonesa da 2ª Grande Guerra" (Japanese Occupation during the Second World War). Additional items can be found through antiquated card catalogs in the reading room.

Instituto dos Arquivos Nacionais / Torre do Tombo (The Institute of National Archives / Torre do Tombo)

The Institute of National Archives / Torre do Tombo (IAN/TT) holds a number of "archives within archives." This is the official description, for example, of the PIDE/PGE secret police files from 1919-1975 which may contain information relevant to Timor in the wartime or prewar period, although the PIDE was not active in Timor until 1960.

The Torre do Tombo archives reading room offers a wealth of archival catalogs. Identifying materials relating to Timor requires an extensive search through many volumes of printed or photocopied catalogs, while identifying materials on the Pacific War period requires parallel searches through library guides and catalogs.

Arquivo Salazar (Salazar Archive)

Located within the IAN/TT is the Salazar Archive, a massive collection of political documents spanning the long period dominated by Salazar and especially the Salazar dictatorship (c. 1926-1974). The Salazar Archive is also rich in official correspondence relating to Timor. One such document is the report on Timor by Captain Silva e Costa, "Inquérito a Timor [Secret Inquiry on Timor] (March 1944). Under pressure from Lisbon, Captain Silva e Costa, then secretary to the Governor of Macau, was granted permission to visit occupied Timor via Tokyo to observe conditions first-hand. Upon his return to Macao he produced this first-hand report on conditions in Timor during 1944.

There is no single catalog guide to the Salazar Archive. One catalog of major interest to the study of wartime Timor found in the Salazar Archive is the *Comissão do Livro Branco do Ministério dos Negócios Estrangeiros* **(Ministry of Foreign Affairs White Book Commission)**. The White Book can be effectively used through an "Index of Documents." Volumes I and II are particularly relevant to Timor, as approximately one third of the index entries relate to negotiations over the Azores bases, one third to Timor, and one third to Germany, Spain and other European affairs. With its sixty pages of closely typed entries, the White Book indexes incoming and outgoing telegrams to the Ministry of Foreign Affairs, ordered chronologically in clusters of 48 per page, with brief descriptions of contents. This is a highly detailed index of diplomatic transactions spanning the war years and therefore an unusually detailed and highly valuable source.

Arquivo Histórico-Diplomático (The Diplomatic Historical Archive)

The Diplomatic Historical Archive houses the major locus of materials relating to foreign relations, including wartime Timor. Some of the significant materials were included in a multi-volume series published by the Ministry of Foreign Affairs, *Dez Anos de Política Externa*. Volume XI (covering 19 February 1942-6 October 1945) deals almost exclusively with Timor, ranging from the consequences of the Japanese landing in Timor, to actions of the "black columns," the bombing of Dili, and the return of Timor to Portuguese sovereignty. It is likely that additional significant documents which were omitted or excluded from the published collection can be found in the archive.

Arquivo Histórico Militar (The Military Historical Archive)

Located within the Museu Militar or Military Museum adjacent to the Alfama quarter of Lisbon, the military archives bring together materials dating back to 1508. One division of the Military Historical Archive is devoted to former colonies. Timor is included as the tenth section of the second division under overseas colonies. From around 2002 all archives pertaining to former colonies were catalogued and this information was compiled in separate catalog booklets. Approximately five entries relate to wartime Timor. The quality of the documentation in one box examined suggested a lack of rigorous record keeping.

The archive also carries holdings of *Revista Militar*, some issues including articles on Timor, as well as a collection of rare monographs on Timor/Macau.

Macau Archives and Libraries

Largely owing to the isolation of Macau from Timor and Portugal during the war years, few if any materials on Timor entered Macau government official files. Political reports from the 1930s in the Arquivo Histórico de Macau (Macau Historical Archive) do track Japanese commercial interest in the colony. Surprisingly Macau archives do not hold documents relating to military matters. Extensive holdings related to Timor will almost certainly not be found in Macau, as many modern political documents held in Macau archives were repatriated to Portugal before the transfer of Macau to China in 1999.

Biblioteca do Edifício do IACM (The ex-Leal Senado Library)

The 250 year-old ex-Leal Senado Library in Macau (now formally known as the Biblioteca do Edificio do IACM) is the major repository of Portuguese language newspapers published during the war years, many carrying wire service reports on occupied Timor. Among the better known is *Renascimento*. The ex-Leal Senado Library also carries extensive runs of the official bulletins of Timor (not published during the war years) along with counterpart bulletins of Angola and Mozambique.

2. A Brief List of Useful Documents and Archival Sources in Portugal

Salazar Archive (AOS)

Garcia, Maria Madalena. 1992. *Arquivo Salazar: inventário e índices* [Salazar Archive: Inventory and indexes]. Lisboa: Biblioteca Nacional. 684 pp.

Timor [Secreto]
AOS/CLB/T-1 1941-1942
AOS/CLB/T-2 1942
AOS/CLB/T-3 1942-1943
AOS/CLB/T-4 1944-1945
AOS/CLB/T-5 1945
AOS/CLB/T-6 1945
AOS/CLB/T-7 1945-1946
AOS/CLB/T-8 1946-1948

AOS/CLB/T-8
   Inquérito a Timor. Missão Silva Costa [Inquiry on Timor: Silva Costa mission]. 1942-1948.

AOS/CO/IN-8C (1936-1948)
   Informação da PIDE sobre o caso Japão-Timor, (1944) [PIDE Information on the Japan-Timor case].
   Situação dos deportados em Timor, (1945) [Situation of the deportees in Timor].

AOS/CO/MA-1B
   Precauções tomadas pela viagem do aviso 《João de Lisboa》, de Macau para Timor, e no regresso a Lisboa, (1942) [Precautions taken for the voyage of notice "João de Lisboa" from Macau to Timor, and in the return to Lisbon].

AOS/CO/NE-2
   Pedido, da Legação da Alemanha, de protecção para os alemães em Timor, (1942) [Request from the German legation, for protection of the Germans in Timor].

AOS/CO/NE-2C

Sargento-aviador Americano Alonso Ackerman, cujo aparelho foi abatido sobre Timor, (1945) [American airman Sergeant Alonso Ackerman, whose equipment went down on Timor].

AOS/CO/NE-2E1

Concessão de facilidades aéreas nos Açores à Inglaterra, ([1943]) [Concession of air facilities in the Azores to England].

Pedido de informação do Estado Maior britânico sobre Timor, Hong-Kong, Singapura e Índias Holandesas, (1944) [Request for information from British Staff on Timor, Hong-Kong, Singapore and the Netherlands Indies].

Negociações, entre Portugal e a Inglaterra, sobre os Açores, ([1944]) [Negotiations between Portugal and England on the Azores].

Uso de facilidades nos Açores pela Inglaterra. Acordo aduaneiro, ([1944]) [Use of facilities in the Azores by England. Customs agreement].

Garantia, do Almirantado inglês, de abastecimento, em Colombo, dos avisos, 《Bartolomeu Dias》, 《Afonso de Albuquerque》, 《Gonçalves Zarco》 e 《Gonçalo Velho》, na viagem para Timor, (1945) [English Admiralty guarantee to supply the "Bartolomeu Dias", "Alfonso de Albuquerque", "Gonçalves Zarco" and "Gonçalo Velho" in Colombo during their voyage to Timor].

AOS/CO/NE-2E3

Perguntas do Embaixador de Inglaterra sobre o cidadão inglês Ross, detido em Timor (?) durante a ocupação deste território, ([entre 1942 e 1945]) [Questions from the Ambssador of England on the English citizen Ross, detained in Timor (?) during the occupation of this territory].

AOS/CO/PC-2D

Sobre o caso de Timor, (1945) [On the case of Timor].

AOS/CO/PC-8D

Serviços de Censura. Corte de artigos sobre Timor, (1945) [Censorship Service. Cutting of articles on Timor].

AOS/CO/UL-10A

Telegramas diversos sobre Timor, (1940-1950) [Various telegrams on Timor].

Ocupação de Timor por forças estrangeiras, (1941-1948) [Occupation of Timor by foreign forces].

Notícias sobre Timor, (1941-1945) [News on Timor].

Agradecimento de um telegrama do Prof. Doutor A. de Oliveira Salazar, enviado após a libertação da ilha de Timor, (1945) [Telegram of grattitude of Prof. Doctor A. de Oliveira Salazar, sent after the liberation of the island of Timor].

Reocupação de Timor, (1945) [Reoccupation of Timor].

Reocupação de Timor-atitude do Comandante em Chefe das forças expedicionárias ao Extremo Oriente perante o Ministro das Colónias, (1946) [Reoccupation of Timor- The attitude of the Commander in Chief of the expeditionary forces to the Far East before the Minister of Colonies].

AOS/CO/UL-10A (Cont.)

Acontecimentos sobre Timor, (1947) [Events on Timor].

AOS/CO/UL-10

Financiamento da reconstrução da capital de Timor, (1950-1952) [Financing for reconstruction of the capital of Timor].

AOS/CO/UL-21

Informação sobre infiltração japonesa em Timor, (1938) [Information on Japanese infiltration in Timor].

AOS/CO/UL-32

Prejuízos derivados da ocupação japonesa em Timor, (1958-1959) [Damages derived from the Japanese occupation in Timor].

AOS/CO/UL-62

Viagem do navio《Gonçalves Zarco》que escolta o vapor《João Belo》, de Moçambique para Timor, (1942) [Voyage of the ship "Gonçalves Zarco" which was escorted by the steamer "João Belo" from Mozambique to Timor].

Rendição de Timor, (1945) [Surrender of Timor].

II. ポルトガル所蔵史料 (Materials in Portuguese Archives)

Arquivo Marcello Caetano

Frazão, António; Filipe, Maria do Céu Barata. 2005. *Arquivo Marcello Caetano: catálogo*, Volume I, Lisboa: Instituto dos Arquivos Nacionais / Torre do Tombo.

Reocupação Administrativa de Timor. [Administrative reoccupation of Timor]

3. Arquivo Histórico Militar (AHM)

Official Index:
Estado Maior do Exército Arquivo Histórico Militar. Timor, 1936-1998. Inventário de Documentos, 2ª Divisão, 9ª Secção. [Inventory of documents, Second Division, Ninth Section] Lisboa, 2002, Maio.
[Second Division/Colonies/Overseas, Ninth Section: Timor, 1936-1998
6 caixas (boxes)]
1936, Janeiro-1939, Março, 21
Pareceres sobre o "Projecto de Reorganização Militar da Colónia de Timor" (cópias). Contém projecto sobre a organização militar da colónia de Timor e os respectivos pareceres da 3ª Direcção-Geral do Estado-Maior do Exército e do Conselho do Império Colonial; nota do Major-General do Exército, Júlio Ernesto de Morais Sarmento e duplicado da nota do Chefe do Estado-Maior do Exército sobre o projecto [Contains plans for the reorganization of the military in the colony].
30 fls. dactilografadas.
Cota antiga: 2/9/2/3.
PT AHM-DIV/2
2/9/1/1

1941, Novembro, 10-Lisboa
Memorando "A Colónia de Timor – Sua importância estratégica no actual momento internacional. [Colony of Timor: Its strategic importance at the present international conjucture]"
15 fls. dactilografadas, 1 recorte de imprensa e 1 mapa.
Cota antiga: 2/9/8/1.
PT AHM-DIV/2
2/9/1/2

1944, Setembro, 18-1946, Janeiro, 30
"Expedição a Timor-1945", pelo general Fernando Louro de Sousa.
Contém documentos respeitantes à expedição a Timor e ao regresso à metrópole das forças expedicionárias estacionadas em Lourenço Marques. [Contains documents relating to the expedition to Timor and the return to metropole of the forces stationed

in Lourenço Marques]
225 fls dactilografadas, 9 fls. impressas e manuscritas e 1 fl. manuscrita.
Cota antiga: 2/9/6/22.
PT AHM-DIV/2
2/9/1/3

1945, Agosto, 19-Dezembro, 27
"De quando fui a Timor" pelo captão José de Freitas Soares, 1° vol.
Contém os seguintes documentos: "Vocabulário Português-Tétum"; ordem-circular da 2ª Repartição do Estado-Maior do Quartel-General das Forças Expedicionárias contendo a constituição, em Lourenço Marques, de um Destacamento Expedicionário a Timor; ordem de embarque das tropas nos vapore "Angola" e "Sofala"; ordens de serviço do Destacamento Expedicionário a Timor a bordo do vapor "Angola" e em Dili; preparação do desembarque do pessoal no porto de Dili; "Cópia do discurso ao Governador de Timor feito pelo Régulo do Reino de Viqueque"; ordens de reconhecimento; tabelas de preços de géneros e artigos a fornecer pelo depósito da cantina; instruções sobre distribuição de fundos às unidades; e ordens de embarque de tropas no vapor "Quanza".
[Contains "Vocabulario Portugues-Tetum" (Portuguese-Tetum dictionary), documents relating to the expeditionary force in Lourenço Marques, and a copy of a document made by the Regulo of the Reino of Viqueque to the Governor.]
149fls dact e 11fls manuscritas.
Cota antiga: 2/9/1/4.
PT AHM-DIV/2
2/9/1/5

1946, Janeiro, 5-Fevereiro, 18
"De quando fui a Timor", pelo capitão José de Freitas Soares, 2º vol.
Contém os seguintes documentos: "Relatório dos trabalhos efectuados em Timor"; "Navios da Marinha Mercante Nacional," características, itinerários, carreiras e tráfego; ordem por que desembarcaram em Díli os efectivos transportados no vapor "Angola"; ordem-circular para o embarque no vapor "Quanza"; "Plano de instalação e manutenção do pessoal a embarcar no vapor Quanza"; e ordens de serviço. [Contains a report on work effected in Timor; ships of the national merchant marine]
114 fls. Dactilografadas e 39 fls manuscritas.
Cota antiga: 2/9/1/5.

PT AHM-DIV/2
2/9/1/6

1945, Abril, 23-1947, Janeiro, 29
"Fundeadouros e Costas de Timor," pelo capitão-de-mar e guerra Humberto Leitão e "Timor (Ventos, clima, pontos conspícuos e descrição da costa e seus fundeadouros)", fornecido pelo Estado-Maior Naval.
Contém a descrição dos aspectos climáticos e geomorfológicos da Costa Sul, Nordeste e Norte e respectivos fundeadouros; notas da Repartição do Gabinete do Ministro para a 2ª e 3ª Repartição do Estado-Maior do Exército remetendo as ditas compilações.
75 fls. dactilografadas.
Cota antiga: 2/9/2/2.
PT AHM-DIV/2
2/9/1/7

III. オーストラリア所蔵史料

Materials in Australian Archives

1. Australian Archives

Australian economic interests and potential competition with Japan resulted in the attention of Australian authorities from the 1930s, visits of consular officials, the stationing of civil aeronautics officials in Dili, and later the stationing of a consul. Following the German occupation of the Netherlands in May 1940, there was also a gradual development of mutual defense agreements between Australia, Britain and the Netherlands East Indies. The small advance parties sent to Kupang and Ambon by the Australian military were dressed in civilian clothes, and were primarily responsible for organizing equipment and supplies. However during 1941, a series of reconnaissance parties also visited Timor (including the group of officers destined for Timor led by Col. Veale and Lt. Col. Youl in October 1941). Finally, in early December 1941 the presence of Australian troops in the Netherlands Indies was authorized, and on about December 7 troops began to depart for the Indies.

In addition to the RAAF units stationed at the Penfoei airfield near Kupang, the 2/40th Australian Imperial Force battalion, and various smaller units, the 2/2nd Independent Company and several hundred KNIL troops were allocated for the occupation and defense of Portuguese Timor. The "Sparrow Force" HQ was initially located in West Timor, although remnants of the west Timor force escaped into Portuguese Timor in early 1941. While not present in Timor, the Royal Australian Navy provided support in transporting men and supplies. This resulted in the loss of the HMAS Voyager on the beach at Betano Bay on 23/9/42 and the Armidale with 61 Indonesian troops on December 1, 1942. The RAAF Hudson squadrons (in particular) based in northern Australia also provided support through supply drops and bombing runs, and were later joined by Beaufighters, Catalinas, and other aircraft.

The prewar concern with Portuguese Timor and the involvement of Australian troops in Timor from 1941-1946 are the primary reasons why substantial archival records remain in Australia, although the presence of officials and family members of Portuguese from Portuguese Timor in Australia was also important. There are many documents related to the pre-invasion negotiations, intelligence, and planning for the Australian side in particular, but there are some bits of information related to Japanese intelligence as well, although it seems to be influenced by paranoia on the Australian side. The failure of the Australian and Dutch forces in Timor to stave off the Japanese landing and several instances of executions were the subjects of both official inquiries and continued discussion by Australians in particular. The inquiry into the Japanese landing in Timor is negligible value, as the Allied informants were not knowledgeable about the situation in Portuguese Timor. Other investigations are perhaps of more value, especially for West Timor. The war crimes investigations into deaths in West Timor, as well as the execution of a group of Australians by Japanese marines near the Dili aerodrome on February 20, 1942 are much better in quality. These include the very vague interrogations of Japanese officers in the AWM, and others in the Melbourne archives. The reports written by 2/2nd IC officers related to initial events are valuable.

While the materials on Timor, especially 1941-1942 are very good and an essential resource for research on this period, there is apparently very little Japanese language material. We also found virtually no Portuguese, Tetum or Dutch language sources in Australian archives. Materials on Portuguese Timor have been collected in several major archives which are detailed below. Smaller private collections do seem to exist, but materials are increasingly concentrated into these major archives.

National Archives of Australia

The National Archives of Australia (NAA) is a network of provincial archives which each hold somewhat different types of materials. Access is through a database which includes not only the holdings of the major NAA branches, but also "official records" (ie. government files) of the Australian War Memorial (see below). A simple search of the *Recordsearch* database conducted in 2004 showed more than 600 files related to Timor during the period 1940-1945, although in fact there are many more relevant files. The majority of these files are held in the Australian War Memorial and the Canberra Branch of the National Archives of Australia, although there are also a significant number held in the Melbourne branch of the National Archives of Australia. While file names can be located through the database, unfortunately the documents are not indexed.

NAA-Canberra

Being the main depository for the federal Australian government, many of the files held in Canberra are from a small set of institutions or related to a few issues:

> Employment/military service records　　Prime Minister's Office
> Defense and Foreign Affairs policy related offices　Immigration and Internment
> RAAF Casualties over Timor　　Censorship
> International Trade

The records thus may be particularly useful for research related to Foreign Relations issues related to East Timor, related to the internment of Portuguese (and others) in Australia during the war, policy decision making related to war and Timor, the service of various individuals (especially in the military), and possibly special operations in Timor from 1943-1945. Materials related to conditions in East Timor and the conduct of the war in East Timor are more limited.

A large number of the records relating to East Timor during the war have been digitized, and are thus available on line. Many other files can be digitized or photocopied upon request, making the Canberra branch of the NAA extremely convenient for researchers who may not be able to spend long periods in Canberra. The list of items which follows is a very small sample of documents and files.

NAA-Melbourne

The main records which deal with Japanese prisoners, war crimes, and military administration are held in the Melbourne archive. Some of these documents are in Japanese, but the majority are in English. Unfortunately, digitization has only just begun, and the Melbourne branch has not allowed patrons to request digitization.

The indexes for many of the military related archives are kept in the Melbourne branch of the NAA. These indexes are likely to lead to more important materials, but would require at least a few weeks in Melbourne. The indexes for the following archival series may provide useful starting points:

MP 742/1 Correspondence series
MP 508/1 Correspondence series
MP 729/6 Secret files section series
MP 729/7 Secret files section series
MP 729/8 Secret files section series

Australian War Memorial

One of the largest collections of documents related to Timor is held at the Australian War Memorial. In addition to a couple of propaganda films, video and audio interviews, unit histories and other publications, and memorabilia, a wide range of documents are collected in the official records collection, the manuscript collections, and the private records collections.

There is also a large collection of photographs, many of them made either during Damien Parer's visit to Timor in late 1942 or in 1945. Most have been catalogued and digitized.

Official Records Collection

These official records of the government contain a large number of reports and other documents related to Timor. However, some files are filled with mixed documents of limited value. The official records include reports, radio messages, notes, plans, orders, maps, and a wide range of other documents. Copies of many of the more significant documents are also held in NAA Canberra. The collection includes the war diaries for the 2/2nd IC, the 2/4th IC, the Sparrow Force and the Lancer Force as well as interrogation reports for Japanese officers based on Timor.

Part of the Official Records Collection are the ATIS documents, Japanese language materials seized by the Allies during and after the war, and turned over to a special unit for translation and analysis. Besides their possible by the military, this information was used for war crimes investigations and trials. There is not much related to Timor.

The Official Records Collection also includes some materials from the War Crimes investigations. These investigations began early in the war and continued well into the postwar era, but as prosecuted cases involved the execution and torture of allied soldiers only, there is little on local society. The best holdings of war crimes documents is in NAA-Melbourne, but the AWM does have an incomplete collection.

Private Records Collections:

There are a number of "private records" archives, collections of materials donated by individuals or their families. The most important are the PRs of former soldiers and official war historians. For example, these materials include an 83 page translation of an autobiographical writing by Antonio de Sousa Santos entitled "Fragments of a Tempestuous Life" (from the Ernest Dudley Francis PR). Some of the most important PR collections are:

Private Records of David Dexter

David Dexter, one of the officers of the 2/2 Independent Company and eventually the officer in charge of special operations in Timor, had a long career as a diplomat, university official, and as a military historian responsible for composing the official history of the New Guinea Campaigns. From the late 1970s until close to his death in 1992, he was working on documenting events in Timor in 1942 and related to Timor from the 1930s until after the end of the war. His files thus include a handwritten "diary" of events in 1942 drawn from the sources he read in 1979-81, as well as a very well organized collection of source documents copied from other archival sources, or in a few cases in original form. These include a few handwritten platoon patrol orders from 1942, situation reports from 1942, Dutch reports (in English), photographs of troops moving near the North coast of Timor, lists of codes, etc.

This is the best starting point for research on Timor during WWII, especially related to military policy and the involvement of Allied troops. While there is open access to readers in the AWM, photocopying items is not allowed.

Private Records of Bernard Callinan

The commanding officer of the 2/2 Independent Company for much of 1942 and eventually the commander of the Lancer Force (the new name for the Timor force), Callinan composed the most important book on the 2/2 Independent Company (published 1953). Following the publication of this book, he was not involved in research related to Timor until he was to present a lecture in the 1970s, at which point other former officers like David Dexter had a much better knowledge of events.

Manuscript Collection:

The manuscript collection includes a number of unpublished manuscripts related to experiences in Timor, as well as draft histories related to other related subjects such as the use of Hudson aircraft in the 1941-43 (the primary Australian plane flown over Timor). Copying from this collection generally requires special permission of the author, depending on the terms of the donation.

The manuscript collection includes, for example, the diaries of Cpl. Wray of the 2/2nd Independent Company.

Films:

There were two films made by an Australian film-maker following a visit to Timor in around November 1942. These propaganda films were then released around November 1943, long after Australian troops had left the island. Much of the content was staged for the camera, including an attack on a village allied to the Japanese in which houses were burned (a similar attack had taken place one day before the film-maker arrived). Nonetheless, this provides a rare view of central East Timor, the Timorese and Aussie soldiers in late 1942.

Australian Guerrillas on Timor. (22 minutes, 12 seconds)
    Original film shot by Damien Parer in Timor between 8-24 November 1942.
    The AWM also has copies of the very important "dope sheets" written by the cameraman (Damien Parer) when filming "Australian Guerillas on Timor," although these are unfortunately not listed in the AWM catalog.

Men of Timor. (8 minutes, 21 seconds)
    This propaganda film was released to the general public in 1943.

AWM posses videotaped interviews with some former soldiers, and some documentary films made in the 1960s-90s. Such items include:

An Emphasis on Training: An interview with Major-General T.F. Cape, CB, CBE, DSO (*in retrospect*). (55 minutes, 51 seconds)
    Cape was the Brigade major for Sparrow Force during early 1942.

Command and Leadership-2/2nd Independent Company Timor, 1942. An interview with Captain Rolf Balwin (*in retrospect*).
    Baldwin was second-in-command of the 2/2nd IC and Sparrow Force during 1942.

Commandos-Timor (Anzac TV Series). 1961. (26 minutes)

Fox Movietone News Vol. 14, No. 9 (12 February 1943).
    Includes a short piece on the awarding of medals to Dutch veterans of the Timor campaign.

Independent Company: The Australian 2/2nd Independent Company, Timor 1941-1942. Written by Philip Dalkin, Colin South; Produced and directed by Colin South, John Tatoulis. Victoria: Media World, 1988. (53 minutes).

Stills and Interview with Pat Penrose. 1991. (38 minutes, 16 seconds).
    Penrose was involved with radio communications for Z Force.

Audio Recordings:

There are also a small number of recorded inserviews, for example with "Doc" Wheatly the Kangaroo shooter and with Keith Hayes who survived the massacre by SNLF troops in February 1942.

National Library of Australia

The National Library of Australia is an important resource for published materials, as well as a more limited number of interviews and other unpublished materials. For example, the NLA has a copy of an interview with Mr. David Dexter, a former platoon commander of the 2/2nd Independent Company, the 2/4th Commando Squadron newsletter, as well as microfilmed items from the US Army/Far Eastern HQ *Japanese* Monographs series related to Portuguese Timor.

III. オーストラリア所蔵史料 (Materials in Australian Archives)

2. National Archive of Australia-

File Number	Author	Title
A816 6/301/332	File	Air Service between Japan and Portuguese Timor
A1196 15/501/222	File	Defence of Portuguese Timor
SP109/3 308/39	File	Dutch forces in and ex Timor
A981Tim P20	File	Japanese activities in Portuguese Timor
A6779 19	File	Miscellaneous Papers Relating to Portuguese Timor 1937-1943
A1838 401/3/6/1/7	File	Netherlands East Indies - Indonesian repatriates Dutch Timor 1946
A816 19/301/820A	File	Occupation of Portuguese Timor - (File 1) to 30-1-1942
A6779 21	File	Portugese Timor December 1941-June 1942. Report by Mr D. Ross, Australian Consul, Dili
A816 19/301/803	File	Portuguese Timor
A1838 376/1/1	File	Portuguese Timor - General Information - Papers & Statistics
A5954 564/2	File	Portuguese Timor File No. 2 (Following Japanese Occuation February, 1942)
A816 19/301/778	File	Report of a visit to Portuguese Timor
A3317 364/1946	File	Timor
A2937 268	File	Timor - Far Eastern Settlement
A981 Tim P 4 Part 2	File	Timor (Portuguese) Political General Part 2
A981 TIM P 4 Part 2	File	Timor (Portuguese) Political General Part 2

Canberra Holdings- Selected List

Date	pp.	Dig.	Contents
1941/11/7	3	•	Report by British consulate in Batavia.
1941/10/15-1942/2/12	106	•	War cabinet meetings, memoranda, communications, and other items related to the December 17, 1941 Dili operation.
1943/2/11	3	•	Contains a letter discussing a proposal for stories about Dutch in Timor, mentioning some of the censorship rules.
1937-1941	260	•	Mixed documents related to Japanese activities on Timor.
1937-1943	137	•	Some documents listed separately.
1945-1946	127	•	Documents related to repatriation of Indonesians in Dutch Timor 1946.
1941-1942	254	•	Department of Defence Coordination files. Includes various cables, the letter presented to the Governor of Timor on December 17, 1941, and other misc. documents.
1941-42	45	•	Report by D. Ross, Australian Consul, Dili. Includes the report, letters, summaries, etc.
1941	21	•	A short Navy report with a series of appendixes related to Australian concerns about Timor: security risks, trade, etc. Also other correspondence.
1937-1950	358	•	Many handwritten notes and reports on telegram charges, Portuguese Timor resources, Public affairs relations over Timor, Defence of Timor, and Trade. Includes a Department of the Navy report, extracts from the Archer and Lambert reports, and an untitled 6 page report from 1942.
1942-43	142	•	File of the Dept. of Defence Co-ordination covering 20/2/42-9/4/43, and including among other thing news clippings, the Callinan report on western Portuguese Timor (Nov. 1942), and other documents detailing either the situation in Timor or related to diplomacy with Portugal.
1941	63	•	Report on the Johnston, Dr. Bradford, Mr. Ross trip on 29 December 1940-1 January 1941 to Timor. Includes various aerial and other photographs.
1944-1946	55	•	Miscellaneous papers related to Portuguese Timor, Timor Oil, Shell, and aerial photographs.
1945/9	145	•	File related to the post-war foreign relations involving a final settlement for Timor. Much on the issue of war crimes.
1936-1941	218	•	Mostly foreign relations between Portugal and Australia, c. 1942.
1942	218	•	Includes the NEFIS Descriptive Report on Timor.

III. オーストラリア所蔵史料（Materials in Australian Archives）

File Number	Author	Title
A1067 PI46/2/9/1	File	Timor, Intelligence and Information
A981 TIM P 3 Part 2	File	Timor:- Portuguese Occupation of. 2
A2671 270/1941	File	War Cabinet Agendum - No 270/1941 and supplements 1-3 - Occupation of Portuguese Timor
A1608 J41/1/9 Part 1	File	War Section - Portuguese Timor Part I
A6779 20	AGS SWPA	Terrain Study Number 50, Portuguese Timor
A981 TIM P 9	Archer, C. H.	File: Timor (Portuguese) Report by C. H. Archer
A 981 Tim P 20	Archer, C. H.	
A816 19/301/1025	Australian Consulate, Dilli	Departmental Dispatch No. 34/47; Subject: Chinese - Tao Chu Fok
A1067 PI 46/2/9/1	Bezarra Dos Santos	To the Prime Minister of Australia
A461 C350/1/9	Bezzera Dos Santos	"To the PM of Australia"
A1067 PI 46/2/9/1	Callinan, B. J. (Major)	Report on:--Situation - Western Portuguese Timor
A816 19/301/1025	Eaton, C.	Department Dispatch No.16
A816 19/301/1025	Eaton, C.	Department Dispatch No.9/47; Subject: Native Census Statistics
A1067 PI46/2/9/1	Johnston, Bradfield and Ross	
A6779 19	Lambert, E. T.	Lambert Report 1937. Japanese Interests

2. National Archive of Australia-Canberra Holdings

Date	pp.	Dig.	Contents
1942-1944	117	●	Political Warfare Department documents, includes report related to Salazar, and the 1942 "Descriptive Report" on Portuguese Timor.
1942	51	●	File related to relations with Portugal over Timor in January-February 1942.
1941-1942	94	●	File of communications and reports related to the planned and implemented occupation of Portuguese Timor.
1941-1942	348	●	Mixed documents related to Japanese activities in Portuguese Timor. Document covers the period from the agreement on Japanese flights to Timor (23 October 1941) to the Japanese announcement to the Portuguese government of its reasons for invading.
1943			AGS Terrain study.
1941/4/29	161	●	Copies of a 29 April 1941 report by Consul C. H. Archer (appx. 50 pp) on his trip to Timor and additional correspondence.
1941/4/29	c.50	●	Report of Consul C. F. Archer dated 29 April 1941.
1947	2		A report on ane extremely influential Chinese man, including mention of the wartime period.
1945	5	●	Letter of protest over internment (original, 3 pp. translation, and other documents).
1945	6+	●	Letter of protest over internment (original, 3 pp. translation, and other documents).
1942/11/3	5	●	A report on the conditions in the western part of East Timor (Same, Ainaro, Rotei and Talo), which had just been visited by Callinan and Pte. P. P. McCabe. Aims to determine a way to counter Japanese activities and support the Portuguese (for Australian benefit).
1946	4		Describes conditions and events in Timor in November 1946, particularly in eastern areas where Eaton had visited, including the Cape Lore Radar Station which he had attacked in December 1944.
1947	3		Data from the 1946 census, along with a cover letter from the Consul discussing the relationship with the Japanese occupation period.
1941	5	●	Report on a trip of Johnston, Dr. Bradfield, and Mr. Ross on 29 December 1940-1 January 1941 to Portuguese Timor.
	2	●	An extract of the section of the Lambert report dealing with Japanese interests in Portuguese Timor (paragraphs 48-50). Found on pp. 54-55 of the digitized NAA file.

III. オーストラリア所蔵史料 (Materials in Australian Archives)

File Number	Author	Title
A981 Tim P4 Part 2	Lambert, E. T.	Report on Portuguese Timor by Consul Lambert
SP109/3 308/30	Marien, Bill	Timor, No. 6
A1067 PI46/2/9/1	NEFIS	Descriptive Report on Timor
A981 TIM P 23	NEFIS	Descriptive Report on Timor-Addendum
SP109/3 308/30	Parer, Damien	Timor, No. 7
A6779 19	Ross, David	Report by Ross 1st September, 1941
A1196 15/501/222	Ross, David	To: The Secretary, Department of External Affairs
A981 Tim P 4 Part 2	Ross, David	
A2937 268	Salazar	
A981 Tim P 4 Part 2	Sluimers, M.	Translation of a Report about a Voyage to Timor, Dilly
A816 19/301/820A	War Cabinet	War Cabinet Agendum - No 270/1941
A2937 268		Note of Agreement concluded between Australian mission at Dilli and Governor of Portuguese Timor
A1838 376/1/1		Photographs
SP109/3 308/30		Timor, No. 8 (By an N.E.I. Army officer who fought in Portuguese Timor)
A1067 PI46/2/9/1		

2. National Archive of Australia-Canberra Holdings

Date	pp.	Dig.	Contents
1938	24	•	Printed copy of the 1937 report on the visit of the outgoing British representative in Batavia, with cover letters from Lambert to Fitzmaurice and Fitzmaurice to Eden. Important pre-war report on visit to Timor. Located on pp. 103-127 of the digitized NAA file.
1943/1/2	4		Typescript of censored text to be published after 3:00 pm January 2, 1943. Based on this journalist's visit to Timor in 1942, this article is a description of the Timorese people, and the Timorese relations with Australians and Japanese.
1942/5/28	55	•	Detailed report, starting of p. 53 of the digitized file.
1942/6/8		•	Addendum signed by van Straaten on 8 June 1942.
1943/1/3	4		Typescript of censored text to be published after 3:00 pm January 3, 1943. Parer tries to describe the coniditions facing troops in Timor, as well as outlining his own experience in Timor. Detailed, but role of propagandist is very clear.
1941	4	•	Report covering coffee, beeswax, shipping, Japanese trade, and the oil survey in around 1940. Focusses on the elimination of Japanese involvement in Timor.
1941/12/22	2	•	Report on events and conditions in Dili and Portuguese Timor since the Allied landings.
1942	4	•	Report on Portuguese Timor by David Ross.
1945/10/6	13	•	English translation of a published statement by Prime Minister Salazar on events in the war, particularly the foreign relationships of Portugal and Timor. Pp. 7-19 of the digitized file.
1941	4	•	A description of the author's observations during a trip to Dili in late October 1941. Mentions most famous individuals, including the Japanese consul Kuroki, the Australian civil aviation personnel (Ross and Wittekes), Brouwer, senior officials, and even visited a Japanese ship in Dili harbor.
1941/8/12	3	•	Details for a meeting, including a summary of the conclusions of the Singapore meeting in 1941.
1945/9	1	•	Located on page 36 of the digitized file.
1945	2	•	Photographs of surrender ceremony of Kupang.
1943/1/4	4		Typescript of censored text to be published after 3:00 pm January 4, 1943. The author builds his discussion of the Dutch in Portuguese Timor around the themes of heroism and being honored by the king/queen.
c.1942	8	•	Untitled report on Portuguese foreign relations 1941-1942 w/re to Timor.

III. オーストラリア所蔵史料 (Materials in Australian Archives)

File Number	Author	Title
A6779 19		

2. National Archive of Australia-Canberra Holdings

Date	pp.	Dig.	Contents
c.1943	10	●	Report about the pre-war and early war context of East Timor, along with notes about the post-war settlement. Probably for Australian diplomatic policy-making purposes.

III. オーストラリア所蔵史料 (Materials in Australian Archives)

3. National Archive of Australia

File Number	Author	Title
MP 742/1 336/1/1724	Abe, Tadaichi	Statement by ABE, Tadaichi
MP 742/1 336/1/1724 MP 742/1 336/1/2073	Arakawa, Kuwakichi	Interrogation of Capt ARAKAWA Kuwakichi of the 228 Inf Regt by WX7309 Capt J. Gerke of War Crimes Section Rabaul on the 14 Oct 1946
MP 742/1 336/1/1724 MP 742/1 336/1/2073	Arakawa, Kuwakichi	Sworn Statement
MP 742/1 336/1/1724	Arakawa, Kuwakichi	Sworn Statement by ARAKAWA Kuwakichi
MP 742/1 336/1/1724 MP 742/1 336/1/2073	Arakawa, Kuwakichi	Translation of a Sworn Statement by ARAKAWA Kuwakichi
MP 742/1 336/1/1724 MP 742/1 336/1/2073	Arakawa, Kuwakichi	Translation of a written Sworn Statement by ARAKAWA Kuwakichi
MP 742/1 336/1/1724	Arakawa, Kuwakichi	Written Sworn Statement by ARAKAWA Kuwakichi. In Japanese
MP 742/1 336/1/1724	Asnawi Koso	Sworn Statement by Asnawi Koso
MP 742/1 336/1/1213	Australian Military Forces	Set of documents related to the war criminal cases on ill-treatment of SRD personnel on Timor
MP 742/1 336/1/1724	Bartolomeu de Almeida, Anselmo	Summary of examination of ANSELMO BARTOLOMEU de ALMEIDA, aged 42 years, occupation, Bank clerk, Portuguese subject residing in DILLI, PORTUGUESE TIMOR
MP 742/1 336/1/1724	Chung Hai Cheng	Summary of examination of CHUNG HAI CHENG, also known as HA HOI, occupation, merchant, aged 24 years, born in CANTON, a Chinese residing during the war in LIQUICA gaol

Melbourne Holdings- Selected List

Date	pp.	Dig.	Contents
1945	6		Testimony of a member of the Tokumu Kikan in Ambon. Much concerns the head of the Tokumu unit, Mr. Kiyokuni, who had extensive experience in China and Manchuria, and was the founder of the "Sonno Juku" (Emperor Worship School). Only marginal reference to Timor, but still aparently some relevance. The primary function was to gather intelligence about Australia.
1946/10/14	2		Question and answer format. Minimal information as the inf was either not knowledgable about the issues raised or evasive.
1949	2		On the 228 landing in Dili, executions, and Rabaul testimonies.
[1949]	4		On the Rabaul meeting, Maeda Eiichiro, executions, etc.
[1949]	3		On the Rabaul meeting, Maeda Eiichiro, executions, etc.
[1949]	5		On his own background, detailed information about the false testimony in Rabaul, and information about personnel.
[1949]	5		On his own background, detailed information about the false testimony in Rabaul, and information about personnel.
1946	1		Testimony of a driver for the Kempeitai in Kupang related to allied servicemen found by Roefoes Takoe.
1946	24		Set of documents related to the war criminal cases on ill-treatment of SRD personnel on Timor. Includes scattered information on the treatment of the SRD personnel after capture and the Fukabori Butai, a Fukumen Butai known as the Tomikikan, testimony of Major TADA Minoru of the 18th Army HQ on Ambon and Capt. Cashman.
1946	1		Testimony of a bank clerk from Dili. About the bank and the Japanese financial relations with the bank and the Portuguese administration (including propaganda leaflets and the robbing of the bank).
1946	2		Testimony of a Chinese man who worked as a interpreter for Kempei unit 1921 in Liquicia from May 1943 to the end of the war. Mentions the Kempeitai members names, several individuals who were tortured and gives a little information about the Ōtori kikan.

III. オーストラリア所蔵史料 (Materials in Australian Archives)

File Number	Author	Title
MP 742/1 336/1/1724	da Silva, Sancha	Summary of examination of SANCHA da SILVA, occupation, clerk to native chiefs, of TIMORESE Nationalisty, born at OSSOROA and 27 years of age, now residing at OSSU, PORTUGUESE TIMOR
MP 742/1 336/1/1724	dos Anjos, Agapito	Summary of examination of AGAPITO dos ANJOS, a Corporal in the Portuguese Army, born in Portugal and 40 years of age and residing in DILLI, PORTUGUESE TIMOR
MP 742/1 336/1/1724	dos Santos, Antonio Augusto	Summary of examination of ANTONIO AUGUSTO dos SANTOS, aged 43 years, occupation, carpenter, Portuguese subject, born in Lisbon, and now residing in Dili, PORTUGUESE TIMOR
MP 742/1 336/1/2073	Gilchrist, A.	Notes of Relevant Information taken from O2E file 145/4/155 on 26 Apr. 46
MP 742/1 336/1/1724	Gomes, Jose Augusto	Summary of examination of JOSE AUGUSTO GOMES, retired Lieutenant of the Portuguese Army, a Portuguese subject, and resides in DILLI and is 63 years of age
MP 742/1 336/1/1724	Goshett, D. Beresford	2 Aust War Crimes Sec SCAP to Army Headquarters, Melbourne; Subject: KIYOKUNI Shigetoshi – FORMER JAPANESE SPECIAL SERVICE AGENT
MP 742/1 336/1/2073	Goslett, D. Beresford	Subject: Execution of Australians – Dilli Area, Timor 20 Feb 42
MP 742/1 336/1/2073	Goslett, D. Beresford	Subject: Execution of Australians – Dilli Area, Timor 20 Feb 42
MP 742/1 336/1/2073	Goslett, D. Beresford	Subject: Execution of Australians – Dilli Area, Timor 20 Feb 42

3. National Archive of Australia Melbourne Holdings

Date	pp.	Dig.	Contents
1946	1		Deals primarily with the 2 Australians brought to the Dili gaol in 1944, but also a little with his own experience of being jailed for more than one year.
1946	1		Testimony of a former member of the police force. Was a prisoner in the Dili gaol in 1942, but by November 1942 he "escaped" and went to "the concentration camp" for his own protection.
1946	2		The testimony of a Portuguese carpenter who had been responsible for the water instillations of Dili up to his arrest on January 5, 1944. He was jailed, tortured and interrogated for 46 days. The bulk of his testimony concerns the jail conditions.
1946	1		A collection of information related to the executions in Dili from various statements of soldiers including a statement of Hayes from 1942.
1946	1		General testimony largely about conditions in the Liquicia camp where he spent the war years.
1949	1		Letter accompanying interrogation reports of the Kiyokuni brothers.
1946	2		Letter WC 439 from 2 Australian War Crimes Sec SCAP concerning the investigations of the executions at Dili in February 1942. Lists individuals interrogated, and those not yet interrogated, with handwritten notes about repatriation in 1947. Tentative lists of units involved in the Dili landing and comanders included, although the commander of the Naval landing force had not been identified.
1947	1		Letter WC 2309 from OC 2 Australian War Crimes Sec SCAP concerning the investigations of the executions at Dili. Mentions that Col. Doi had conducted an investigation of whether there were grounds for Australian claims that if surrendered they would be killed anyway. As a result they found the Army had not conducted killings, but that Navy personnel had killed some Australians.
1949	3		Letter WC 533 from OC 2 Australian War Crimes Sec SCAP concerning the investigations of the executions at Dili in February 1942. Very clear about interviews conducted, responsibility for the executions, details about unreliable testimony.

III. オーストラリア所蔵史料 (Materials in Australian Archives)

File Number	Author	Title
MP 742/1 336/1/2073	Goslett, D. Beresford	Subject: Execution of Australians - Dilli Area, Timor 20 Feb 42
MP 742/1 336/1/1724 MP 742/1 336/1/2073	Goto, Takezu	Sworn Statement
MP 742/1 336/1/1724	Graca, Sebastiao	Summary of examination of SEBASTIAO GRACA, Telephone Chief
MP 742/1 336/1/2073	Hayes, K. M.	Missing Personnel - 2/2 Ind Coy - WX 12316 Pte AIREY D. H.
MP 742/1 336/1/1724 MP 742/1 336/1/2073	Hondo, Mitsuyoshi	Sworn Statement
MP 742/1 336/1/1724 MP 742/1 336/1/2073	Ishiwata, Asakichi	Sworn Statement
MP 742/1 336/1/1724	Ito, Takeo	Interrogation of LT GEN ITO, Takeo AT RABAUL on 9 OCTOBER 46
MP 742/1 4/7 (Ito Intero) MP 742/1 336/1/2073	Ito, Takeo	Interrogation of Lt-Gen ITO Takeo by Lt. R.S. Tuck of War Crimes Section HQ 8 MD, through interpreter Army Capt SUSUKI Hachiro, at RABAUL on 27 Nov 46.
MP 742/1 4/7 (Ito Intero)	Ito, Takeo	War History of Lt. Gen. Ito Takeo....
MP 742/1 336/1/1724 MP 742/1 336/1/2073	Iwata, Seiichi	Interrogation of Major IWATA Seiichi of 228 Inf Regiment by WX7309 Capt J Gerke "A" Branch, War Crimes Section, Rabaul on 10 day of Oct 1946
MP 742/1 336/1/1724	Iwata, Seiichi	Report on Interrogation of IWATA Seiichi conducted in Japanese at Meiji Bldg. TOKYO on 3 Nov 47
MP 742/1 336/1/1724 MP 742/1 336/1/2073	Iwata, Seiichi	Notes on Interrogation of IWATA Seiichi conducted in Japanese at Meiji Bldg. TOKYO on 20 Apr 49
MP 742/1 336/1/1724 MP 742/1 336/1/2073	Iwata, Seiichi	Sworn Statement
MP 742/1 336/1/1724 MP 742/1 336/1/2073	Iwata, Seiichi	Translation of Sworn Statement made by IWATA Seiichi regarding conversations that he had with OZAWA Kunio

3. National Archive of Australia Melbourne Holdings

Date	pp.	Dig.	Contents
1949	3		Letter WC 329 from OC 2 Australian War Crimes Sec SCAP concerning the investigations of the executions at Dili in February 1942 from 5 Dec 1947 to 24 March 1949. Very clear about interviews conducted, and presents the then current best information about the initial landings in Dili and the killing of Asutralian prisoners.
1949	1		On the Navy landings in Dili.
1946	3		Testimony of a portuguese man. Much is questionable, either chronologically or in some other way, but it is also of interest. Brief note related to native girls geing "forced to sleep with the Japanese."
1946	1		The statement describes Hayes' experiences and details information about missing soldiers who were probably executed.
1948	5		Detailed statement on the Navy landings and personnel in Dili.
1949/4/8	2		On the 228 landing in Dili and the executions. Mentions postwar contact with other officers.
1946/10/9	3		On Navy and Army relationships, responsabilities, etc. Mentions roles of Kempeitai, including to train police.
1946/11/27	4		Primarily asscertains the major commanders on Timor during 1942, but includes various miscellaneous information.
1946/11/24	4		Taken under oath at RABAUL on 26 Nov 46 by Lt. R.S. Tuck of War Crimes Section HQ 8 MD through interpreter Army Capt SUSUKI Hachiro. Explicitly states he did not visit Dili.
1946/10/10	6		Question and answer form yields some information, but inf was either not knowledgable about the issues raised or evasive.
1947/11/13	1		On the executions, personnel and Rabaul interrogations.
1949/4/20	3		On the executions and a list of Doi Butai personnel.
1949	2		On the landing in Dili, executions, Rabaul investigations, and postwar contacts.
1949	1		On the contents of his 1947 meeting with Ozawa Kunio (1st lt., intelligence officer)

Ⅲ. オーストラリア所蔵史料 (Materials in Australian Archives)

File Number	Author	Title
MP 742/1 336/1/1724	Johannes Adoe	Sworn Statement by Johhannes Adoe
MP 742/1 336/1/1724 MP 742/1 336/1/2073	Kasai, Tomojiro	Sworn Statement
MP 742/1 336/1/1724 MP 742/1 336/1/2073	Kasai, Tomojiro	Sworn Statement
MP 742/1 336/1/1724 MP 742/1 336/1/2073	Kasai, Tomojiro	Sworn Statement
MP 742/1 336/1/1724	Kasai, Tomojiro	Sworn Statement by KASAI, Tomojiro. In Japanese
MP 742/1 336/1/1724	Kasai, Tomojiro	Sworn Statement by KASAI, Tomojiro. In Japanese
MP 742/1 336/1/1724 MP 742/1 336/1/2073	Kasai, Tomojiro	Translation of a Sworn Statement by KASAI, Tomojiro
MP 742/1 336/1/1724 MP 742/1 336/1/2073	Kimura, Eijiro	Sworn Statement
MP 742/1 336/1/1724	Kiyokuni, Seiji	Report on Interrogation of KIYOKUNI Seiji conducted in Japanese through Interpreter Sgt Horace K. NAKAMURA at Meiji Bldg. TOKYO on 27 Dec 48
MP 742/1 336/1/1724	Kiyokuni, Shigetoshi	Report on Interrogation of KIYOKUNI Shigetoshi Conducted in Japanese through Interpreter Sgt Fred OSHIMA at MEIJI Bldg. TOKYO on 20/21 Dec 48
MP 742/1 336/1/1724 MP 742/1 336/1/2073	Kojima, Shinichi	Interrogation of Capt KOJIMA Shinichi of the 228 Inf Regt by WX7309 Capt J. Gerke of War Crimes Section Rabaul on the fifteenth day of October 1946
MP 742/1 336/1/1724	Kojima, Shinichi	Sworn Statement
MP 742/1 336/1/1724 MP 742/1 336/1/2073	Kojima, Shinichi	Sworn Statement
MP 742/1 336/1/1724	Luz, Patricio	Summary of examination of PATRICIO LUZ, age 32 years, occupation, wireless operator, a Portuguese subject, born in Portuguese Timor and now residing in DILLI, PORTUGUESE TIMOR
MP 742/1 336/1/1724 MP 742/1 336/1/2073	Matsumoto, Bunjin	Interrogation of Capt MATSUMOTO Bunjin of the 228 Inf Regt by WX7309 Capt J. Gerke of War Crimes Section Rabaul on the fifteenth day of Oct 1946

3. National Archive of Australia Melbourne Holdings

Date	pp.	Dig.	Contents
1946	1		Testimony of a witness to the killing of 2 Australians near Kupang (Oesapa Ketjil).
1949/3/3	2		On the initial Dili landing and executions in 1942, and personnel in Dili.
1949/3/2	2		Correction of false testimony. On the executions in 1942.
1949/1/2	2		Statement on the Navy landings and executions. Detailed.
1949	6		On the initial Dili landing in 1942.
1949/3/3	5		Sworn statement (March 3, sic) which was apparently not translated because the information was the same as a March 3 English Statement.
1949	3		On the initial Dili landing in 1942.
1949	2		On the 228 landing in Dili and executions. Major Kimura was the acting commander during the landing.
1948/12/27	?		Testimony by a member of the Otori Kikan (also brother of the commander). Denied being a member of the subsequent Nishiki-tai established by the Navy after his brother "resigned" from service or being based in the Aroe islands. Initially based in Kupang.
1948/12/21	5		Report by Otori Kikan head about his general activities and the organization of his interlligence unit. Personally went to Kupang several times.
1946/10/15	2		Question and answer format. Basic information.
1947	3		Relatively detailed statement on his service history, invasion of Dili, personnel, prisoner of war compound, etc.
1949	2		A statement supplementing his 1947 sworn statement listing 228 personnel and his observations during first days in Dili.
1946	3		Covers many subjects like the attack on Aileu and other towns, names of officers and units (e.g. DAICHOMEHO Company), prewar residents turned guides (Nawata, Tokiwa, Inokuchi), killing of chiefs, Nanyo Kohatsu and SAPT, etc. Luz became a member of Z Force, which makes the ultimate source of his data difficult to determine. Much may derive from suspect intelligence operations of Z Force.
1946/10/15	2		Question and answer format. Light artillery platoon commander, ordered to prepare for tanks and pillboxes.

File Number	Author	Title
MP 742/1 336/1/1724	Matsumoto, Bunjin	Sworn Statement
MP 742/1 336/1/1724	Moriyama, Miyoshi	Sworn Statement
MP 742/1 336/1/2073	Moro, Hajime	Sworn Statement
MP 742/1 336/1/1724 MP 742/1 336/1/2073	Moro, Hajime	Sworn Statement
MP 742/1 336/1/1724 MP 742/1 336/1/2073	Moro, Hajime	Sworn Statement
MP 742/1 336/1/1724 MP 742/1 336/1/2073	Nakajima, Yasushi	Interrogation of Capt NAKAJIMA Yasushi of 228 Inf Regt by WX7309 Capt J. Gerke, War Crimes Section Rabaul on the 14 Oct '46
MP 742/1 336/1/1724 MP 742/1 336/1/2073	Nakajima, Yasushi	Sworn Statement
MP 742/1 336/1/1724	Nakajima, Yasushi	Sworn Statement by NAKAJIMA Yasushi. In Japanese.
MP 742/1 336/1/1724 MP 742/1 336/1/2073	Nakajima, Yasushi	Translation of a Sworn Statement by NAKAJIMA Yasushi
MP 742/1 336/1/1724 MP 742/1 336/1/2073	Nawata Hisakasu	Sworn Statement
MP 742/1 336/1/1724 MP 742/1 336/1/2073	Okamura, Toshio	Sworn Statement
MP 742/1 336/1/1724	Okamura, Toshio	Sworn Statement by OKAMURA, Toshio. In Japanese
MP 742/1 336/1/1724 MP 742/1 336/1/2073	Okamura, Toshio	Translation of a Sworn Statement by OKAMURA, Toshio
MP 742/1 336/1/1724	Oliveira, Mario Borges	Affidavit
MP 742/1 336/1/1724 MP 742/1 336/1/2073	Ono, Mitsuji	Interrogation of Capt ONO Mitsuji of 228 Inf Regiment by WX7309 Capt J. Gerke, War Crimes Section Rabaul on the 14 Oct '46
MP 742/1 336/1/1724 MP 742/1 336/1/2073	Onogi, Isamu	Interrogation of Major ONOGI Isamu of the 228 Inf Regiment by WX7309 Capt J. Gerke, War Crimes Section Rabaul on the 14 Oct 1946
MP 742/1 336/1/1724 MP 742/1 336/1/2073	Onogi, Isamu	Sworn Statement

3. National Archive of Australia Melbourne Holdings

Date	pp.	Dig.	Contents
1949	1		On the Dili landing, executions, and concocted stories.
1949	1		On the killing of Indonesians and execution of prisoners.
1948/8/2	2		Statement by the surgeon attached to the Nomber 3 Air Force (Kamei Butai). Mentions a lot of naval personnel, but has no recollection of ever hearing of executions.
1949/2/4	2		On the initial Dili landing and executions.
1949	2		Additional information added to 4 February statement.
1946/10/14	2		Question and answer format. Mostly on invasion and prisoners, but unlike other officers admits seeing about 15 Indonesian prisoners.
1949	1		On the Dili landing, executions, and concocted stories.
1949	2		On the discussions in Rabaul about Dili executions.
1949	2		On the discussions in Rabaul about Dili executions.
1949	2		Brief statement by a civilian guide for the 228th Inf. Reg. who had been Nanyo Kohatsu employee in Dili 1936-1938. He was only attached to the Army unit for a few days.
1949/2/15	2		On the initial Dili landing and executions in 1942. Signed 15 February 1949 after his attempted suicide.
1949	4		On the initial Dili landing in 1942 and executions.
1949	4		On the initial Dili landing in 1942 and executions.
1946	3		Testimony of the Portuguese physician of the Dili hospital (a captain in the army). Provides a wide range of somewhat vague information, much of it probably second hand information from his patients, family, or friends. Went to Osso in 1942, where his son was Chef de Posto. Gives a date of 31 August for the Aileu attack.
1946/10/14	2		Question and answer format. Vetinary surgeon who knew little of what was happening.
1946/10/14	3		Question and answer format. Medical officer at Dili from 23 Feb to 7 Sept 1942. Mostly on invasion and prisoners.
1949	2		On the 228 landing in Dili, the executions, and the Rabaul meeting with 9 officers. Capt. Onogi was a medical officer.

III. オーストラリア所蔵史料 (Materials in Australian Archives)

File Number	Author	Title
MP 742/1 336/1/1724 MP 742/1 336/1/2073	Onuki, Shigenobu	Interrogation of Capt ONUKI Shigenobu of 228 Inf Regt by WX7309 Capt J. Gerke of War Crimes Section Rabaul on the fifteen day of Oct 1946
MP 742/1 336/1/1724 MP 742/1 336/1/2073	Onuki, Shigenobu	Sworn Statement
MP 742/1 336/1/1724 MP 742/1 336/1/2073	Ozawa, Kunio	Sworn Statement
MP 742/1 336/1/1724	Quinton, N. F.	Cover letter: to Consul for Australia, Dilli
MP 742/1 336/1/1724	Rodrigues, Luis Antonio Nunes	Summary of examination of LUIS ANTONIO NUNES RODRIGUES, occupation, doctor's clerk, of Portuguese nationality and born in Portuguese Timor, and 30 years of age, and residing at DILLI, PORTUGUESE TIMOR
MP 742/1 336/1/1724	Roefoes Takoe	SWORN STATEMENT BY ROEFOES Takoe
MP 742/1 336/1/2073	Ross, David	War Crimes - Portuguese Timor
MP 742/1 336/1/1724	Simoes, Ernesto	Summary of examination of ERNESTO SIMOES, aged 29 years, born at HATOLIA, Portuguese Timor, a Portuguese subject, a driver and now residing in DILLI, Portuguese Timor
MP 742/1 3/7	Takeuchi, Tatsuo	Full translation of statement by TAKEUCHI, Tatsuo
MP 742/1 3/7	Takeuchi, Tatsuo	Statement/Affidavit (in Japanese)
MP 742/1 336/1/1724 MP 742/1 336/1/2073	Taniguchi, Tadamitsu	Full translation of a statement by TANIGUCHI, Tadimitsu dated 30 March 1949
MP 742/1 336/1/1724	Taniguchi, Tadamitsu	Statement by TANIGUCHI, Tadimitsu dated 30 March 1949
MP 742/1 336/1/1724 MP 742/1 336/1/2073	Taniguchi, Tadamitsu	Sworn Statement

3. National Archive of Australia Melbourne Holdings

Date	pp.	Dig.	Contents
1946/10/15	2		Question and answer format. Communications officer in the second wave landing west of the airport.
1949	2		On the 228 landing in Dili, the executions, and the Rabaul meeting with 9 officers.
1949/4/12	2		On the 228 landing in Dili and the executions. Mentions postwar contact with other officers.
1946	1		Cover letter to consul related to investigations of war crimes. Includes clear statement about suppression of information and obstruction.
1946	3		This testimony covers a lot of subjects, including various attacks by Japanese and their "black" troops, destruction of hospitals, torturing of individuals including native chiefs, the threats made to induce chiefs to arrange women for Japanese brothels, etc. Was generally precise about what he saw or who told him. Seems to have traveled widely, thus was a good informant.
1946	1		Testimony of a Kupang based Kempeitai "secret agent" whose job was to find allied servicemen.
1946	1		An undated statement from 1946 about the killing of Australian prisoners, the POWs in Dili, and Ross's discussion with the Japanese OC in Dili.
1946	2		Testimony of a Portuguese soldier about the Japanese occupation of Aileu in late September and the October 1, 1942 attack by "black" troops backed unoffically by Japanese which resulted in the deaths of most Portuguese and the interment of the others. Seems failrly reliable.
1947	3		ATIS translation. Document numner 37159. "AFFIDAVIT (Details regarding prisoners, witnessed at KOEPANG on the island of TIMOR)."
1947	7		Statement related to prisoners at Kupang.
1949/3/30	4		On his meeting with Lt. Hondo in 1948, his correspondence with the same person. Related to the execution of prisoners by the unit under his command, and his effort to cover up his role.
1949/3/30	4		On his meeting with Lt. Hondo in 1948, his correspondence with the same person. Related to the execution of prisoners by the unit under his command, and his effort to cover up his role.
1949	1		Brief statement mostly on postwar contacts with other officers. Includes and written addition.

III. オーストラリア所蔵史料 (Materials in Australian Archives)

File Number	Author	Title
MP 742/1 336/1/1724	Tilman de Ataide, Francisco	Summary of examination of FRANCISCO TILMAN de ATAIDE, aged 41 years, a TIMORESE and Portuguese subject, born in MOTAEL, Portuguese Timor and native chief of MOTAEL....
MP 742/1 336/1/1724	Tindale, M. B.	Report on Interrogation of GOTO, Hikobachi
MP 742/1 336/1/1724 MP 742/1 336/1/2073	Tokiwa, Moriaki	Sworn Statement
MP 742/1 336/1/2073	Wheatley, Mervyn	Handwritten Letter
MP 742/1 336/1/2073	Wheatley, Mervyn	Letter
MP 742/1 336/1/2073	Williams, H. S.	Report on Further Interrogation of TOSAKU Susumu Formerly Brigade Major of Ito Bde at Koepang
MP 742/1 336/1/2073	Williams, H. S.	Report on Interrogation of HANADA Yukitake (Formerly Rear Admiral) at Meiji Building, 5 Nov 46
MP 742/1 4/7 (Ito Intero)	Williams, H. S.	Report on Interrogation of HANADA Yukitake at Meiji Building, 5 Nov 46
MP 742/1 336/1/2073	Williams, H. S.	Report on Interrogation of KIMURA Eijiro at Meiji Bldg on 4 Nov 46
MP 742/1 3/7	Williams, H. S.	Report on Interrogation FUJITA Yoshio conducted in Japanese at MEIJI Bldg, TOKYO 24 Jun 47
MP 742/1 336/1/1724 MP 742/1 336/1/2073	Williams, H. S.	Report on Interrogation of KUROKI, Tokitaro at MEIJI Bldg. TOKYO on 15 and 16 Dec 47
MP 742/1 336/1/1724 MP 742/1 336/1/2073	Williams, H. S.	Report on Interrrogation of TOKIWA, Moriaki conducted in Japanese at MEIJI Bldg. TOKYO on 23 & 24 Dec 47
MP 742/1 336/1/1724 MP 742/1 336/1/2073	Williams, H. S.	Notes on Interrogation of KASAI Tomojiro
MP 742/1 336/1/1724	Williams, H. S.	Notes on Interrogation of MORIYAMA Miyoshi

3. National Archive of Australia Melbourne Holdings

Date	pp.	Dig.	Contents
1946	1		A series of short statements related to the occupation by the Japanese. Schools where boys would learn Japanese taught by Japanese teachers, and orders to find women were among the subjects mentioned.
1949	1		On the Dili executions.
1948	2		Statement by the second civilian guide for the 228th Inf. Reg. who had been Nanyo Kohatsu employee in Dili 1940. He was in Dili until the end of March.
1946	2		Letter written in response to question related to a Dili Police Captain and the killing of Australians. Not dated, but probably 1946.
1946	1		Letter written in response to question related to certain Portuguese officers and the killing of Australians.
1946	1		A second interrogation made regarding the Dili landing, the Kempeitai and treatment of PW. Tosaku was not in Dili.
1946/11/5	2		While this report contains little directly on East Timor since the informant was not on Timor until June 1942, and then only in Kupang, it still is of some interest for the movement of this officer and his reference to naval units. A full interrogation report, if exitant, would be more interesting.
1946/11/5	2		About the Navy personnel and units in Kupang and Dili in 1942.
1946/11/4	2		Report on the interrogation of No. 2 Battalion, 228th Rgt commander. Injured in mid-April 1942, and eventually repatriated on a hospital ship. Provides information about initial landing, including the ship and and units. A note states that all but around 10 members of the No. 2 Battalion reportedly died in Guadacanal.
1947/6/24	2		Prewar resident of Surabaya, was translator for several months in West Timor. Nonetheless, the short report is of some interest.
1947/12/16	2		On his assignment as Consul to Dili (1941-2) and the situation he faced there.
1947/12/24	2		Information from a former Nanyo Kohatsu employee who was briefly attached to the 228th Inf. Reg. as a translator. Much focusses on the executions, but there is a little information on another translator (English) named Nawata. Tokiwa was a Portuguese translator.
1949	1		On executions, previous lies and Naval Air Force officer names.
1949	1		On executions and various personnel.

III. オーストラリア所蔵史料 (Materials in Australian Archives)

File Number	Author	Title
MP 742/1 336/1/2073	Williams, H. S.	Notes on Interrogation of OKAMURA Toshio at YOKOSUKA KYOSEI Hospital 15 Feb 49
MP 742/1 336/1/1724 MP 742/1 336/1/2073	Williams, H. S.	Notes on Interrogation of OKUMURA & KASAI
MP 742/1 336/1/1724	Williams, H. S.	Notes on Re-interrogation of ISHIWATA Asakichi
MP 742/1 336/1/1724	Williams, H. S.	Notes on Re-interrogation of TANIGUCHI Tadamitsu
MP 742/1 336/1/1213	Wynne, P.	Report of Treatment of SRD Prisoner in Japanese Hands
MP 742/1 336/1/1724	Yacob Mozes	Sumary of Examination of YACOB MOZES, residing on board the Dutch ship "MERAUKE"
MP 742/1 336/1/1724	Yamada, Nobuyoshi	Sworn Statement made by YAMADA Nobuyoshi. In Japanese
MP 742/1 336/1/1724 MP 742/1 336/1/2073	Yamada, Nobuyoshi	Sworn Statement
MP 742/1 336/1/1724 MP 742/1 336/1/2073	Yamada, Nobuyoshi	Translation of a Sworn Statement made by YAMADA Nobuyoshi regarding contacts that he made with former members of 228 Infantry Regiment after cessation of hostilities
MP 742/1 336/1/1724 MP 742/1 336/1/2073	Yokouchi, Keisuke	Sworn Statement
MP 742/1 336/1/2073	Yoshiyasu, Tatsuo	Interrogation of Capt YOSHIYASU Tatsuo of 228 Inf Regt by WX7309 Capt J Gerke; War Crimes Section 8 Military District. RABAUL
MP 742/1 336/1/1724 MP 742/1 336/1/2073	Yoshiyasu, Tatsuo	Sworn Statement
MP 742/1 336/1/1724 MP 742/1 336/1/2073	Yoshiyasu, Tatsuo	Sworn Statement
MP 742/1 336/1/1724	Yutani Yujino	Interrogation of Lt-Col YUTANI Yujino by Capt R L WATTS, at Rabaul on the 16th July 1946 to ascertain any knowledge of Cpl SAKAI in answer to signal AG2424990
MP 742/1 336/1/2073		Report on murder of Australian POW by Japanese troops near Dilli. Timor 20 Feb 1942

3. National Archive of Australia Melbourne Holdings

Date	pp.	Dig.	Contents
1949/12/15	2		This interrogation is particularly critical as it was conducted at a hospital after Okamura tried to commit suicide. He provides information about the executions.
1949	1		On Naval officer names.
1949	1		On the executions and warrant officer Kubo.
1949	1		On Naval Air Force officer names.
n.d.	2		Detailed statement about Capt. Wynne's treatment, interrogations, the information he provided to the Japanese, etc.
1946	1		Testimony of the chief of Lebelan on Kisar related to the forced recruitment of men and women for Lautem. Two women from his village were taken, and forced to work in the "Restaurants" in Lautem (according to "reliable sources").
1949	2		On contact with former members of 228 Infantry Regiment after the war.
1949/4/27	2		On his landing in Dili, his interrogation of a prisoner, the execution of prisoners, and postwar contacts with other 228 officers.
1949/4/25	1		On contact with former members of 228 Infantry Regiment after the war.
1949	1		Brief testimony mentioning his meeting an Australian prisoner.
1946	3		A report in question-answer form. Deals with initial landing in Dili. Only moderately interesting.
1947	1		A brief statement on the Dili landing and the first he heard of the executions.
1949	1		A brief statement on his involvement in the Dili landing and postwar contacts with other officers from Dili.
1946/6/16	3		Testimony of the former commander of the 1 Sec 5 Jap FD Military Police in Kupang. Mentions 6 Section as being the Dili based unit under the command of Capt Akuzawa which arrived on around 23 March 1943.
1946	1		A short summary of events, the state of the investigation, and prospects.

III. オーストラリア所蔵史料 (Materials in Australian Archives)

File Number	Author	Title
MP 742/1 336/1/1213 Timor 5		Original Documents (Statements, affidavits, translations, interrogation reports, photostat copies etc.) relating to Dilli, Timor, File 46C, Subject capture of two SRD Parties
MP 742/1 4/7 (Ito Intero)		List of names of Japanese Kempeitai in Timor Obtained by Capt. Pos, N.E.I. Army

3. National Archive of Australia Melbourne Holdings

Date	pp.	Dig.	Contents
1948	69		Set of documents related to the war criminal cases on ill-treatment of SRD personnel on Timor. Includes copies of material in other sub-files, but also additional correspondence and interviews. Includes 2 statements by Capt. Kitano Tomotsu of the 5 military Police Unit, L/Cpl S. Kamimoto, translator of the 48th Div. HQ, Capt Abe Raisaku of the 47th Inf regt, Capt Siki Kasukane, Sgt Maj Arai Taizo of the Akuzawa Tai (Kempeitai), Capt Akuzawa Kisaburo of the 5 Field Military Police, Capt Mori Teishu of the 2 Formosan Inf Regt, Sgt. Maj. Haraguchi Kunio, and Sgt. Maj. Naruta Eigi of the 5 Field Military Police.
	1		

III. オーストラリア所蔵史料 (Materials in Australian Archives)

4. Australian War Memorial

File Number	Author	Title
PR 00249 (item 91)	2/2nd Aust. Ind. Coy.	2/2 Aust Indep Coy (now 2/2 Aust Commando SQN) Outline of Activities
AWM 52 2/2/52	2/2nd Austr. Ind. Coy.	2/2nd Australian Independent Company AIF
AWM 52 2/2/54	2/4th Austr. Ind. Coy.	2/4th Australian Commando Squadron AIF
PR 00249.099-.109 (item 88)	Aitkins, R. L. (Lt.)	Paymaster's Report
F 355-47183 T323 no. 50	Allied Geographical Section	Portuguese Timor
AWM 54 1010/9/67	Arakawa, Kuwakichi	Interrogation of Capt ARAKAWA Kuwakichi of the 228 Inf Regt by WX7309 Capt J. Gerke of War Crimes Section Rabaul on the 14 Oct 1946
AWM 54 571/4/34 AWM 54 571/4/45 PR 00249.299	Arnold, G. J.	Interview 16 Jul. 42 with Capt. G. J. Arnold, Staff Capt. Sparrow Force by M. O. 1. (O)
PR 00249.099-.109 (item 88)	Arnold, G. J. (Capt.)	Supplies, Rationing, etc. Appendix 1. Administration Instruction No. 1, Timor
AWM 54 571/3/3 (1B)	Baldwin, R. R.	Report on the Transport Situation, Portuguese Timor
PR 00249.056-.087 (item 86)	Baldwin, R. R. (Capt.)	Deterioration in Situation from 1 Aug – 15 Aug and from 25 Sep – 15 Oct 42
PR 00249.056-.087 (item 86)	Baldwin, R. R. (Capt.)	Situation Report 9 Dec – 13 Dec (inclusive)
PR 00249 (item 91)	Baldwin, R. R., D. Dexter and C. W. Vernede	Report on the Coastal Topography of the Dilli Area, Portuguese Timor
AWM 54 571/4/45 PR 00249.056-.087 (item 86)	Bamford, A. E. (Lt. Col.)	Brief Review of Ops in Timor to 12 Dec 42

Selected List

Date	pp.	Dig.	Contents
	27		2/2 Australian Independent Company Outline of Activities 20 September – 20 December 1942. Typed and handwritten manuscripts for each unit in the 2/2nd.
1941–1942			The unit diaries for the 2/2nd Australian Independent Company.
1942–1943			The unit diaries for the 2/4th Australian Independent Company.
1942/5/19	2		Report describing payments and paybook situation as best as possible given the loss of records and money when his boat capsized.
1943/3/11	1		1:250,000. Based on 1:250,000 reprint of Asia Investment Co. Map by Chief Engineer U.S.A.F.I.A. May 1942. Amended by Allied Geographical Section in Cooperation with Central Interpretation Unit D.ofI. A.A.F. from air photographs, Dutch charts, 2/2 Independent Coy. sketches and reports, Shell Co. topographical engineers, personnel of Sparrow Force, and former residents.
1946/10/14	2		Question and answer format. Minimal information as the informant was either not knowledgable about the issues raised or evasive.
1942/7/16	3		Statement about conditions and prospects in Portuguese Timor.
1942/4/17	2		Instructions on supply procedures, signed by Capt. J. T. Read for Capt. G. J. Arnold. This copy appended to a report by Brig. Veale of June 1942.
1942/11/17	4		Report on the transportation situation in November, with explicit reference to the changes following the collapse of the Portuguese administration.
1942/10/20	4		Handwritten copy of report. At the time of writing, supplies still obtainable with money, but general conditions expected to worsen.
1942/12/14	2+1		Describes the location of the various Sparrow Force units. The general sense is that Allied units are only functioning defensively.
1942	7 +1 +4 +6		A Recce report by Capt. R. R. Baldwin and D. Dexter on the Dili area, with 6 map sketches and 7 photographs by Pte. C. W. Vernede (and a cover letter by Brig. Veale), May 1942.
1942/12/14	3		Information covers one year, but the focus is on the later period. Information unreliable.

III. オーストラリア所蔵史料 (Materials in Australian Archives)

File Number	Author	Title
PR 00249.180-.214 (items 92-94)	Berryman (Maj. Gen.)	Subject: Relief of Netherlands Forces in Timor
AWM 113 MH1/121 pt.2	Blamey, T. A. (Commander in Chief)	Rabaul, Timor and Ambon Operations
AWM 54 571/4/45 PR 00249.180-.214 (items 92-94)	Breemour, J.	Translation of a letter from the C. O. Dutch Forces in Timor to G. O. C. Netherlands Army Forces in Australia (van Straten)
AWM 54 571/4/28	Brigadier i/c Administration, Northern Territory Force	Evacuations and Strength Sparrow Force
PR 00684 1 of 3	Brigadier, Director of Military Intelligence	
F 940.5425092 B86w	Brodie, A. J. (Ben)	We Fought in the Jungle of Timor
PR 00249.180-.214 (items 92-94)	Bruin, de (Sgt.)	Report on Dutch Area by Sgt. De Bruin (Dutch Forces)
PR 00249.056-.087 (item 86)	Callinan, B. J. (Major)	Appreciation of the Situation in Portuguese Timor
PR 00249.056-.087 (item 86)	Callinan, B. J. (Major)	Report on Dispositions of Sparrow Force Consequent on NORFORCE message O/4196
AWM 54 571/1/11 AWM 54 571/4/28 AWM 54 571/4/36	Callinan, B. J. (Major)	Report on:--Situation - Western Portuguese Timor
AWM 54 571/4/28 AWM 54 571/4/36 PR 00249.180-.214 (items 92-94)	Callinan, B. J. (Major)	Report on:--Situation - Western Portuguese Timor. Appendix One: List of Portuguese Killed in Portuguese Timor since May 1942
PR 00249.056-.087 (item 86)	Callinan, B. J. (Major)	Situation Report - Sparrow Force 18 - 28 Nov 1942
PR 00249.056-.087 (item 86)	Callinan, B. J. (Major)	Situation Report 29 Nov - 8 Dec (incl)
AWM 54 571/4/51 AWM 54 722/4/38	Cape, T. F.	Allied Operations in Timor
PR 00249 (item 87)	Cape, T. F.	Instructions to Capt Francis

4. Australian War Memorial

Date	pp.	Dig.	Contents
1942/10/19	1		Ref. GHQ Secret Memo 1754 of 15 Oct. (See Sutherland entry). Finalizes replacement plan. Signed for the Commander, Allied Land Forces.
1942/7/29	2		The cover letter for reports on the "Court of Inquiry with Reference to Landing of Japanese Forces in New Britain, Timor and Ambon."
1942/9/12	5		Letter describing the conditions of the Dutch troops, events from August-September, irritation at the praise for Australians, and expressing a need for support. Translated by NEFIS and provided to the Australian military.
1942/9/10	2		
1943/9/27			Letter including "The latest G-2, GHQ, estimate of the enemy forces in TIMOR".
	6		Short narrative by a KNIL sgt.
1942/8/20	1		Covers events in the Dutch area of East Timor during the previous days.
1942/12/8	1+4+1		Very clear discritpion of the situation and goals, including a title page and a map. Appendix 1 covers ships seen at Dili from 17 Oct - 2 Dec 1942.
1942/12/9	2		Handwritten report, signed by Maj. Callinan and forwarded to NORFORCE by Capt. R. R. Baldwin. Focuses on the possibility of moving A Platoon, which would leave the entire unit on the defensive.
1942/11/3	3 or 4		A report on the conditions in the western part of East Timor (Same, Ainaro, Rotei and Talo), which had just been visited by Callinan and Pte. P. P. McCabe. Aims to determine a way to counter Japanese activities and support the Portuguese (for Australian benefit).
1942/11/3	1		Includes an appendix (list of Portuguese killed in Portuguese Timor since May 1942).
1941/11/28	3+1		Handwritten report, including a sketch of the general extent of patrolable areas in East Timor as of Nov. 27.
1942/12/8	3		Describes the location of the various Sparrow Force units and the situation in Timor.
1942	5		Review of situation in Timor and possible courses of action in the future. Cape was a Brigade Major for Sparrow Force. Probably written in June 1942.
1942	1		Instructions (27 March 1942) for the organization of the remnant troops into 3 or more platoons, under the command of Maj Chisholm.

III. オーストラリア所蔵史料 (Materials in Australian Archives)

File Number	Author	Title
PR 00249 (item 86) PR 00249 (item 88)	Cape, T. F. (B.M. Sparrow Force)	Conference at GOC's Mess 0900 Hrs 23 Aug 42
AWM 54 571/4/34	Cape, T. F. (B.M. Sparrow Force)	Situation Report - Sparrow Force. 06 Jul - 13 Jul 42 + Appendixes
AWM 54 571/4/34	Cape, T. F. (B.M. Sparrow Force)	Situation Report - Sparrow Force. 21 Jun - 5 Jul 42
AWM 54 571/4/34 PR 00249 (item 95)	Cape, T. F. (B.M. Sparrow Force)	Situation Report--Sparrow Force 1 Jun - 20 Jun 42.
AWM 54 183/5/19	Clarke, A. C.	To GSI HQ lof Coan Victoria Barracks, Brisbane
AWM 54 471/4/51 MSS 1468 4 of 4	Command Paymaster, N. T. Force (Lt. Col.)	Field Returns and Reports
AWM 54 571/1/3 AWM 54 471/4/51	Commander, N.T. Force	Propaganda -- Timor
AWM 54 571/3/3 (1B)	Costelloe, P.	Report on visit to Sparrow Force by Maj P. Costelloe, EQ, NT Force, 12-27 Sep 42
PR 00249 102.278	d'Abreu da Silva-Marq, Jose Eduardo	Dialects of Portuguese Timor
AWM 54 571/4/29	Desandre, G. H. J. (Sgt.)	Intelligence Report Timor
AWM 54 571/4/45 PR 00090/184	Desandre, G. H. J. (Sgt.)	Military Intelligence Report on Timor
AWM 54 571/4/29 MSS 1468 4 of 4	Desandre, G. H. J. (Sgt.)	Report
PR 00249.260-.277 (item 101)	Dexter, David	Timor 1942. Some Press Items
PR 00249 102.220	Dexter, David.	Esqueleto das Linhas Telefonicas
PR 00249.180-.214 (items 92-94)	Dexter, David.	Report on Memo Conference, 30 July 42
PR 00249 (item 91)	Dexter, David.	Reports on Jap Activities

4. Australian War Memorial

Date	pp.	Dig.	Contents
1942/8/23	3		Contents of a meeting with Lt. Gen Sturdee, Maj. Gen. Stevens, Brig. Sutherland, Col. Rogers. Primarily an explanation of the events and situation in Timor.
1942/7/15	3+2		Appendix A listed separately. See Laidlaw entry. Appendix B and C are maps.
1942/7	2		
1942	5+7		Includes a description of conditions of Dili, and the author's own experience being caught obtaining benzine for Australians. AWM 54 571/4/34 copy has appendixes A, B (Laidlaw platoon report 12-16 Jun 1942), C, D, E (Japanese propaganda and translations), PR 00249 copy has "Appendix D: Copy of letter received from Portuguese Subject - May 42".
1942/12/7	2		Letter related to Capt Oliviara of the Red Cross of Dili.
1942/8/4	1		A letter to the Paymaster, Sparrow Force, commending his work in Timor.
1943/1/12	1		Table detailing Allied propaganda pamphlet drops over Timor up to January 7, 1943.
1942/9/29	9		Report on plans for the arrival of the 2/4th IC on September 21, with detailed discussions of supply requirements, many of which show clearly the particular circumstances in Timor.
	1		Map, copied by N. C. McGan from a Portuguese original.
1941	2+1+1		A report or part of a report obtained by Sgt. Desandre from the commanding officer of the 2/1 Heavy Artillery Battery in December 1941.
1942/8/8	4		
1941/12/20	1+5+1		A report from the Sparrow Force Intelligence Section in Koepang. Includes a cover letter to Lt. Col. W. J. R. Scott, of the Special Operations Section, Army H. Q. Appended is a translation of instructions issued by the Dutch Navy to private ship captains.
1943-1967			A collection of press clippings on the Timor campaign, some from old issues of veteran newsletters.
1942	1		Telephone map of East Timor coped by David Dexter from a Portuguese original.
1942/7/31	1		Report on a meeting between A Platoon and Dutch troops, aiming to improve cooperation and communication.
1942/9/28	1+4		Dexter's reports on Japanese activities in the Ainaro area 24-25 September, 1942. Probably copied from AWM 54 571/4/18.

File Number	Author	Title
PR 00249.056-.087 (item 86)	Doig, C. D. (Lt.)	Report on Interview with Port. Sgt. Martin
AWM 54 571/4/34	Dowman, S. J. (Lieut.)	Report on suggested landing ground sites at Beco and Camnassa, Portuguese Timor
AWM 27 118/12	East, Fred G. (Capt.)	Report on Activities and Observations with Sparrow Force, Dutch Timor, from 19 Jan 42 to 23 Sep 42 and consequency
AWM 54 183/5/18 PR 00249 (item 92-94)	Edwards, A. W.	Evaluation of Portuguese nationals from Timor
PR 00249 102.283	Foster, Thomas Albert	Cailaco - Rita Bau - Bobonaro
PR 00249 102.282	Foster, Thomas Albert	South-East of Kablak Range including Same
PR 00249 102.287 PR 00249 102.288	Foster, Thomas Albert	
AWM 54 571/4/29	Francis, E. D. (Capt.)	Report by Capt. E. D. Francis A. I. F. Dated 27 Nov. 1941 re. Roads
PR 00684 3 of 3	Francis, E. D. (Capt.)	Report by Capt. E. D. Francis A. I. F. Dated 27 Nov. 1941 re. Roads
PR 00249 (item 95)	G-2, GHQ	Timor - An Estimate of the Enemy Strength
AWM 54 571/4/45 PR 00091/076	GHQ, SWPA, Military Intelligence Section, General Staff	Timor Situation, August 16, 1942
AWM 54 424/2/3	GS INT NT Force	Timor, Enemy Strengths and Dispositions by Areas
PR 00249.180-.214 (items 92-94)	GS NT Force	Intelligence Notes 1720 Hrs 19 Nov 42
PR 00249.180-.214 (items 92-94)	HQ N.T. Force	Targets in Timor
PR 00249.056-.087 (item 86)	HQ Northern Territory Force	Enemy Dispositions - Dilly Area (GSI/5579)
AWM 54 722/4/38	HQ Timor Force	Copies of Organization Charts of Japanese Army and Navy Forces, Timor, Together with lists of personalities
AWM 54 1010/9/67	Ito, Takeo	Interrogation of LT GEN ITO, Takeo AT RABAUL on 9 OCTOBER 46

Date	pp.	Dig.	Contents
1942/10/20	2		Handwritten report on interview with the former Portuguese commander at OSSU, who had been at Ailieu during the Japanese push, and then brought to Dili. Mentions that hotels in Dili seem to be devoted to prostitution and that as there are about 50 women, bombing them would kill many Japanese soldiers.
1942/6/24	2+2		Includes 2 hand-drawn maps of proposed sites.
1945/10/29	9+1		Detailed report on time in Timor and in POW camps. Includes 1 page index (by paragraph number). Includes details like v.d. rate, leaflet contents, information from Japanese, and news from Asia Raya and Jawa Shinbun.
1943/1/18	5		A description of the activities surrounding the arrival of the Portuguese evacuees from Timor.
1942/8/7	1		Sketch map
1942/10/6	1		Sketch map, apparently updated in November or Decembar 1942.
1942	1		Untitled sketch map from A Platoon of 2/2 IC, probably of Betano-Mape area.
1941/11/27	5		
1941/11/27	5		Attached to a report by Major Wilson, and issued by A.H.Q. (M.I.) in Melbourne under the title "Secret Report on Communications in Portuguese and Dutch Timor".
1943	9		Detailed estimates of Japanese troop strength in Timor with clearly dated information.
1942/8	1		Map. "To Accompany Intelligence Summary No. 147. Enclosure no. 1"
1945/8/27	1		Map with delails in Table form.
1942/11/19	1		A note related to the results of several attacks by Australian air forces. Includes a handwritten question about whether they wee supposed to be avoiding attacks against the Administrative house and native huts in Baucau.
1942/11/16	1		A note on the targets in Timor, including a note about not attacking the Baucau-Beaco road.
1942/10/27	1		Provides intelligence on the current utilitation of various sites in Dili. 16 locations mentioned.
1945	8		
1946/10/9	3		On Navy and Army relationships, responsabilities, etc. Mentions roles of Kempeitai, including police training.

III. オーストラリア所蔵史料（Materials in Australian Archives）

File Number	Author	Title
AWM 54 1010/9/67	Iwata, Seiichi	Interrogation of Major IWATA Seiichi of 228 Inf Regiment by WX7309 Capt J Gerke "A" Branch, War Crimes Section, Rabaul on 10 day of Oct 1946
AWM 54 571/4/45 PR 00090/184	Jana, Jose Alves	Objection no. 20. In the Matter of An Objection by Jose Alves Jana. (February 1, 1944)
AWM 54 492/4/46 AWM 54 1010/1/28	Kaida Tatsuichi	Japanese Military Operation
AWM 54 492/4/46 AWM 54 1010/1/28	Kaida Tatsuichi	日本軍の作戦に就いて　（戒田達一）
AWM 54 1010/9/67	Kojima, Shinichi	Interrogation of Capt KOJIMA Shinichi of the 228 Inf Regt by WX7309 Capt J. Gerke of War Crimes Section Rabaul on the fifteenth day of October 1946
AWM 54 571/4/34	Laidlaw, G. G. (Capt.)	Appendix A. Enemy organization etc. in Dili as at 3 Jul 42
AWM 54 571/1/11 AWM 54 571/4/36	Laidlaw, G. G. (Major)	Report by Maj G. J. Laidlaw on the present fighting efficiency and general physical condition within No 2 Aust Ind COY. (354/SPO)
AWM 54 571/4/18 PR 00249.180-.214 (items 92-94)	Laidlaw, G. G. (Major)	Report on Killing of Portuguese by Japanese Troops
AWM 52　1/5/49	Lancer Force	Lancer Force Unit Diary
AWM 54 571/2/5	Landforces Melbourne	Message to Norforce Darwin (G 59329)
AWM 54 571/2/5	Landforces Melbourne	Message to Norforce repeated Landops Brisbane (G 59459)
AWM 54 571/2/5	Landforces Melbourne	Message to NT Force repeated Landops Brisbane (G 59579)
AWM 54 571/4/29	Leggatt, W. W. (Lt.Col.)	General Report
PR 00249 (item 91)	Lilya, Des L.	Des Lilya narrative
AWM 54 571/4/29 PR 00684 3 of 3	Lt. Col., G. S., L. H. Q.	Senhor Sousa Santos – Ex Timor
PR 00249 (item 92-94)	Marcal, Vasco de	Letter to Capt. Dexter

4. Australian War Memorial

Date	pp.	Dig.	Contents
1946/10/19	6		Question and answer form yields some information, but inf was either not knowledgable about the issues raised or evasive.
1944/2/1	5		National Security Regulations, Advisory Committee. Transcript of the testimony by Jose Alves Jana. Interrogation related to the prewar and early occupation periods, and the supplying of cattle to the Japanese.
1946/1/25	1+5		English translation and cover letter for Brig. Dyke. Japanese listed separately.
1946/1/25	9+1		This text was translated and is listed as "Japanese Military Operation." Original letter also attached.
1946/10/15	2		Question and answer format. Basic information.
1942/7/3	1		Notes marines well educated and that some had lived in Brazil so could speak Portuguese. Laborers and some infantry from Manchuria.
1942/11/2	2		A report of November 2, 1942 by the commander of the 2/2nd IC, explaining the conditions in Timor, and the actual conditions of the troops. Argues for rest and reorganization.
1942/10/10	1		A report based on Portuguese sources about the Aileau massacre on October 2, 1942. This information was passed back to Australia very quickly.
1942-1943		●	The unit diaries for Lancer Force.
1942/10/30	1		Message regarding possible reinforcement of Timor garrison and arming of Portuguese.
1942/10/31	1		Message to General Stevens regarding bombing of Dili and other targets by 12 B-26 bombers.
1942/10/31	2		Message regarding possible reinforcement of Timor garrison and arming of Portuguese.
1941/12/19	4		General report on deployment of Sparrow Force.
1943/11/8	6		An account of Des Lilya's escape from Timor to Darwin in early 1942 written by request of David Dexter while on Timor.
1944/3	6		On Sousa Santos' background, the author's impression of him unpon meeting him in Melbourne, on possible decorations, and on possible usefulness for the Allies.
1947	2		Letter from the translator of A Platoon, Vasco, to Dexter. After returning to Portugal he had been punished, presumably for leaving Timor.

III. オーストラリア所蔵史料 (Materials in Australian Archives)

File Number	Author	Title
AWM 54 571/4/45 PR 00091/076	Martin, Gordon John	Letter to Normal Campbell
AWM 54 1010/9/67	Matsumoto, Bunjin (Capt.)	Interrogation of Capt MATSUMOTO Bunjin of the 228 Inf Regt by WX7309 Capt J. Gerke of War Crimes Section Rabaul on the fifteenth day of Oct 1946
AWM 54 571/1/3 AWM 54 471/4/51	McCabe, P. P.	Report on Portuguese and Natives -- Portuguese Timor
AWM 54 571/1/3 AWM 54 471/4/51	McCabe, P. P.	Report on Portuguese Timor
PR 00249 (item 91)	McKenzie, C. F. G. (Lt.)	Report on Interrogation of Ex-Portuguese Soldier by Lieut. McKenzie
AWM 54 571/1/11 AWM 54 571/4/36	McKenzie, C. F. G. (Lt.)	Report to OC No. 2 Aust Ind COY by Lieut C. F. G. McKenzie - 'C' PL No. 2 Aust Ind COY
AWM 54 1010/1/12 PR 00249 (item 95)	Milford, Gen.	Japanese Dispositions in Timor August 1942
AWM 54 492/4/52 AWM 54 1010/6/16	Military History Section, LHQ	The Campaign in Timor: Brief History of the AIF in Timor from 8 December 41 - 8 December 42
PR 00123	Milsom, George	
AWM 54 1010/9/67	Nakajima, Yasushi	Interrogation of Capt NAKAJIMA Yasushi of 228 Inf Regt by WX7309 Capt J. Gerke, War Crimes Section Rabaul on the 14 Oct '46
PR 00085/023	Neave, R. C. (Capt.)	Diary
AWM 54 571/4/34	Neave, R. C. N. (Capt.)	Copy of letter from Capt. Neave to the controller, KISSAR
AWM 54 571/4/34 PR 00249.233-.247 (item 97)	Neave, R. C. N. (Capt.)	Report on reconnaisence of East Portuguese Timor by Capt. R. C. N. Neave. 2 May - 4 July
AWM 54 571/2/5	Norforce	Message to Landforces Melb. rptd Landops Brisbane (GSI 5655)

4. Australian War Memorial

Date	pp.	Dig.	Contents
1943/4/9	12		Original handwritten letter written by Lt. G. J. Martin of the 2/4th AIC to Staff Sergeant Norman Campbell (his uncle) describes his training, posting to the Gulf of Carpentaria, then Timor and work with locals, observing Japanese.
1946/10/15	2		Question and answer format. Light artillery platoon commander, ordered to prepare for tanks and pillboxes.
1942	3		Undated report to "CO Sparrowforce" by Pte P. P. McCabe (NX73234).
1942/12/8	8		Handwritten note indicates that this report was written by Lt. McCabe, attached to Far Eastern Liaison Office.
1942/10/10	3		Report on an interrogation in Same on 10-11 October 1942. Handwritten copy, possibly from AWM 54 571/4/18.
1942/11/3	1		A short report on the very poor conditions and morale of the C Platoon dated November 3, 1942.
1945	25+		Data extracted from other sources by Gen. Milford. Original held in AWM 54 1010/1/12. Includes photographs of several Australians and Timorese, as well as the surrender ceremony. Finally data and lists of Japanese suspects in war crimes investigations are listed.
1943/1	24		A report written primarily based on unit diaries. Designed for the use of R.A.A.F. but then sought by A.G.S.
			Private record of George Milson. Includes patrol orders from Lt. McKenzie in Ainaro (August 1942) and a leaflet obtained from the Chefe di Posto in Ermera in 1945.
1946/10/14	2		Question and answer format. Mostly on invasion and prisoners, but unlike other officers admits seeing about 15 Indonesian prisoners.
1941-1942			Private record of Capt. R. C. Reave. Four notebooks used as diaries of his time in Timor, from arrival in Kupang until evacuation in Ausgust 1942. Almost every entry has a sketch of the route travelled and the mountain.
1942/6/1	1		Related to stores on Kisar.
1942/7/6	8		Part of the report deals with Kisar island, with other parts deal with the conditions and individuals in eastern Timor.
1942/10/28	2		Message regarding possible arming of Portuguese before interned. Mentions an Allied initiated native vs. native attack as an example.

III. オーストラリア所蔵史料 (Materials in Australian Archives)

File Number	Author	Title
AWM 54 571/2/5	North Force	Message to Landforces rptd Landops (GSI/5608)
AWM 54 571/2/5	Northern Territory Force	Message to L.H.Q. Melb. rptd Landops Brisbane
AWM 54 571/2/5	Northern Territory Force	Message to L.H.Q. Melbourne rptd Land Operations Brisbane
AWM 54 183/5/19	NT Force HQ	Evacuees from Timor
AWM 54 1010/9/67	Ono, Mitsuji	Interrogation of Capt ONO Mitsuji of 228 Inf Regiment by WX7309 Capt J. Gerke, War Crimes Section Rabaul on the 14 Oct '46
AWM 54 1010/9/67	Onogi, Isamu	Interrogation of Major ONOGI Isamu of the 228 Inf Regiment by WX7309 Capt J. Gerke, War Crimes Section Rabaul on the 14 Oct 1946
AWM 54 1010/9/67	Onuki, Shigenobu	Interrogation of Capt ONUKI Shigenobu of 228 Inf Regt by WX7309 Capt J. Gerke of War Crimes Section Rabaul on the fifteen day of Oct 1946
PR 00249.056-.087 (item 86)	Parker, G. E.	Appendix "A": Destruction of Wireless Equipment
PR 00249.180-.214 (items 92-94)	Parker, G. E.	Report by Capt. G. E. Parker. Report on activities of Special W/T section
AWM 54 571/4/15 PR 00249.180-.214 (items 92-94)	Pires, Manoel de Jesus	Communication from the administrator Sao Domingos Province Portuguese Timor
AWM 54 183/5/19	Portuguese Party in Timor	Information Report No. 274
AWM 54 571/4/45 PR 00090/184	Prieto, Francisco Unera	Objection no. 21. In the Matter of An Objection by Francisco Unera Prieto. (February 1, 1944)
AWM 54 571/4/29 MSS 1468 4 of 4	R. A. A. F. A. O. B. Koepang	Weekly Intelligence Summary
AWM 54 571/3/31A	Read, J. F. (Capt)	Re Supplies, Transport, Accounting, etc.

4. Australian War Memorial

Date	pp.	Dig.	Contents
1942/10/28	1		Message relayed from "Z Black" regarding meeting between Portuguese governor and Japanese, and the plans to establish concentration zaones.
1942/10/28	1		Message relaying Sparrow request for permision to arm Portuguese in Fronteira and Suro provinces with Bren guns and Thompson submachine guns.
1942/10/30	1		Urgent message requesting further consideration of request to arm Portuguese.
1943/8/24	4		A list of evacuees from Timor who left Darwin for Bob's farm on August 23, 1943, with cover letter.
1946/10/14	2		Question and answer format. Vetinary surgeon who knew little of what was happening.
1946/10/14	3		Question and answer format. Medical officer at Dili from 23 Feb to 7 Sept 1942. Mostly on invasion and prisoners.
1946/10/15	2		Question and answer format. Communications officer in the second wave landing west of the airport.
	1		Appendix to Webster report of 1942/8/20.
1942/5/13	8		Includes cover letter from Brig. Gen. Veale, and various appended reports and diagrams.
1942/7	1+1		Portuguese language message to Lisbon on the maltreatment of Portuguese citizens. Includes a cover letter from Lt. Col. Spence.
1943/4/18	1		Partially corrupt message from Timor from April 1943, including information about the supplying of women to the Japanese in Viqueque.
1944/2/1	3		[National Security Regulations, Advisory Committee.] Transcript of the testimony by Francisco Unera Prieto. Interrogation related to the prewar and early occupation periods.
1941/12/15	2		
1942/5/31	2		A report about the current status of supply acquisition and accounting, including the issue of local administration of supplies at the posto level, payment frequency, and availability of supplies.

III. オーストラリア所蔵史料 (Materials in Australian Archives)

File Number	Author	Title
PR 00249.180-.214 (items 92-94)	Reinderhoff, G. L. (Capt.)	[Report on interview with Capt. Reinderhoff]
AWM 54 183/5/19	Roberts, C. G.	Subject: Timor
PR 00684 3 of 3 PR 00249.180-.214 (items 92-94)	Roberts, C. G.	Subject: Timor
AWM 54 571/4/34	Roberts, C. G. (Controller, A.I.B.)	Information Report No. (AIB) 1
PR 00249 (item 91)	Robinson, S. A.	The Australian Campaign in Portuguese Timor
AWM 54 571/3/3 1A	Rodd, C. (Lt.)	Report on Rubber Supplies in Portuguese Timor
AWM 54 571/1/3	Ross, David	Report by D. Ross (Quantas) dated 25 November 41, Road from Atamboea to Dilli
PR 00684 3 of 3	Ross, David	Report by D. Ross (Quantas) dated 25 November 41, Road from Atamboea to Dilli
AWM 54 571/4/45 AWM 54 561/4/34 PR 00684 1 of 3	Ross, David	Report on Interview of D. Ross, Esq, British Consul Dilli, at Mape, 27 Jun 42
AWM 54 571/4/45 PR 00090/184	Ross, David	Summary of a General Report on Portuguese Timor during the Period December 1941 to June 1942, Made by Mr. D. Ross, Australian Consul at Dilli, Who Arrived in Darwin From Timor on July 10th
MSS 1565	Sadler, Stanley	War Service 1941-1945. Stanley Sadler WX 11372, Charles Sadler WX 11374 with the 2nd Aust Independent Company (Section 8) and the 2/2nd Commando Squadron (Section 8)
AWM 54 627/16/1	Services Reconnaissance Department	Operation - Sunlag. Intelligence Report

4. Australian War Memorial   *261*

Date	pp.	Dig.	Contents
1942/10/19	5		Report on an interview with Capt. Reinderhoff about Japanese military practices, in which Japanese use of elephants was mistakenly included. Includes his letter explaining the mistake. The original interview was conducted on March 8, 1942.
1943/2/25	3		A note from the Allied Intelligence Bureau summarizing information from 12-23 February 1943, and comments from "Major Oldham's organization in Melbourne."
1942/11/22	2		A secret note from Col. C. G. Roberts, Controller, Allied Intelligence Bureau regarding A. de Sousa Santos, his information and recommendations on Timor, and his anticipated activities in Australia.
1943/8/17	1		Misc. intelligence information.
c.1946	142+5		A historical narrative of the conflict in Portuguese Timor focussing on the 2/2nd IC, based largely on interviews with soldiers in Rabaul immediately following the end of the war. The author is a member of the Historical Section.
1942/7/25	1		
1941/11/25	2		
1941/11/25	2		Attached to a report by Major Wilson, and issued by A. H. Q. (M. I.) in Melbourne under the title "Secret Report on Communications in Portuguese and Dutch Timor".
1942/7	3		Includes a transcript of letter from the Japanese Consul (Saita) and Japanese Army C. O. (Doi) dated June 17, 1942.
1942/8/3	3		Covers subjects like natives' attitudes, Japanese behavior, Portuguese attitude, and the military situation.
1993	1+20 +1		Manuscript compiled from the writings of Stanley Sadler. Describes service of Stanley and brother Charles, including enlistment and training with 2/2 Independent Company, No.8 Section, C Platoon. Details experience in Portugese Timor, including recreation in Deli, Japanese invasion, patrols and ambushes, arrival of 2/4 Independent Company, and relations with natives. Also briefly mentions return to Australia, and experiences at New Guinea and New Britain.
1945	8		This report deals with local conditions before and during the operation.

III. オーストラリア所蔵史料 (Materials in Australian Archives)

File Number	Author	Title
AWM 54 571/4/29 PR 00090/184	Silva, Manriel da	Statement by Manriel da Silva, Retired Captain in Portuguese Army. (February 7, 1944)
AWM 54 471/4/51 AWM 54 571/6/1	Sinclair, F. R. (Secretary, Department of Defence Coordination)	Report on Occupation of Dilli - Portuguese Timor
PR 00249.056-.087 (item 86)	Smyth (Lt.)	Situation Report Sparrow Force 22 Sep 42 - 19 Oct 42
AWM 54 571/4/34	Smyth, N. W.	Report by Sgt. N. W. Smyth on interview with Ans. Brat de Almeida at Same
PR 00684 2/3	Sousa Santos, Antonio Policarpo de	Fragments of a Tempestuous Life or Fragments of Six Years of Struggles
AWM 54 571/4/18 PR 00249.180-.214 (items 92-94)	Sousa Santos, Antonio Policarpo de	Information regarding Timor Supplied by Senor Sousa Santos - 19 Nov 42 & 20 Nov 42
PR 00249.180-.214 (items 92-94)	Sousa Santos, Antonio Policarpo de	Letters from Sousa Santos - Mainly to David Dexter related to return to Timor under SRD
AWM 54 571/4/29 PR 00684 3 of 3	Sousa Santos, Antonio Policarpo de	List of the Portuguese in Timor, whose help the Allied Forces there since Japs landing
AWM 54 571/3/3 1A PR 00249.056-.087 (Item 86)	Sparrow Force	Message to Norforce. In reply to Number GSI/4662
AWM 54 571/3/3 1A	Sparrow Force	Message to Norforce. Strength return.
AWM 54 571/3/3 1A	Sparrow Force	Ref Supplies of Rubber in Port Timor
AWM 52 1/5/55	Sparrow Force	Sparrow Force Unit Diary
MSS 1468 1 of 4	Sparrow Force, Koepang	General Report
AWM 54 571/3/3 1A	Spence, Alan (Lt. Col.)	Administrative Report
PR 00249.056-.087 (item 86)	Spence, Alan (Lt. Col.)	Appendix "B": Present Position
AWM 54 571/4/21 PR 00249.180-.214 (items 92-94)	Spence, Alan (Lt. Col.)	Santos Family/ Message 3764/Sparrow to Norforce in response to message 02415/2 of 30 Aug 42

4. Australian War Memorial   263

Date	pp.	Dig.	Contents
1944/2/7	6		[National Security Regulations, Advisory Committee. Transcript of the testimony by Manriel da Silva. Interrogation related to the prewar and early occupation periods, mentions supplying cattle and women to the Japanese.
1944/8/2	3+3		Extracts from the CO AIF Timor report of December 19, 1941, with three appendicies (statements by the allied commanders and the Portuguese government with translation)
1942/10/20	4+1		Includes a cover letter by Lt. Col. Spence, and originally contained the report of deterioration of the situation by R. R. Balwin (see also).
1942/7/3	1+2		Includes 2 maps of Dili. Informant was a radio operator. Contents related to radio issues and the conditions in Dili.
1944	83		Translated from Portuguese. Apparently also held in WM 54 571/1/3.
1942/11/20	2		
1944-1948	9		
1945	2+1		2 pages but with an extra annotation by a reader.
1942/10/8	1		Answers to questions in earlier message. The bulk of the message relates to relations with natives after Japanese advances.
1942/10/28	1		Message listing numbers of officers and men from all the Sprarrow Force compunent units. Total force 47 officers, 776 inlisted men.
1942/8/4	1		Letter from the commander of Sparrow Force to N.T.F. suggesting purchase of the SAPT supplies of rubber. 3 samples were also sent.
1941-1942		●	The unit diaries for Lancer Force.
1941/12/19	4		
1942/6/26	4		Covers personnel (32 officers and 429 enlisted men plus the constantly increasing numbers of Dutch troops, having recently risen from 10+250 to over 300), stores, rations, finance, medical, stores returned, Dutch requirements, mail, and personnel returned.
	1		Appendix to Webster report of 1942/8/20. Thus deals with the post-push conditions.
1942/8/31	1		Related to the effort to remove the family of Sousa Santos from Baucau to Betano while he was in Bobonaro.

III. オーストラリア所蔵史料 (Materials in Australian Archives)

File Number	Author	Title
AWM 54 571/4/15	Spence, Alan (Lt. Col.)	Situation Report, Sparrow Force, 1-11 Sep 42
AWM 54 571/4/28	Stevens (Major General)	Situation in Timor (SM/4064/6/SP)
PR 00249 (item 93)	Straten, N. L. W. van	Appreciation of the situation at Timor at the end of May 1942
PR 00249.180-.214 (items 92-94)	Sutherland, R. K. (Maj Gen.)	Memorandum to: Commander, Allied Land Force. Subject: Relief Netherlands Forces in Timor (Secret Memo 1754)
AWM 54 571/4/36	Sutherland, R. K. (Maj Gen.)	Relief of 2 Indep COY in Timor (SM/3641/SP)
AWM 54 571/4/45 AWM 54 1010/1/28	Takahashi (Senior Staff officer, SE Japanese Forces, Rabaul)	Location of Japanese in Timor in Aug 42 and Comds Names
AWM 423/4/155	TANAKA Toru	Report by Major General Tanaka Toru, dated 11 January 1946 which includes a brief history of the operations in which he took part
AWM 54 571/3/3 1A	Thorpe (Asst Secretary Supplies)	Message to Norforce from Landforces
AWM 54 571/1/11 AWM 54 571/4/36	Trebeck, N. B. (Capt.)	Report on liaison visit to Lancer Force by Capt N. B. Trebeck 20 Oct - 9 Nov 42
AWM 54 571/4/34	Turton, D. K.	Summary of Report by Lieut. D. K. Turton, Ind. Coy, on visit to Hatolia and Ermera 10-12 Jul 42
AWM 54 571/4/45 PR 00684	van Straten, N. L. W.	Appreciations of the Situation at Timor at the End of May 1942
PR 00249.099-.109 (item 88)	Veale, W. C. D.	Finance - Sparrow Force
AWM 54 571/4/45	Veale, W. C. D.	Information Relating to Timor Obtained from Brigadier W. C. D. Veale - 5/6/42
PR 00249.099-.109 (item 88)	Veale, W. C. D.	Movements No. 2 Ind. Coy. Following Japanese Landing in Dilli 19-20 Feb. 42

4. Australian War Memorial   265

Date	pp.	Dig.	Contents
1942/9/18	3+2		Handwritten and typed versions, slightly varient.
1942/12/2	3		A brief summary of conditions on Timor and strategic options. Sent by the C.O. N.T. Force HQ to HQ Allied Land Forces.
1942/6	7		This report provides some information about the personnel and organization of the NEI troops, as well as a Dutch perspective on conditions in Timor. Includes a sketch of the Western part of Portuguese Timor.
1942/10/16	1		Related to querries from Rear Admiral Coster of the Royal Netherlands Forces in Timor about the number of troops to be replaced, and the training of troops.
1942/11/12	2		Letter from the OC Allied Land Headquarters explaining policy decisions related to the relief or withdrawal of the 2/2nd IC in December 1942. Letter dated November 12, 1942.
1945/11/2	3+2		Includes cover letter.
1946/1/11	13		Report covers various aspects of military activities (intelligence, obtaining supplies, etc.). Handwritten in English with seal.
1942/9/28	3		Message requesting the purchase of crude rubber for transshipment to Australia, and even the obtaining of rubber from other islands by prahu. Even hint at bribing Japanese to allow plan to work.
1942/11/11	4		A report on the conditions in Timor and the supply situation. Trebeck concludes the 2/2nd must be withdrawn and need not be replaced.
1942/7/15	2		Includes information about the Japanese who had recently visited those places.
1942/6/1	1+6+1		No. 339/R. Copy of a report sent to the Australian Director of Military Intelligence on July 1, 1942 by NEFIS. States Timorese to give women to Japanese and take paper money. Includes a map of the border region. Explains units and officers, numbers of men, and ratio of "Europeans" to "natives" (3/2).
1942/6	2		Brig. Veale's financial report, including details of money received from the Dutch, explanation of lost financial records (by Lt. Atkins), etc.
1942/6/5	9		
1942/6	4		

III. オーストラリア所蔵史料 (Materials in Australian Archives)

File Number	Author	Title
PR 00249.099-.109 (item 88)	Veale, W. C. D.	Stores - Sparrow Force
PR 00249.099-.109 (item 88)	Veale, W. C. D.	Supplies, Rationing, etc.
PR 00249.099-.109 (item 88)	Veale, W. C. D.	Supplies, Rationing, etc. Appendix no. 2. Proforma Demand
PR 00249.056-.087 (item 86)	Wadey (F/O)	Report from F/O Wadey - 27.9.42
PR 00249.233-.247 (item 96)	Walker, E. McD. (Major)	2/4 Aust Independent Company, Summary of Unit History
PR 00249.056-.087 (item 86)	Webster, P. G. (Capt.)	Report on Present Conditions Sparrow Force
AWM 54 571/4/29 MSS 1565	Weidner, Ch. T.	To The Inhabitants of the Town of Koepang
PR 00684 3 of 3	Wilson, A. J. (Major)	Report by Major A. J. R. Wilson, 2/1 HY. BTY. A. I. F. on Communications in Portuguese and Dutch Timor
AWM 54 805/5/4	Wood, R. C. (Sgt.)	An Account of the Experiences of the "Sparrow" Force
MSS 1468 1 of 4	Wray, Arthur H. K.	[Untitled manuscript]
AWM 54 571/4/29	Wray, Arthur H. K.	Handwritten copies of propaganda flyers from Japanese military
PR 00083/237	Wray, Arthur H. K.	Surrender Propaganda
PR 00249.056-.087 (item 86)	Wylie (Capt.)	Report by Capt. Wylie Taken on 22 Aug.
AWM 54 1010/9/67	Yoshiyasu, Tatsuo	Interrogation of Capt YOSHIYASU Tatsuo of 228 Inf Regt by WX7309 Capt J Gerke; War Crimes Section 8 Military District. RABAUL
PR 00249.056-.087 (item 86)	Z Special Unit	Special Information Report from Timor
AWM 54 183/5/19	Z Unit (Quere)	To Landops for GHQ SWPA, for Roberts
PR 00249.299		[Hand-drawn map of border region]
AWM 54 571/4/45		[Untitled map of border region and list of 3 letter place name designations]

4. Australian War Memorial   267

Date	pp.	Dig.	Contents
1942/6	5		Detailed report on supplies situation.
1942/6	2		Narrative introduction requesting approval for actions taken to establish a supply system. See also Appendix 1 listed under Capt. G. J. Arnold.
1942/6	2		A copy of a standard form requisitioning goods from Chef de Posto, along with a brief statement noting that Dutch currency was no longer recognized and that paybooks had been lost.
1942/9/27	2		Interrogation report by the Air Intelligence Section of F/O Wadey who had been shot down over eastern East Timor, badley burned.
1943/5/29	5		A short summary of the unit history and current conditions written by the commander 4-5 months after evacuation from Timor.
1942/8/20	5		Report after a short visit to Timor of a GIII Capt. 2 appendixes were attached (see Parker and Spence reports).
1941/12/15	2		Translation of an official announcement by the Dutch government.
1941/12/29	5+8		Includes 8 photographs and 4 maps on unnumbered pages. Issued by A. H. Q. (M. I.) in Melbourne under the title "Secret Report on Communications in Portuguese and Dutch Timor".
1943/1/8	7		First-person account for popular publication. Heavily marked, probably by censors, as most details of any kind were deleted.
	181+4		A narrative of his experiences from joining the AIF to the end of the Timor campaign.
	13		This is probably the same as the 7 page copy from PR 83/237....Originally 13 pages of handwritten text.
1942	13		Handwritten copies of propaganda flyers from the Japanese military in 1942.
	4+1		
1946/10/14	3		A report in question-answer form. Deals with initial landing in Dili. Only moderately interesting.
1942/10/23	2		Intelligence about Dili from a Portuguese man present 3-16 October. 18 points.
1943/2	2		Summary of messages 12 to 20 February 1943 transmitted in Portuguese. Seems to have much unreliable information.
1942	2		
[1942]	2		

III. オーストラリア所蔵史料 (Materials in Australian Archives)

File Number	Author	Title
AWM 54 571/4/45		Activities in Timor
PR 00684 1 of 3		Appendix "B" to Operational Instructions - No. 15. Notes on Portuguese Timor, Dutch Timor, Amboina (With Maps Attached)
AWM 54 805/5/4		Australian Guerillas in Timor
PR 00249.056-.087 (item 86)		Conference on Sparrow Force held in GOC's Mess 19 Aug 42
AWM 54 1010/6/16		Court of Inquiry with Reference to Landing of Japanese Forces in New Britain, Timor and Ambon. Volume I. Reports
PR 00249.180-.214 (items 92-94)		Declaration of Open Towns in Timor June/July 1942
AWM 54 571A/4/4		Details of Proposed Expedition to Portuguese Timor by Military History Field Team
AWM 54 805/5/4		Highlights of Timor Jungle Warfare. N.E.I. troops always outnumbered - never out-generalled
AWM 54 805/5/4		Importance of Timor
PR 00249.056-.087 (item 86)		Jap Actions
AWM 54 571/6/1		Japanese Behaviour in the Occupied Areas
AWM 54 805/5/4		Japanese Savagery in Island War
F 355-47183 T323 no. 50		Keine Soenda-Eilanden en Aangrenzenden Vaarwaters. Blad V. 1:510,000
AWM 54 571/1/11 PR 00249 (item 92-94)		List of Portuguese Killed in Portuguese Timor since May, 1942
AWM 54 571/3/3		Maintenanca of Lancer Force

4. Australian War Memorial

Date	pp.	Dig.	Contents
1942	8		Covers events and actions on Timor from 12/12/42 to 23/4/42.
1941	14		Sections on Portuguese Timor and Dutch Timor, including maps and title page 14 p.
	6		Journalistic report. Probably pre-release.
1942/8/19	6+1		Present were Maj. Gen. Stevens, Air Commodore Bladin, Brig. Sutherland, Brig. Sneed, G II (O), G II (I), Maj. Chisholm, and Capt. Wylie. Capt. Webster was not listed, but was apparently there, as he presented a report as well.
1942/7/8-16	1+4 +24+5 +9		Of special interest are parts a (general report), c (Timor), and d (Ambon). These sections appx. 18 p.
1942/6- 1942/7	7		A collection of Australian communications related to a Portuguese request that the Allies respect Baucau and Lautem as open cities and not bomb them.
1945/11/26			
1943	3		A report based on an interview with Dutch troops who had returned to Australia. Dateline is "Somewhere in Australia – Thursday". Obviously post-censor as no names, dates or places are mentioned, and as a release date is handwritten at the top.
	4+2		A report by a journalist who travelled to Timor in October 1942. Obviously not yet censored.
1942/11	3		A table of Japanese activities covering 27 October – 14 November 1942. Not dated or titled, but possibly related to the Dexter report on activities in the Ainaro area.
	7+14		This report from Dili (7 pp.) was accompanied by a cover letter from the Far Eastern Liaison office (1 page), an account of the "Co-Prosperity Sphere" (1 pg.), and "'Co-Prosperity Sphere,' 'The New Order in Asia,' 'The Pan-Asian Movement'" (12 pp.).
1943/1/2	6		Final version of one story for publication in early 1943 based on a visit to Timor. Includes reports about demands for women, rapes, and establishment of brothels (perhaps with women from Japan).
1943	1		Republication (Sydney) of a Dutch government map originally published in 1925 (1928 revision). Apparently included in AGS publication no. 50.
1942/10	1		A short list written as an appendix to a report in early October 1942. Short descriptions of events at Ainato and Aileu on Oct. 2 are appended.
	2		Undated description of the supply problems and strategies adopted for and by "Lancer Force". Written after evacuation.

III. オーストラリア所蔵史料 (Materials in Australian Archives)

File Number	Author	Title
AWM 54 571/4/28		Missing Personnel - Timor
AWM 54 805/5/4		N.E.I. Commandos had World's Smallest Daily. Journalistic feat in Timor's Jungle
MSS 1468 4 of 4		Nominal Roll of Ex Koepang Personnel Attached to 2 Ind Coy
PR 00249.180-.214 (items 92-94)		Note for DCGS. Dutch Troops Timor
PR 00249.056-.087 (item 86)		Operations in Timor
AWM 54 471/4/51		Organization Charts of the Japanese Army and Navy Forces on Timor, together with lists of personalities
PR 00249.296-.307 ([59 of 60), item 102)		Papers of David Dexter. Maps and Sketches
AWM 54 571A/4/4		Places of Historical Interest in Portuguese Timor
PR 00249 (item 92-94)		Sao Domingos Corridor, Portuguese Timor. Native Arms Question
PR 00249.180-.214 (items 92-94)		Sao Domingos Corridor, Portuguese Timor: Native Arms Question
PR 00249 (item 91)		Signal (Message to K-N from J)
PR 00249.180-.214 (items 92-94)		Signal Abbreviations Used in Timor 1942
PR 00249 (item 92-94)		Signals ref. relief and reinforcement of Dutch 2 Oct 42 - 13 Jan 43
AWM 54 571/4/34		Situation Report - Sparrow Force. Appendix E: Japanese Propaganda
AWM 54 571/4/51		Situation Report Timor to 11 Jan
AWM 54 571/4/51		Situation Report Timor to 7 Dec
AWM 54 571/4/51		Situation Review of Timor from 10 Aug to 24 Aug
AWM 54 571/4/51		Situation Review of Timor from 10 Aug to 24 Aug

4. Australian War Memorial

Date	pp.	Dig.	Contents
1942	1		A list of missing personnel, units, as well as the dates and the reporting officer. Probably compiled in around April 1942.
1943	4		A report based on an interview with Dutch troops who had returned to Australia. Dateline is "Somewhere in Australia - Wednesday". One copy of the Dutch troops' "News Bulletin Aneta" was apparently brought to Australia by KNIL troops.
1942	2		Second page in bad condition with institutional affiliations unreadable in some cases.
1942/9/10	1		Report of a request by Lt. Col. Sandberg of the Dutch LO GHQ to replace the Dutch troops on Timor with a party of around 50.
1942/10/2	2		Brief narrative overview.
1945/11	9 (A4)		Charts are broken up into two pages each.
			A collection of maps and sketches, may of them documenting weekly changes in the positions of Allied and Japanese troops.
1945	1		
	2		An undated, anonymous report on Pires and the arms for Timorese problem.
1942/10	2		Discussion of Pires and the native arms question. Dexter suggests it might be an AIB report, but is not sure.
1942	2		Signal to A and D Platoons ordering the first movements towards leaving Timor. 27 November 1942.
1905/4/25	4		Handwritten list of codes.
1942-1943	10		Various signals related to the relief and reinforcement of the Dutch 2 October 1942 - 13 January 1943.
1942/7	20+3		A summary set of translated propaganda used in West Timor as well as copies of propaganda in orginal language and English translation. Some are actually not propaganda but forms for reporting livestock ownership, etc.
1943/1	1		
1942/12	1		
1942	9		Includes the Supplementary Reports A-G (covering up to November 12, 1942).
1942-1943	13+1		Includes a large map of Timor showing Allied areas, supplementary reports (to 12 Nov) and other situation reports to 11 January 1943.

Ⅲ. オーストラリア所蔵史料（Materials in Australian Archives）

File Number	Author	Title
AWM 54 571/4/36		Some aspects of the Portuguese and native offer of anti-Japanese co-operation in Eastern Timor
AWM 54 805/5/4		Some Individual Stories of Outstanding Exploits
PR 00249.180-.214 (items 92-94)		Sousa Santos in Australia - AGS + SRD 1944
AWM 54 471/4/51 MSS 1468 4 of 4		Sparrow Force - Nominal Roll
PR 00249.056-.087 (item 86)		Summary of Casualties Inflicated on Enemy at Timor Since 18 Sep 42
AWM 54 424/2/3		Summary of Intelligence Information (Enemy)
PR 00249.056-.087 (item 86)		Summary of Operations in Timor
PR 00249.056-.087 (item 86)		Summary of Reports of Jap Movement from Dilli to East Since 15 Sept 1942
PR 00249.056-.087 (item 86)		Summary of suggested targets, Timor Island
AWM 54 571/4/51		Telephone Communication Scheme of the Island of Timor
AWM 67 3/346		Telephone Communication Scheme of the Island of Timor
PR 00249 (item 93)		The Action in Timor from December 1941 - December 1942
AWM 54 571/4/51		Timor
AWM 54 571/4/51		Timor Operations to 26 Nov
AWM 54 1010/1/12		War Crimes Trial of Accused
AWM 54 183/5/19		
AWM 54 41/4/55		
AWM 54 41/4/55		
AWM 54 571/4/28		

4. Australian War Memorial 273

Date	pp.	Dig.	Contents
1942	4		Report and appendix largely deal with Sao Domingos, with specific reference to the Lizard party. Mentions conditions and personalities in various areas.
	4		A report by a journalist who travelled to Timor in October 1942. Obviously not yet censored.
1905/4/27	11		A collection of correspondence related to Sousa Santos in Australia and his employment by AGS and SRD in particular.
1942	2		Nominal roll of unknown date for Sparrow Force (does not include 2/2nd Ind. Coy.).
1942/11/27	1		Covers estimated casualties from September 18 - November 27, listed by location, and with separate figures for Japanese and natives. Allied casualties and material losses are marginally noted.
1945	15		A collection of reports on Japanese troops in Timor.
1942/10/1	4		Review of events in Timor from 10 Dec. 1941 to 28 September.
1942/11/27	2+2		Final report listed from November 27 was handwritten. Second set of pages detail movement in and out of 5 towns in eastern Timor.
1942/12	4		Intelligence dates include information as late as 1942/12/2.
1942/9/3	2		Schema showing telephone connections between various settlements. One (undated) in km, the other in miles.
c.1941			Single page original copied on to two pages. Second copy on larger paper. Covers only the Netherlands Indies part of Timor (and links to Portuguese Timor).
	13		An undated Dutch report about events in Timor.
1942	1		Large format map, little detail. May have been appended to a report.
1942	1		
1945/12/27			Cover letter and various documents related to the trials of 8 Japanese/Taiwanese and 2 Timorese. Includes mug-shots and basic personal data.
c.1943	2		A timeline of events relaed to evacuees covering 1942-1943.
1945			Docments related to surrender. Includes a map and description of the hierarchy of command.
1945			Description of a visit to West and East Timor by a doctor, along with the surrender cerimonies and a copy of the Portuguese speech.
			[Miscellaneous documents on relief of 2/2nd IC and Dutch]

III. オーストラリア所蔵史料 (Materials in Australian Archives)

File Number	Author	Title
AWM 54 571/4/36		
AWM 54 627/16/1		

Date	pp.	Dig.	Contents
			A large file of communications from and about conditions in Timor and the 2/2nd IC until its return to Australia. Some documents listed separately.
1945/8/21	12		SRD Salary Report.

Ⅳ. イギリス所蔵史料

Materials in British Archives

1. United Kingdom [London Archives]

The primary collection of material on Timor during WWII is in the National Archive (Public Records Office) in a suburb of London, In this section, we list some of the archival collections and file series which contain Timor-related documents, providing a few detailed examples of interesting items in each archive. A slightly longer list of easily identifiable materials held in the National Archives/PRO follows. It is hoped that this will provide researchers with sufficient guidance about the relative strengths of the collection, and a starting point for more thorough archival research.

IV. イギリス所蔵史料 (Materials in British Archives)

CAB [Cabinet]

One of the largest collections related to East Timor is that of the Records of the Cabinet Office. There are a number of different files which include relevant materials. As the contributing institutions were primarily those directly involved in the War Cabinet, most documents are related to diplomatic relations (especially with respect to Portugal) or policy making. Notably, the Historical Section also collected several interesting documents related to British and Australian involvement in Portuguese Timor.

65	War Cabinet and Cabinet: Minutes (WM Series)
66	War Cabinet and Cabinet: Memoranda (WP Series)
79	War Cabinet and Cabinet: Chiefs of Staff Committee: Minutes
80	War Cabinet and Cabinet: Chiefs of Staff Committee: Memoranda
84	War Cabinet and Cabinet: Joint Planning Committee, later Joint Planning Staff, and Sub-committees: Minutes and Memoranda (JP, JAP and other Series)
106	War Cabinet and Cabinet Office: Historical Section Files: Archivist and Librarian Files: (AL Series)
121	Cabinet Office: Special Secret Information Centre: Files
122	War Cabinet and Cabinet Office: British Joint Staff Mission and British Joint Services Mission: Washington Office Records

Selected list of Timor-related items from CAB files

CAB 106 26	Account of Operations of 2nd Australian Independent Company in Timor 1941-42	c. 1943	A narrative about the 2/2nd IC involvement in Timor written by Pte. W.H. Rowan-Robinson. Place names left out due to an assumption that readers would be uninterested in the names and confused by orthographic problems. They may also have been omitted due to security concerns. (119pp.)
CAB 106 135	Operation of Allied Forces in the Netherlands East Indies during the Period from 8th December, 1941 to 8th March, 1942	1947	Largely a copy of Lt-Col. Leggatt's report (Sparrow Force (Timor)-Account of Action) upon returning to Australia in 1942, compiled by the AWM in 1947.

1. United Kingdom [London Archives]

CAB 106 135	The Action in Timor from Dec. 1941 until Dec. 1942		Narrative in English and a map of Portuguese Timor provided by the Dutch Military War Section.
CAB 122 8	Anglo-Dutch-British Conference at Singapore, April 1941 [file]	1941-42	Miscellaneous documents from or on the conference. Timor is mentioned as a geographical point, but it is given only slight attention as a politically distinct part.
CAB 122 8	Draft Agreement on the Outline Plan for the employment of American, Dutch and British Forces in the Far East Area in the event of War with Japan	1941	A Japanese invasion of Portuguese Timor was mentioned as a possible grounds for military counter-action (p. 14). Plans for Australian ground troops to be sent to Kupang are also mentioned.
CAB 122 148	Anglo-Dutch-British Conference at Singapore Feb. 1941 [file]	1941-42	Reports on conference. A Japanese attack on Portuguese Timor was mentioned as a possible aggressive move, but apparently no concrete actions were discussed.
CAB 122 201	Portuguese Timor [file]	1941-42	Communications related to the defence of PT and presence of Allied troops. USGCS 25 shows US/Britain considered Timor worthy of defending; other documents from December 1941-February 1942 related to Portuguese-Dutch negotiations and the arrival of a Portuguese liaison in Batavia on February 8.
CAB 122 513	Reoccupation of Portuguese Timor [file]	1945-46	FO and DO telegrams; largely debate over Japanese surrender.
CAB 122 966	Portuguese Timor [file]	1943-46	Diplomatic communications related to Portuguese requests to be included in the liberation of Portuguese Timor, and to minimize bombing of Portuguese Timor. Finally, documents related to Australian withdrawal from West Timor in 1946.

DO [Dominion Office]

The records with DO item numbers were created or owned by the Dominion Office, the Commonwealth Relations Office, or the Foreign and Commonwealth Offices. Most documents examined were related to Australia and oil or mining rights in Portuguese Timor before the war.

35   Dominions Office and Commonwealth Relations Office: Original Correspondence

Selected list of Timor-related items from DO files

DO 35 557/7	Situation in Portuguese Timor-Information from Mr. Max Sander, a resident	1939	Information from the British Consul General H. Fitzmaurice in Batavia.
DO 35 557/7	Visit of the Governor of Portuguese East Timor to Batavia	1939	Information from the British Consul General H. Fitzmaurice in Batavia.
DO 35 557/7	Oil resources of Portuguese East Timor	1939	Information obtained by the British Consul General H. Fitzmaurice in Batavia from the Portuguese Governor General Maj. A.E. Neves da Fontoura.
DO 35 557/7	Letter	1939	Letter from the British Ambassador in Lisbon (W. Selby) to Viscount Hallifax concerning oil concessions and the Japanese.
DO 35 557/7	Telegram	1939	Telegram from the British Ambassador in Lisbon (W. Selby) concerning Wittouck and oil concessions.
DO 35 557/7	Oil concessions [File]	1939	[sub-file entry]
DO 35 557/7	Oil concessions in Portuguese East Timor	1939	A copy of a telegram sent by the Government of the Commonwealth of Australia to Lisbon.
DO 35 557/7	Old Staughton Oil Concessions, Australia	1939	A copy of a telegram sent by the Commonwealth of Australia to the British Ambassador in Lisbon.
DO 35 557/7	Serge Wittouck and Portuguese Timor	1939	An updated FO report on Serge Wittouck.
DO 35 557/7	Set of letters	1939	Letters on Wittouck and mining investments.
DO 35 1720	Reoccupation of Timor		File name. A thick file of documents related to the reoccupation of Timor, including translations of Portuguese statements, Australian parliamentary statements, explanations of diplomatic stands by the Portuguese government, etc. Very interesting.

FO [Foreign Office]

From the late 1930s, the Foreign Office collected information on Portuguese Timor and Japanese involvement, and was an interested party in oil and mining rights negotiations, as well in negations over trade and landing rights. During the war and early postwar period, the Foreign Office was the primary party in various negations with Portugal. Some of the Eden papers (FO 954) are also available in digitized form on-line.

93	Foreign Office and Foreign Commonwealth Office: Protocols of Treaties
115	Embassy and Consulates, United States of America: General Correspondence
371	Political Departments: General Correspondence from 1906-1966
850	Foreign Office and Diplomatic Service Administration Office: Communications Department: General Correspondence from 1906 (Y DSY series)
925	Library: Maps and Plans
954	Private Office Papers of Sir Anthony Eden, Earl of Awon, Secretary of State for Foreign Affairs

Selected list of Timor-related items from FO files

FO 371 27792	Portuguese Timor: Japanese Activities [file]	1941	File 222 (to pp. 1996). File of various typed and handwritten documents concerning oil concessions, flights to Dili, and Archer's visit (but not his report). Many of the files have extensive handwritten notes.
FO 371 27793	Portuguese Timor-Japanese activities [file]	1941	File 222 (pp. 2054-7333). Much on the Archer trip, also alarm from Portuguese residents of Timor (including the SAPT director) who concluded the new GG was pro-Japanese. SAPT director hoped the Japanese air service would not materialize. Hudson Fysh report. More on the manganese and coffee exports to Japan, as well as oil concessions.
FO 371 27794	Portuguese Timor-Japanese activities [file]	1941	File 222 (pp. 7403-10890). Includes the Archer report and his 4 page cover letter (typed and printed copies), as well as FO comments. There is also much on the purchase of manganese and coffee by Japanese. There is a document from October 1941 which seems to be the start of discussion on preemptive occupation of Timor, but it is not clear when discussions with the NEI on this issue would be held. By October 28, the US State Dept had been informed and was to raise the issue of "outside help" with Portugal.
FO 371 31758	Japanese subversive activities in the Netherlands East Indies	1942	Much of this report (judged to be of little value to the British FO) was from Java Bode. Includes cover letter and file notes.
FO 371 31758	Japanese Intelligence Service in the Netherlands East Indies	1941	Translation of a Dutch report on the Japanese Intelligence services in Indonesia. Includes Portuguese Timor. [4p. + sketch maps; original and other copy included, as well as a cover letter and the file cover with notes.]
FO 925 19010	Portuguese Timor, topographical map (1: 250,000)	1940	Fotostat copy, 1/2 scale. AIC, printed by G. Kolff, Batavia, 1940.

HS [Records of the Special Operations Executive]

Only one Special Operations Executive file was listed in the catalog, a file with several documents related to the SOE Australia operations, including the operations in Timor. It is likely that a more thorough search would yield additional information related to the various SOE missions to Timor.

Selected list of Timor-related items from HS files

| HS 1 246 | SOE Far East: Australia [file] | 1942-45 | Items 9-10 are related to Timor – largely cables and information about Santos and others being helpful but forced into hiding. Item 13 is a status report on operations. |

HW [Records Created or Inherited by the Government Communications Headquarters (GCHQ)]

Files in the HW series were created or held by the Government Communications Headquarters, and thus largely consist of intercepted and decoded diplomatic messages. Relevant messages are indexed on the on-line catalog, but mistakes do exist, and some relevant messages are not listed under obvious topics.

1   Government Code and Cypher School: Signals Intelligence Passed to the Prime Minister, messages and correspondence.

12   Government Code and Cypher School: Diplomatic Section and predecessors: Decrypts of Intercepted Diplomatic Communications (BJ Series)

Selected list of Timor-related items from WO files

| HW 1 391 | Spanish ambassador, London: Allied failure to resist in Timor, Mar 1; Japanese minister, Madrid: Spanish-Portuguese relations over Timor, Feb 28 | 1942 | Intercepted messages from the Spanish rep. in London stating that the Portuguese Defence attaché had remarked on the lack of spirit of Australian troops and their failure to defend Timor, and from the Japanese ambassador in Madrid related to Portuguese-Spanish defence agreements which were limited to European territories. |
| HW 1 411 | Portugal: Lisbon report continued Australian resistance in Timor, Mar 11 | 1942 | Intercepted message dated 11 March 1942 from MFA to Portuguese Ambassador in London stating that negotiation with Japan over Timor were failing due to continued Australian resistance in PT. |

1. United Kingdom [London Archives]

HW 1 571	Portuguese ministry of foreign affairs comment on conduct of Japanese in Timor, May 10	1942	Intercepted message to the Portuguese Minister in Tokyo about the conduct and difficulties of Japanese in Timor. The message is corrupted.
HW 1 580	Portuguese report of situation in Timor, May 18	1942	Intercepted message from MFA Lisbon to Portuguese Ambassador London about the situation in Portuguese Timor. Somewhat detailed.
HW 1 633	Lisbon to Portuguese ambassador, Tokyo: part of report on situation in Timor, June 6. 105382	1942	Intercepted message from MFA Lisbon to Portuguese Minister in Tokyo dated June 6, 1942. Relates to the situation in Timor.
HW 1 639	Japanese Consul, Dili, Reports situation in Portuguese Timor. 105453	1942	Intercepted message dated June 3, 1942 from the Japanese Consul in Dili to the Foreign Minister.
HW 1 673	Japanese determination to clear Australian and Dutch forces from Timor. 106103	1942	Intercepted message from the Foreign Minister, Tokyo to the Japanese Minister, Lisbon, dated June 26, 1942 related to the determination to clear Timor of Allied troops, following which an understanding could be reached with the Portuguese.
HW 12 273	Japanese landing in Portuguese Timor. Portugal: 101612, 101613, 101623 and 101803	1942	Intercepted diplomatic messages from February 1942, includes one message not in index.
HW 12 274	Japanese views on delivery of Portuguese reinforcements to Timor. Japan: 101869, 101902, 101906, 101907, 101940, 101945, 102014, 102027, 102092, 102600; Troops for Timor. Portugal: 101909, 102465; Added 101904, 101905	1942	Intercepted diplomatic messages from March 1942. 2 messages not found in index.
HW 12 275	Portuguese Timor. Japan: 103299; Portugal: 102999, 103000 103061		Intercepted diplomatic messages from April 1942. Messages are general except one (103061) from Lisbon which mentions Japanese air attacks of Er… and Hatolia. During the former, 7 natives, 1 Chinese woman, and 1 half-caste child were killed and 9 natives, 7 Chinese and 1 half-caste child wounded. In the later, 1 native was killed.
HW 12 276	Portuguese Timor. Japan: 104066, 104404; Portugal: 104431, 104489, 104633, 104831	1942	Intercepted diplomatic messages from May 1942.

HW 12 277	Japanese forces in Timor. Japan: 105364, 105453, 105505, 105542, 105584, 105606, 105627, 105662, 105820, 105972, 105974, 106054, 106103, 106141; Portugal: 105373, 105382, 105403, 105466, 105467, 105517	1942	Intercepted diplomatic messages from June 1942. Several item numbers corrected.
HW 12 278	Japanese occupation of Portuguese Timor. Portugal: 106213, 106274, 106277; Italy: 107099; Japan: 106268, 106427, 106614, 106956, 106957, 107157	1942	Intercepted diplomatic messages from July 1942.
HW 12 279	Portuguese Timor. Japan: 107638, 107717, 107808, 108073, 108253, 108309; Portugal: 107727	1942	Intercepted diplomatic messages from August 1942.
HW 12 280	Portuguese Timor. Japan: 108703, 108795, 109103, 109359; Portugal: 109067, 109243	1942	Intercepted diplomatic messages from September 1942.
HW 12 281	Portuguese Timor. Japan: 109881, 109907, 109975, 110060, 110144, 110339, 110475, 110532, 110538, 110540; Portugal: 110242, 110352	1942	Intercepted diplomatic messages from October 1942. Intercepted diplomatic communiques, mostly dealing with the unsafe situation and need for protection of Portuguese officials in Timor, the refusal of Japan to allow cyphered messages to be sent to and from Timor, and a US statement on Timor. Little concrete information on the situation in Timor.
HW 12 290	Portuguese Timor. Portugal: 119833	1943	Message from Portuguese Ambassador in London to the MFA in Lisbon. Item 119833, messages 249 and 251, 2 July 1943 and 6 July 1943.
HW 12 291	Japanese concern over reports of murders of Portuguese in Timor and Macao. Japan: 121607; Portuguese Timor. Japan: 121724, 121831	1943	Intercepted diplomatic messages from August 1943.

PREM [Records of the Office of the Prime Minister]

A very limited number of documents are available in the Records of the Prime Minister's Office. Only one file was located through the catalog.

PREM 3   Prime Minister's Office: operational Correspondence and Papers

Selected list of Timor-related items from PREM 3 files

| PREM. 3. 361 2 | Protection of Portuguese Timor. | 1941-42 | File. A collection of documents on diplomatic relations with Portugal related to Timor and its defence. |

WO [War Office]

Responsible for planning and military operations during the war, the War Office compiled numerous materials which are another major source of materials on Timor-related affairs during the war.

106   Correspondence and papers concerning various theatres of war....
193   Director of Military Operations: Collation Files.
203   War of 1939-45 military headquarters papers, Far East, including South East Area Command (SEAC), covering Burma, Malaya and Indo-china, and Allied Land Forces South East Asia.
208   War Office: Directorate of Military Operations and Intelligence, and Directorate of Military Intelligence, Ministry of Defence, Defence Intelligence Staff: Files
252   Admiralty, Inter-service Topographical Department, and Ministry of Defence, Joint Intelligence Bureau Library: Surveys, Maps and Reports

Selected list of Timor-related items from WO files

| WO 106 3328A | Allied guerilla operations in Portuguese Timor [file] | 1941-43 | A mixed set of documents which includes parts of prewar intelligence reports, wartime intelligence, diplomatic exchanges, information from Dutch military sources, newspaper clippings, etc. |
| WO 106 3328B | Allied guerilla operations in Portuguese Timor [file] | 1941-42 | Two documents related to Timor. One is a 1941 Straits Settlement Police report on Portuguese Timor, while the other relates to the return of Ross from Timor in 1942. |

Ⅳ. イギリス所蔵史料 （Materials in British Archives）

WO 106 3441	Acquisition of Timor for Commonwealth Defence [file]	1943-45	Two documents, one concerning a proposal for 4000 Portuguese troops to be concentrated in Australia for invasion of Timor (March 1945). A second relates to Roosevelt's suggestion that Australia might want to buy Timor from the Portuguese (1943).
WO 203 4892	Timor and Amboina	1945	Documents related to the surrender of Japanese in Timor, the movement of Portuguese Ships, and the question of authority in West Timor.
WO 208 852	Relations with and activities in Portuguese and Dutch Timor [file]	1939-42	Folders related to Japanese activities and British/Australian relations with Portuguese Timor. Includes a copy of *Diario do Governo* (27 Oct 1941) with treaty texts (with Australia in Portuguese and English; with Japan in Portuguese and French). There is also a copy of intercepted messages on oil concessions between the Japanese Minister in Lisbon, the Japanese Foreign Minister, and the Japanese Minister in Sydney (1939).
WO 208 1124	Order of Battle: Timor and Celebes [file]	1944	Little on Timor. One map shows Japanese troop deployments in 1944, another document describes conditions in Indonesia by RNEI Sgt-maj de Haas, however information on Timor is clearly second hand.
WO 208 1124	Identification & Distribution of Japanese Forces in NW Sector as at 2 Jan 44	1944	Map. (Secret: Appendix "C" to AMF Weekly Intelligence Review (number unclear)). This map shows Japanese troop deployments in January 1944.
WO 208 1633	General information and evacuation by Japanese	1943-45	A set of mostly geographical documents, including one from the Japanese Domei English language news service, describing efforts to improve agriculture on the island.
WO 208 1693	Netherlands (Possessions) Intelligence Report	1945	Geographical information, including on the border between Portuguese and Dutch Timor.
WO 252 698	Terrain Study: Portuguese Timor	1943	Published AGS study.
WO 252 1638	Terrain Study: Portuguese Timor	1943	Published AGS study.

2. Files and Items in the Public Records Office Collection of the National Archives

Reference Number	Title	Covering Dates
AIR 23 7717	Bases in Celebes, Borneo, Java, Lesser Soenda and Timor	1944
CAB 65/20/24	5. Timor	1941/12/19
CAB 65/20/27	2. Timor	1941/12/24
CAB 65/20/28	4. Timor	1941/12/26
CAB 65/20/29	5. Timor	1941/12/29
CAB 65/25/1	3. Timor	1942/1/1
CAB 65/25/9	6. Timor	1942/1/19
CAB 66/21/27	Portuguese Timor. Memorandum by the Secretary of State for Foreign Affairs, includes Letter from His Majesty's Ambassador at Lisbon	1942/1/29
CAB 66/27/31	Australian Troops in Portuguese Timor, Telegram from the Minister for External Affairs, Canberra, to the High Commissioner for Australia in London	1942/8/11
CAB 79/16/21	9. PORTUGUESE TIMOR. COS(41)741	1941/12/13
CAB 79/16/36	11. PORTUGUESE TIMOR	1941/12/27
CAB 79/16/41	3. PORTUGUESE TIMOR	1941/12/30
CAB 79/17/ 2	7. PORTUGUESE TIMOR. COS(42)4	1942/1/2
CAB 79/17/12	11. POSITION IN PORTUGUESE TIMOR	1942/1/12
CAB 79/17/17	4. PORTUGUESE TIMOR	1942/1/16
CAB 79/17/23	8. PORTUGUESE TIMOR. COS(42)30(Revise)	1942/1/21
CAB 79/21/34	2. TIMOR	1942/6/20
CAB 79/30/11	3. Information on Timor for the Netherlands Government. JP(45)50(Final)	1945/3/08
CAB 79/31/5	6. Information on Timor for the Netherlands Government	1945/3/29
CAB 79/35/4	7. Portuguese Participation in Operations for the Recapture of Timor	1945/6/18
CAB 79/35/5	4. Portuguese Participation in Operations for the Recapture of Timor	1945/6/19
CAB 79/35/8	12. Portuguese Participation in Operations for the Re-capture of Timor	1945/6/21
CAB 79/36/1	2. Portuguese Participation in Operations for the Recapture of Timor. JP(45)151	1945/7/3
CAB 79/37/16	3. Portuguese Participation in Operations for the Recapture of Timor. COS(45)169	1945/8/13
CAB 79/38/ 7	1. Portuguese Timor	1945/8/29
CAB 79/38/11	15. Portuguese Timor	1945/9/3

IV. イギリス所蔵史料 (Materials in British Archives)

Reference Number	Title	Covering Dates
CAB 79/38/12	4. Portuguese Timor	1945/9/4
CAB 79/38/13	6. Portuguese Timor	1945/9/5
CAB 79/39/2	1. Portuguese Timor	1945/9/12
CAB 79/46/1	4. TRANSFER OF DUTCH TIMOR TO SEAC	1946/5/13
CAB 79/67/19	9. Portuguese participation in the capture of Timor. JP(43)368	1943/11/15
CAB 79/68/2	8. Portuguese participation in the capture of Timor. COS(43)734(O)	1943/11/30
CAB 79/79/11	8. Portuguese Declaration of War against Japan. COS(44)698(O). 9. Bombing of Portuguese Timor	1944/8/10
CAB 80/32/61	PORTUGUESE TIMOR. Memo. by Foreign Office	1941/12/11
CAB 80/33/4	PORTUGUESE TIMOR. Letter dated 1.1.42 from Foreign Office covering Memorandum	1942/1/1
CAB 80/33/30	PORTUGUESE TIMOR. Note by Secretary. Annex I. Prime Minister's Personal Minute, Serial No. M 3/2. Annex II. Draft telegram to Supreme Commander, S. W. Pacific	1942/1/20
CAB 80/34/29	KOEPANG (TIMOR). DEFENCE PLAN FOR BASE AT: Memo. by Ad Hoc Sub-Committee on Defence Arrangements for the Indian Ocean Area	1942/2/13
CAB 80/49/1	PORTUGUESE PARTICIPATION IN OPERATIONS FOR THE RECAPTURE OF TIMOR. Copy of letter (Z.9050/50/G) dated 10th August, 1945 from the Foreign Office to the Secretary, Chiefs of Staff Committee	1945/8/11
CAB 80/76/84	PORTUGUESE PARTICIPATION IN THE CAPTURE OF TIMOR. Copy of a letter (O.13582/166/G) dated 26th November, 1943, from the Foreign Office to the Secretary	1943/11/27
CAB 84/58/9	PORTUGESE PARTICIPATION IN THE CAPTURE OF TIMOR	1943/10/14
CAB 84/70/22	INFORMATION ON TIMOR FOR THE NETHERLANDS GOVERNMENT. Note by Secretary	1945/3/3
CAB 84/70/23	INFORMATION ON TIMOR FOR THE NETHERLANDS GOVERNMENT. Report by J.P.S. C.O.S. Meeting 1945: 63rd	1945/3/6
CAB 106/26	Account of operations of 2nd Australian Independent Company in Timor 1941-1942, by Private W. H. Rowan-Robinson	[1945]
CAB 106/135	Australian and Netherlands accounts of the action in Timor 1941 Dec.-1942 Dec.	[1947]
CAB 121/772	Proposed Portuguese participation in the defence and liberation of Timor	1941/12 - 1944/1

2. Files and Items in the Public Records Office Collection of the National Archives

Reference Number	Title	Covering Dates
CAB 122/ 8	Anglo-Dutch-British Conference at Singapore, April 1941	1941
CAB 122/148	Anglo-Dutch-British Conference at Singapore Feb. 1941	1941 - 42
CAB 122/201	Portuguese Timor	1941 - 1943
CAB 122/513	Reoccupation of Portuguese Timor	1945
CAB 122/966	Portuguese Timor	1943 - 1946
DO 35/ 372/6	Oil and agricultural concessions in Portugese Timor	1935 - 1936
DO 35/ 557/5	Portuguese Timor	1938
DO 35/ 557/6	Portuguese Timor	1938 - 1939
DO 35/ 557/7	Portuguese Timor	1939 - 1940
DO 35/ 589/1	Timor: Japanese trade relations	1937
DO 35/1718	Consultations with Dominion Governments regarding the setting up of staff talks on possible Portuguese participation in any allied operation for the occupation of Timor	1943 - 1946
DO 35/1720	Re-occupation of Timor - surrender of Japanese troops to Australian armed forces	1943 - 1946
DO 35/1721	Australian hopes for early negotiations with Portugal under the 1943 Azores Agreement about Timor defence, commerce and civil aviation	1943 - 1946
FO 115/4016	Portugal's participation in operations relating to the re-occupation of Timor: Portuguese agreement to construction of an airport Santa Maria by the United States: Anglo-American agreements with Portugal	1944
FO 371/22165	Japanese interest in Portuguese Timor	1938
FO 371/22166	Japanese interest in Portuguese Timor	1938
FO 371/23541	Oil concessions in Portuguese Timor	1939
FO 371/23549	Visit of Japanese consular official to Port Darwin and Timor	1939
FO 371/24705	Portuguese Timor: oil concessions Japanese activities	1940
FO 371/24706	Portuguese Timor: oil concessions Japanese activities	1940
FO 371/25041	Japanese air service to Timor	1940
FO 371/27792	Portuguese Timor - Japanese activities	1941
FO 371/27793	Portuguese Timor - Japanese activities	1941
FO 371/27794	Portuguese Timor - Japanese activities	1941
FO 371/27795	Portuguese Timor - Japanese activities	1941
FO 371/27796	Portuguese Timor - Japanese activities	1941
FO 371/27797	Portuguese Timor - Japanese activities	1941
FO 371/27798	Portuguese Timor - Japanese activities	1941
FO 371/27799	Portuguese Timor - Japanese activities	1941

IV. イギリス所蔵史料 (Materials in British Archives)

Reference Number	Title	Covering Dates
FO 371/27800	Portuguese Timor - Japanese activities	1941
FO 371/27821	Japanese air service to Bangkok and Timor	1941
FO 371/28720	Portuguese Timor	1941
FO 371/31727	Portuguese Timor - Anglo-Portuguese negotiations	1942
FO 371/31728	Portuguese Timor - Anglo-Portuguese negotiations	1942
FO 371/31729	Portuguese Timor - Anglo-Portuguese negotiations	1942
FO 371/31730	Portuguese Timor - Anglo-Portuguese negotiations	1942
FO 371/31731	Portuguese Timor - Anglo-Portuguese negotiations	1942
FO 371/31732	Portuguese Timor - Anglo-Portuguese negotiations	1942
FO 371/31733	Portuguese Timor - Anglo-Portuguese negotiations	1942
FO 371/31734	Portuguese Timor - Anglo-Portuguese negotiations	1942
FO 371/31764	Timor Oil Concession	1942
FO 371/35913	Portuguese Timor	1943
FO 371/39586	Portuguese-Japanese relations: Timor	1944
FO 371/39587	Portuguese-Japanese relations: Timor	1944
FO 371/39588	Portuguese-Japanese relations: Timor	1944
FO 371/39589	Staff talks regarding recovery of Timor	1944
FO 371/39590	Staff talks regarding recovery of Timor	1944
FO 371/39591	Staff talks regarding recovery of Timor	1944
FO 371/49492	Portuguese Timor: preparations for re-occupation: accidental bombing of Macao	1945
FO 371/49493	Portuguese Timor: preparations for re-occupation: accidental bombing of Macao	1945
FO 371/49494	Portuguese Timor: preparations for re-occupation: accidental bombing of Macao	1945
FO 371/49495	Portuguese Timor: preparations for re-occupation: accidental bombing of Macao	1945
FO 371/60311	Disciplinary proceedings against certain former Portuguese officials in Timor	1946
FO 371/60319	Oil concessions in Mozambique and Timor	1946
FO 371/67857A	Oil concessions in Timor and Mozambique	1947
FO 371/73307	Surrender of oil concession in Portuguese Timor	1948
FO 373/4/11	Dutch Timor and the Lesser Sunda Islands	1919/5
FO 373/4/19	Portuguese Timor	1919/5
FO 850/145	Communication with British Mission proceeding to Lisbon for talks with Portuguese Government on the subject of Timor	1944
FO 925/19010	Portuguese Timor. Topographical map. 1:250,000. Photostat copy of half-scale. Asia Investment Co, Ltd. Printed by G. Kolff & Co, Batavia	[1940]

2. Files and Items in the Public Records Office Collection of the National Archives

Reference Number	Title	Covering Dates
FO 925/7938	Carta da Provincia de Timor. 1:1,000,000. Portuguese Ministry of Colonies	1927
FO 93/77/119	Notes. Timor Garrison.	1942/1/22
FO 954/16A	Netherlands: To Sir N. Bland (despatch No 83). Talk with Dutch Minister for Foreign Affairs (Japanese move in Timor)	1941/10/20
FO 954/21	Portugal: Foreign Office despatch to Lisbon, No 427. Aerodrome facilities in Timor given by Portuguese to Japan	1941/10/21
FO 954/21	Portugal: Foreign Office despatch to Lisbon, No 453. Timor	1941/11/4
FO 954/21	Portugal: Foreign Office despatch to Sir N. Bland (No 97). Timor	1941/11/6
FO 954/21	Portugal: Foreign Office despatch to Lisbon, No 6. Landing of Allied troops in Timor	1942/1/1
FO 954/21	Portugal: From Sir R. Campbell. Agreement on Timor. Character of Salazar	1942/1/23
FO 954/21	Portugal: Foreign Office despatch to Lisbon, No 74. Japanese invasion of Timor. Internal condition of Portugal	1942/2/23
FO 954/21	Portugal: Foreign Office telegram to Washington, No 4115. President to Prime Minister No 292. Timor and Macao	1943/6/22
FO 954/21	Portugal: Foreign Office minute. Draft reply to 43/25 (Timor and Macao)	1943/6/24
FO 954/21	Portugal: Foreign Office telegram to Washington, No 4258. Prime Minister to President, No 331 (of 27/6) Timor and Macao (Reply to 43/25)	1943/6/28
FO 954/21	Portugal: Foreign Office minutes about President Roosevelt's views on Timor	1943/7/23
FO 954/21	Portugal: Foreign Office despatch to Lisbon, No 286. Talk with the Portuguese Ambassador (Azores-Timor Post-War Civil Aviation)	1944/7/3
FO 954/4B	Dominions: Secretary of State Minute to Prime Minister No 43/184. Possibility of Australia purchasing Timor from Portugal	1943/6/25
HS 1 246	SOE Far East: Australia	1942 - 1945
HW 1/391	Spanish ambassador, London: Allied failure to resist in Timor, Mar 1; military failings in India, Feb 27	1942
HW 1/391	Japanese minister, Madrid: Spanish-Portuguese relations over Timor, Feb 28	1942
HW 1/411	Portugal: Lisbon report continued Australian resistance in Timor, Mar 11	1942

IV. イギリス所蔵史料 (Materials in British Archives)

Reference Number	Title	Covering Dates
HW 1/ 568	Japanese foreign minister informs Lisbon of actions of Australians, Dutch and Portuguese in Timor, May 9	1942
HW 1/ 571	Portuguese ministry of foreign affairs comment on conduct of Japanese in Timor, May 10	1942
HW 1/ 580	Portuguese report of situation in Timor, May 18	1942
HW 1/ 633	Lisbon to Portuguese ambassador, Tokyo: part of report on situation in Timor, June 6	1942
HW 1/ 639	Japanese consul, Dili: situation in Portuguese Timor, June 3	1942
HW 1/ 649	Japanese Ministry of Foreign Affairs complaint to Lisbon about non-cooperation of Portuguese authorities in Timor and pro-Australian activities, June 8	1942
HW 1/ 673	Japanese Minister of Foreign Affairs reiterates determination to rid Timor of Australian and Dutch forces, suspects Portuguese of giving friendly assistance June 26	1942
HW 1/ 677	Japanese Minister of Foreign Affairs' statement of Japan's intentions to remove Australian and Dutch forces from Timor, and his view of Portuguese responsibilities in the area	1942
HW 1/2587	Minister of Foreign Affairs, Tokyo: Japan and Portuguese mission to Timor, Mar 2	1944
HW 1/3072	Portuguese minister, Pretoria: report of July 10 following meeting with General Smuts, discussion of the war in Europe, South African pressure for Portugal to join the war on Allied side, to stand up and declare war on Japan for seizing its colony of Timor	1944
HW 1/3072	The question of Portuguese Timor, message of July 1 from German legation in Lisbon to Berlin on talks between Salazar and Japanese minister in Lisbon, Portuguese pressure for Japanese to leave Timor and return it to Portugal	1944
HW 1/3536	Japanese Minister, Lisbon, informed of impossibility of withdrawing Japanese troops from Timor	1945
HW 1/3774	Japanese Minister for Foreign Affairs to Minister, Lisbon: Authority to negotiate withdrawal of Japanese troops from Timor, May 16	1945
HW 1/3774	Japanese minister, Lisbon: urges conciliation over Timor, Apr 12 and 13	1945
HW 12/273/17	Japanese landing in Portuguese Timor. Portugal: 101612 101623 and 101803	1942/2/1 - 1942/2/28

Reference Number	Title	Covering Dates
HW 12/274/1	Japanese views on delivery of Portuguese reinforcements to Timor. Japan: 101869, 101902, 101906, 101907, 101940, 101945, 102014, 102027, 102092, 102600	1942/3/1 - 1942/3/28
HW 12/274/2	Troops for Timor. Portugal: 101909, 102465	1942/3/1 - 1942/3/28
HW 12/275/7	Portuguese Timor. Japan: 103299; Portugal: 102999, 103000 103061	1942/4/1 - 1942/4/30
HW 12/276/10	Portuguese Timor Japan: 104066, 104404; Portugal: 104431, 104489, 104633, 104831	1942/5/1 - 1942/5/31
HW 12/277/12	Japanese forces in Timor. Japan: 105364, 105453, 105505, 105542, 105584, 105606, 105627, 105662, 105820, 105972, 105974, 106054, 106103, 106141; Portugal: 105373, 105382, 105403, 105466, 105467, 105517	1942/6/1 - 1942/6/30
HW 12/278/3	Japanese occupation of Portuguese Timor. Portugal: 106213, 106274, 106277; Italy: 107099; Japan: 106268, 106427, 106614, 106956, 106957, 107157	1942/7/1 - 1942/7/31
HW 12/279/6	Portuguese Timor. Japan: 107638, 107717, 107808, 108073, 108253, 108309; Portugal: 107727	1942/7/1 - 1942/8/31
HW 12/280/4	Portuguese Timor. Japan: 108703, 108795, 109103, 109359; Portugal: 109067, 109243	1942/9/1 - 1942/9/30
HW 12/281/10	Portuguese Timor. Japan: 109881, 109907, 109975, 110060, 110144, 110339, 110475, 110532, 110538, 110540; Portugal: 110242, 110352	1942/10/1 - 1942/10/31
HW 12/282/2	Portuguese Timor. Japan: 110603, 110627, 110652, 110655, 110722, 110748, 110752, 110785, 110859, 111003, 111183, 111184, 111279, 111671; Portugal: 110610, 110757, 110862, 110960, 111206	1942/11/1 - 1942/11/30
HW 12/283/3	Portuguese Timor. Japan: 111742, 111772, 111801, 111911, 111915, 111990, 111994, 112368, 112431; Portugal:112003, 112464	1942/12/1 - 1942/12/31
HW 12/284/10	Portuguese Timor. Portugal: 112792, 112893, 112944, 112946, 113095; Japan: 112890, 113191, 113400; Brazil: 112947, 113052	1942/12/5 - 1943/1/31
HW 12/285/6	Portuguese Timor. Vatican: 113866; Portugal: 113952, 114294, 114454, 114736; Italy: 114535; Germany: 114564	1943/2/1 - 1943/2/28
HW 12/286/11	Portuguese Timor. Japan: 114888, 115098, 115313, 115428; Portugal: 115130, 115215, 115251, 115749	1943/3/1 - 1943/3/31
HW 12/287/16	Portuguese Timor. Japan: 116329, 116503; Portugal: 116917	1943/4/1 - 1943/4/30
HW 12/288/7	Portuguese Timor. Italy: 117264	1943/2/19 - 1943/5/31

IV. イギリス所蔵史料 (Materials in British Archives)

Reference Number	Title	Covering Dates
HW 12/289/12	Portuguese Timor. Portugal: 119051	1942/11/3 - 1943/6/30
HW 12/290/11	Portuguese Timor. Portugal: 119833	1943/5/20 - 1943/7/31
HW 12/291/21	Japanese concern over reports of murders of Portuguese in Timor and Macao. Japan: 121607	1943/7/7 - 1943/8/31
HW 12/291/22	Portuguese Timor. Japan: 121724, 121831	1943/7/7 - 1943/8/31
HW 12/293/1	Japanese-Portuguese relations; Macao (Sian incident) and Portuguese Timor. Japan: 123217, 123345, 123350, 123565, 123801; Portugal: 123234, 123376, 123537, 123638, 123731, 123735, 124036; Bulgaria: 124227	1943/9/15 - 1943/10/31
HW 12/294/13	Portuguese-Japanese relations (Portuguese Timor and 'Sian' incident in Macao). Japan: 124724, 125451; Portugal: 124999	1943/11/01 - 1943/11/30
HW 12/295/2	Japanese-Portuguese relations (Portuguese Timor and Macao). Japan: 125592, 125595, 125740, 125743, 125785, 126051, 126102, 126334, 126367, 126474, 126507, 126511, 126595, 126597, 126617, 126619; 126649; Portugal: 125878, 125979, 126117, 126531-126532, 126614; Thailand: 125655	1943/12/01 - 1943/12/31
HW 12/296/1	Japanese-Portuguese relations (Portuguese Timor). Japan: 126726-126728, 126828, 126833, 126865, 126950, 127130, 127157, 127617, 127707; Portugal: 126821, 127174, 127283, 127487, 127565; China: 127505	1944/1/1 - 1944/1/31
HW 12/297/5	Japanese-Portuguese relations (Portuguese Timor and Macao). Japan: 127789, 128259, 128304, 128340, 128444, 128449, 128479, 128510, 128548, 128621; Portugal: 127990, 128120, 128289	1944/2/1 - 1944/2/29
HW 12/298/4	Japanese-Portuguese relations (Portuguese Timor). Japan: 128846, 128951, 128990, 129056, 129490, 129540; Portugal: 128884, 129192, 129194, 129271, 129294-129296, 129332, 129609, 129689, 129827	1944/3/1 - 1944/3/31
HW 12/299/1	Japanese-Portuguese relations (Portuguese Timor). Japan: 129937, 130160, 130330, 130646, 130781, 130943; Portugal: 130015, 130050, 130116, 130219, 130281-130282, 130414, 130620, 130707, 130806, 130895, 130932, 130966, 130996	1944/4/1 - 1944/4/30
HW 12/300/8	Japanese-Portuguese relations (Portuguese Timor). Portugal: 131097, 131235, 131260, 131298, 131330, 131400, 131438, 131472, 131505, 131577, 131579, 131661, 131697, 131726, 131760, 131798, 131836, 131838, 131876, 131943, 132004; Japan: 131379	1944/5/1 - 1944/5/31

Reference Number	Title	Covering Dates
HW 12/301/6	Japanese-Portuguese relations (Portuguese Timor). Japan: 132055, 132701; Portugal: 132076, 132172, 132204, 132238, 132278, 132315, 132400, 132440, 132486, 132524, 132560, 132605, 132646, 132726, 132805, 132845, 132895, 132039-132040, 133076, 133118	1944/6/1 - 1944/6/30
HW 12/302/14	Japanese-Portuguese relations (Portuguese Timor). Japan: 133230, 133518, 133907, 134080, 134276; Portugal: 133240, 133242, 133274, 133542, 133926, 134254; France: 133343	1944/7/1 - 1944/7/31
HW 12/303/12	Portuguese-Japanese relations (Portuguese Timor). Japan: 134357, 134566, 134665, 134783, 135090, 135406, 135446; Portugal: 134475, 134601, 134617, 134653-134654, 134657, 134731-134732, 134801, 134986	1944/8/1 - 1944/8/31
HW 12/304/11	Japanese-Portuguese relations (Portuguese Timor). Japan: 135524, 135566, 135643, 136049, 136543; Uruguay: 135595; Brazil: 135662; Portugal: 135691, 135763, 135990, 136271, 136437; Germany: 136096; China: 136638	1944/9/1 - 1944/9/30
HW 12/305/4	Portuguese-Japanese relations (Portuguese Timor). Portugal: 136708, 136947, 137285, 137319, 137466, 137506, 137713, 137817; Japan: 136730, 136999, 136069-137070, 137110, 137476, 137601, 137606, 137728; Turkey: 137642; Brazil: 137754	1944/10/1 - 1944/10/31
HW 12/306/22	Japanese-Portuguese relations (Portuguese Timor). Brazil: 138234; Portugal: 138416, 138555, 138666, 138889; Japan: 138605	1944/11/1 - 1944/11/30
HW 12/307/12	Japanese-Portuguese relations (Portuguese Timor). Portugal: 138989, 139479, 139670; Japan: 139011, 139077, 139249, 139771	1944/12/1 - 1944/12/31
HW 12/308/6	Portuguese-Japanese relations (Portuguese Timor). Portugal: 139900, 140125, 140515, 140584, 140815; Japan: 140529, 140559, 140660, 140794	1945/1/1 - 1945/1/31
HW 12/309/3	Japanese-Portuguese relations (Portuguese Timor). France: 140867; Portugal: 140961, 141073, 141201-141202, 141239, 141242, 141523; Japan: 141021, 141053, 141258, 141304, 141567, 141643, 141762	1945/2/1 - 1945/2/28
HW 12/310/2	Japanese-Portuguese relations (Macao and Portuguese Timor). Japan: 141976, 141867, 141942, 142051, 142093, 142165; Portugal: 141992, 142113, 142355	1945/3/1 - 1945/3/15

Ⅳ．イギリス所蔵史料（Materials in British Archives）

Reference Number	Title	Covering Dates
HW 12/311/8	Japanese-Portuguese relations (Macao and Portuguese Timor). Japan: 142416, 142423, 142558, 142607, 142787, 142830, 142872, 142959; Portugal: 142446, 142538, 142541, 142589-142590, 142667, 142739, 142861	1945/3/16 - 1945/3/31
HW 12/312/4	Japanese-Portuguese relations (Macao and Portuguese Timor). Portugal: 143074, 143160, 143296, 143394, 143444; Japan: 143144, 143316	1945/4/1 - 1945/4/10
HW 12/313/13	Japanese-Portuguese relations (Macao and Portuguese Timor). Japan: 143555, 143605, 143680, 143742, 143746, 143820; Germany: 143661, 143787; Portugal: 143670, 143738, 143765	1945/4/11 - 1945/4/20
HW 12/314/12	Japanese-Portuguese relations (Macao and Portuguese Timor). Japan: 143944; Portugal: 144010-144011	1945/4/21 - 1945/4/30
HW 12/315/12	Japanese-Portuguese relations (Macao and Portuguese Timor). Japan: 144329, 144331, 144413-144414, 144541; Portugal: 144347	1945/5/1 - 1945/5/10
HW 12/316/9	Japanese-Portuguese relations (Macao and Portuguese Timor). Portugal: 144701, 144704; Japan: 144757, 144874, 144926	1945/5/10 - 1945/5/20
HW 12/317/1	Japanese-Portuguese relations (Macao and Portuguese Timor). Japan: 145007, 145009-145010, 145081, 145120, 145169, 145286, 145291, 145322, 145367; Portugal: 145151, 145223, 145357	1945/5/21 - 1945/5/31
HW 12/318/6	Japanese-Portuguese relations (Macao and Portuguese Timor). Portugal: 145457; Japan: 145511, 145557, 145713	1945/6/1 - 1945/6/8
HW 12/319/2	Japanese-Portuguese relations (Macao and Portuguese Timor). Japan: 145746, 145814; Portugal: 145870, 145943	1945/6/9 - 1945/6/17
HW 12/320/10	Japanese-Portuguese relations (Macao and Portuguese Timor). Portugal: 146103, 146217, 146252, 146293; Brazil: 146109	1945/6/18 - 1945/6/24
HW 12/322/13	Japanese-Portuguese relations (Macao and Portuguese Timor). Portugal: 146619, 146694, 146729; Japan: 146815	1945/7/1 - 1945/7/8
HW 12/323/11	Japanese-Portuguese relations (Macao and Portuguese Timor). Portugal: 146905, 146987	1945/7/9 - 1945/7/15
HW 12/324/12	Japanese-Portuguese relations (Portuguese Timor). Japan: 147197, 147366; Portugal: 147273	1945/7/16 - 1945/7/22
HW 12/325/3	Japanese-Portuguese relations (Macao and Portuguese Timor). Japan: 147443, 147521, 147525; Portugal: 147468, 147501-147502, 147539, 147542	1945/7/23 - 1945/7/28
HW 12/326/11	Japanese-Portuguese relations (Macao and Portuguese Timor). Portugal: 147684, 147715, 147760	1945/7/29 - 1945/7/31

Reference Number	Title	Covering Dates
HW 12/327/8	Japanese-Portuguese relations (Macao and Portuguese Timor). Portugal: 147807, 147850, 147894, 147896, 148037; Japan: 147979	1945/8/1 - 1945/8/7
HW 12/328/9	Japanese-Portuguese relations (Portuguese Timor). Portugal: 148081, 148123, 148266, 148309, 148312, 148314-148315; Japan: 148280	1945/8/8 - 1945/8/14
HW 12/329/1	Japanese-Portuguese relations (Macao and Portuguese Timor). Japan: 148332, 148392, 148464, 148533; Portugal: 148367, 148369-148371, 148413, 148443, 148445, 148477, 148522, 148524, 148568, 148601-148603; France: 148551	1945/7/5 - 1945/8/21
HW 12/330/8	Japanese-Portuguese relations (Macao and Portuguese Timor). Portugal: 148641-148643, 148646, 148648, 148691, 148737, 148739-148741, 148743-148746, 148785, 148824-148825, 148869, 148871-148872, 148874, 148908, 148910-148911; France: 148677; Japan: 148707, 148713, 148757	1945/8/22 - 1945/8/28
HW 12/331/9	Japanese-Portuguese relations (Macao and Portuguese Timor). Portugal: 148940, 148980-148983, 149014-149016	1945/8/29 - 1945/8/31
PREM 3. 361/2	Protection of Portuguese Timor	1941 - 1942
WO 106/3328A	Allied guerilla operations in Portuguese Timor	1941/4 - 1943/1
WO 106/3328B	Allied guerilla operations in Portuguese Timor	1941/4 - 1942/9
WO 106/3441	Acquisition of Timor for Commonwealth defences	1943/6 - 1945/3
WO 106/3495	Portuguese Timor: telegrams in and out	1941/9 - 1945/9
WO 193/871	Netherlands and Portuguese East Indies	
WO 203/4892	Timor and Amboina	1945/8 - 1945/9
WO 203/6067	Dutch Timor: responsibility for territory handed over to Royal Netherlands Indies Army	1946/3 - 1946/6
WO 208/ 852	Relations with and activities in Portuguese and Dutch Timor	1939/5 - 1942/8
WO 208/1124	Timor and Celebes	1942/9 - 1944/12
WO 208/1125	Timor and Celebes	1945/1 - 1945/6
WO 208/1126	Timor and Celebes	1945/7 - 1945/9
WO 208/1633	Portuguese Timor: general description with maps; Allied relations with the Portuguese Government and evacuation of the Japanese	1943/1 - 1945/10
WO 208/1638	Terrain study; Portuguese Timor	1943/2
WO 208/1684	Dutch Timor and Lesser Soenda Islands; military geography and topography	1944/5 - 1945/5
WO 208/1693	Netherlands (Possessions) Intelligence Report; Java, Lesser Soenda Islands, Dutch Timor, Borneo, Celebes, Boeroe Island, Amboina Island and Ceram	1945/1

IV. イギリス所蔵史料 (Materials in British Archives)

Reference Number	Title	Covering Dates
WO 252/698	Portuguese Timor	1943/2
WO 252/718	Netherlands East Indies: Dutch Timor	1943/8
WO 373/65	Recommendation for DSO for Lt. Col. William Walt Leggatt	1947

V．オランダ所蔵史料

Materials in the Archives of the Netherlands

1. Archives in the Netherlands

The Netherlands East Indies administration was very interested in events on the eastern half of Timor, primarily due to concerns that it could become a foothold in the Indies for an expanding Japanese empire. Accordingly KNIL troops and an Australian unit moved into Portuguese Timor from west Timor in December 1941, with Dutch ships providing transportation and Col. Van Straten commanding the combined force. During the guerrilla war of 1942, a varying number of Dutch troops remained in the western part of Portuguese Timor as part of the Sparrow Force. It is primarily this history which has resulted in materials being collected in Dutch archives.

The following list represents a substantial portion of the materials held in Dutch archives, materials primarily preserved in seven institutions. A more detailed investigation will likely uncover additional materials in these archives, while other institutions like the Royal Tropical Institute (KIT) with its collection of maps and photographs, the Museum Bronbeek, and perhaps even the KITLV in Leiden hold relevant materials but could not be surveyed here. Additionally, some materials may have been moved since this data was compiled in late 2004, more being concentrated at the National Archives. Nonetheless, the following list provides access to a large range of important research materials, both original Dutch materials held exclusively in the Netherlands, and copies of materials also in Australian, British, or American archives.

Materials are listed by archive, with the archive number, title of the document or file, and a rough translation of this title on separate lines. Holding institutions are labelled in bold-face type, while collections and archives within those institutes are in italics.

Instituut voor Maritieme Historie [Institute for Naval History], The Hague

The Instituut voor Maritieme Historie in The Hague is a small archive which holds archival materials related to the Dutch Navy and Dutch Marines.

V. オランダ所蔵史料（Materials in the Archives of the Netherlands）

Collectie Tweede Wereldoorlog [*Second World War Collection*]

BC 8-4
Kort overzicht van de Timor-actie 1942, mei 1943.
Short review of the Timor action 1942, May 1943.

BC 8-14
Stukken betreffende de ondergang van het H.M.A.S. Armidale met aan boord een aflossingsdetachement voor de Nederlandse troepen op Timor, februari 1943.
Documents concerning the sinking of the H.M.A.S. Armidale, with a detachment of reinforcements for the Dutch troops on Timor on board, February 1943.

BC 8-15
Stukken betreffende H.M.A.S. Armidale, december 1942.
Documents concerning H.M.A.S. Armidale, December 1942.

BC 8-21
Brief van de onderbevelhebber Strijdkrachten in het Oosten, F.W. Coster, aan BSO, 4 februari 1943. Met bijlagen.
Letter of the Vice Commander of the Armed Forces in the East, F.W. Coster, to the Commander of the Armed Forces in the East, 4 February 1943. With appendices.

CA 1-64
Japanese studies in World War II, no. 30. Eastern Detachement. [Japanese] Invasion operation of Ambon and Timor 1942, June 1947.

Instituut voor Militaire Geschiedenis van de Koninklijke Landmacht [Institute for Military History], The Hague

This is a small institute located in the Hague which holds archival materials related to the Dutch Army. This institute thus holds a major collection of Dutch materials related to the military experience and situation "on-the-ground" in Timor especially during 1942.

Collectie 'Nederlands-Indië contra Japan' [*Collection 'Netherlands East Indies versus Japan'*]

001/1
Bundel bescheiden omtrent gebeurtenissen op de Kei, Aroe en Tanimbar eilanden, inclusief informatie over Timor.
A bundle of documents concerning events on the Kei, Aroe and Tanimbar islands, including information on Timor.

001/7
Situatierapporten Timor augustus-november 1942; Verslag Timor-actie, december 1941-december 1942.
Situation reports on Timor August-November 1942; Report on Timor action, December 1941-December 1942.

001/11
Inlichtingenrapporten over januari 1942, party Starfish Timor en Koepang, met verslag van ir. Hees.
Intelligence reports on January 1942, the Starfish party Timor and Koepang, including report by ir. Hees.

005/2
Bescheiden betrekking hebbende op de Nederlandse troepen in Timor, september-december 1942.
Documents concerning the Dutch troops in Timor, September-December 1942.

005/5
Inlichtingenrapporten 22 tot en met 28 over de maanden september, oktober en november 1942 met betrekking tot de toestand op Timor.
Intelligence reports 22 to 28 for September, October and November 1942 concerning the situation on Timor.

10/1
Brieven en telegrammen van regering Nederlands-Indië aan legercommandant betreffende maatregelen ten aanzien van Portugees Timor.
Letters and telegrams from the Netherlands East Indies government to the Army Commander concerning measures regarding Portuguese Timor.

V. オランダ所蔵史料 (Materials in the Archives of the Netherlands)

10/2

Publicatie van krijgsgeschiedkundige gegevens van de actie op Timor van december 1941 tot december 1942.

Publication of military history information on the Timor action of December 1941 to December 1942.

10/3

Overzicht in duplo van de Timor actie in 1942 door lt. kol. N.L.W. van Straten, 17 mei 1943.

Survey of the Timor action in 1942 by Lt. Col. N.L.W. van Straten, 17 May 1943.

10/4

Brief van Japanse commandant met betrekking tot overgave van Nederlandse troepen te Timor, 12 april 1942.

Letter by the Japanese commander concerning the surrender of Dutch troops on Timor, 12 April 1942.

10/5

Verslag van de militaire acties in gewest Timor en onderhorigheden door lt. kol. W. Detiger; Verslag van de gevoerde onderhandelingen met de gouverneurs van Portugees Timor op 15 december 1941.

Report of the military actions in the Timor territory and its dependencies by Lt. Col. W. Detiger; Report of the negotiations with the governors of Portuguese Timor on 15 December 1941.

10/6

Gevechtsverslag van de kapitein C.L.E.F. van Swieten omtrent het detachement Atamboea over de periode 8 december 1941-20 augustus 1942, 16 juni 1946.

Fighting report of Captain C.L.E.F. van Swieten concerning the Atamboea detachment in the period 8 December 1941-20 August 1942, 16 June 1946.

10/7

Dagboek van lt. adjudant Timorese troepen Th. de Winter over de periode 28 maart-11 december 1942.

Diary of Timorese troops Lt. Adjutant Th. de Winter for the period 28 March-11 December 1942.

10/10
Verslag van Lt. ter zee W.J. Kruys, commandant van de HrMS 'Tjerk Hiddes,' betreffende de evacuatie van 952 personen van Timor in de periode 10-18 december 1942.
Report of Naval Lt. W.J. Kruys, Commander of the HRMS 'Tjerk Hiddes,' concerning the evacuation of 952 people from Timor from 10-18 December 1942.

10/14
Brief van generaal majoor N.L.W. van Straten over betaling voeding Timorese troepen.
Letter of General
Major N.L.W. van Straten concerning payment for food for Timorese troops.

10/15
Krantenknipsel over geallieerde troepen in Portugees Timor, 22 februari 1942.
Newspaper clipping on Allied troops in Portuguese Timor, 22 February 1942.

10/16
Brief van kolonel J. Breemouwer met inlichtingen over Portugese personen die diensten hebben verricht voor de Nederlands-Indische troepen op Timor van maart tot december 1942.
Letter by Colonel J. Breemouwer with information on Portuguese persons who provided services for the Netherlands East Indies troops on Timor from March to December 1942.

10/17
Opgave van vermiste, gewonden en overleden militairen en een opgave van krijgsgevangen militairen op Timor, 1942.
Statement of missing, wounded and deceased soldiers and a statement of military prisoners of war on Timor, 1942.

10/19
Verslag van de verrichtingen van het detachement Atamboea, Garnizoensbataljon van Timor en Onderhoorigheden, later ten deele ingedeeld bij de gereorganiseerde troepenmacht op Timor, 16 juni 1946; Verslag 1e luitenant J.C.L. Stoll aangaande geallieerde troepen op Timor, 7 mei 1942; Verslag dr. Bloemsma over gebeurtenissen

op Timor in februari 1942; Verslag van lt. kol. N.L.W. van Straten over de expeditie naar Timor-Dilly van 19 februari 1942 tot en met 31 mei 1942, 31 mei 1946; Dagboeken Nederlandsche troepen op Timor, 28 maart 1942-11 december 1942; Kort overzicht van de Timor-actie 1942; Verslag omtrent de verrichtingen van kapitein infanterie C.L.E.F. van Swieten gedurende Timor guerilla, 24 april 1946; Stukken betreffende verleende onderscheidingen aan deelnemers Timor-actie; Verslag lt. kol W. Detiger van de militaire actie in het gewest Timor en onderhoorigheden, 10 april 1946; interrogations of deelnemers Timor-actie.

Report of the activities of the Atamboea detachment, the Garrison Batallion for Timor and its Dependencies, later making up part of the reorganized military force on Timor, 16 June 1946; Report by first Lieutenant J.C.L. Stoll concerning Allied troops on Timor, 7 May 1942; Report by dr. Bloemsma on events on Timor in February 1942; Report by Lt. Col. N.L.W. van Straten on the Timor-Dilly expedition from 19 February 1942 to 31 May 1942 (31 May 1946); Diaries of Dutch troops on Timor, 28 March 1942-11 December 1942; Short survey of the Timor action 1942; Report on the action of Infantry Captain C.L.E.F. van Swieten during the Timor guerilla war (24 April 1946); Documents concerning decorations granted to participants in the Timor campaign; Report by Lt. Col. W. Detiger on the military campaign in the province of Timor and its Dependencies subordinates, 10 April 1946; Interrogations of participants of the Timor action.

10/19

Bundel t.b.v. commissie beloningen en gedragingen inzake de strijd in Timor van december 1941 tot december 1942.

Bundle for the behavior and rewards commission concerning the conflict in Timor of December 1941 to December 1942.

10/20

Schrijven van generaal majoor N.L.W. van Straten en majoor C.L.E.F. van Swieten met aanbieding voordracht koninklijke onderscheiding voor Portugezen welke bijzondere diensten hebben bewezen aan de Nederlands-Australische troepen op Timor, 2 mei 1949.

Letter by Major General N.L.W. van Straten and Major C.L.E.F. van Swieten including recommendations for royal honors to Portuguese who performed special services to the Dutch and Australian troops on Timor, 2 May 1949.

10/21

Verslag in duplo van de adjudant onderofficier infanterie A. Hoornweg over de strijd op Timor.

Report by infantry Warrant-officer A. Hoornweg on the fighting on Timor.

10/22

Verslag in duplo omtrent de toestand op Timor eind mei 1942 door lt. kol. N.L.W. van Straten.

Report on the situation on Timor at the end of May 1942 by Lt. Col. N.L.W. van Straten.

10/28

Aantekeningen over de Japanse bezetting van Timor door L.E. Brouwer (Nederlands consul te Dilly), 1 oktober 1942.

Notes on the Japanese occupation of Timor by L.E. Brouwer (Dutch consul in Dilly), 1 October 1942.

10/29

Brief nr. B/6923 van Netherlands Military liaison officer, 18 november 1942 met als bijlage 'Report of operations in Timor 19 February-31 May 1942 by lt. kol. N.L.W. van Straten.'

Letter no. B/6923 of Netherlands Military Liaison Officer, 18 November 1942 with the appended 'Report of operations in Timor 19 February-31 May 1942 by Lt. Col. N.L.W. van Straten.'

10/31

NEFIS rapport van P. Reimer omtrent gebeurtenissen in Timor tijdens de strijd tegen Japan in 1942, 7 mei 1946.

NEFIS report of P. Reimer concerning events in Timor during the fight against Japan in 1942, 7 May 1946.

10/33

Krantenknipsel over Portugese versterking op weg naar Portugees Timor, Lissabon 4 februari 1942.

Newspaper clipping on Portuguese reinforcements on their way to Portuguese Timor, Lisbon 4 February 1942.

V. オランダ所蔵史料（Materials in the Archives of the Netherlands）

10/34

Brief van kabinet Legercommandant Batavia met als bijlage afschriften van Japanse documenten afkomstig van Timor tijdens de strijd tegen Japan in 1942, 14 juni 1946.

Letter by Cabinet Army Commander Batavia with copies of Japanese documents from Timor during the fight against Japan in 1942, 14 June 1946.

10/36a

Stukken betreffende de uitreiking van de Timor gesp 1942.

Documents concerning the conferring of the Timor buckle 1942.

11/4

Korte inlichtingen over de situatie op Timor betreffende Japanse activiteiten aldaar van oktober 1941 tot november 1942.

Short inquiries concerning the situation on Timor with respect to Japanese activities from October 1941 to November 1942.

11/5

Bescheiden van de liaison officer general headquarters te Brisbane, lt. kol. jhr. J.M.R. Sandberg, betreffende de strijd tegen Japan op Timor.

Documents by the Liaison Officer to General Headquarters in Brisbane, Lt. Col. esquire J.M.R. Sandberg, concerning the fight against Japan on Timor.

11/6

Brief van Marine en Leger inlichtingendienst nr. 574/I met bijlage 'Notes on Portuguese Timor by L.E.I. Brouwer, former Dutch consul Dilly,' 27 juli 1942.

Letter from Navy and Army Intelligence Service no. 574/I with appended 'Notes on Portuguese Timor by L.E.I. Brouwer, former Dutch consul Dilly,' 27 July 1942.

11/7

Brief van hoofdkwartier KNIL te Melbourne met bijlagen omtrent 'summary of the general report on Portugese Timor during the periode december 1941 to June 1942,' door D. Ross van het Australisch consulaat te Dilly, 25 augustus 1942.

Letter from KNIL Headquarters in Melbourne with appendices concerning 'summary of the general report on Portugese Timor during the periode december 1941 to June 1942' by D. Ross of the Australian consulate in Dilly, 25 August 1942.

11/8

Rapport inzake de acties op Timor in de maanden augustus, september en oktober door de commandant N.I. troepen Timor, J. Breemouer, 11 oktober 1942.

Report concerning the actions on Timor during the months August, September and October by the Commander of NEI troops on Timor, J. Breemouer, 11 October 1942.

11/9

Rapport opgemaakt door de Marine/Leger inlichtingendienst over de Japanse troepen, ontleend aan het optreden der Japanners.

Report on Japanese troops. by the Navy/Army Intelligence Service based on the conduct of Japanese.

11/10

Summary of a general report on Portuguese Timor during the period December 1941-June 1942, D. Ross, Australian consul at Dilly who arrived in Darwin from Timor on 10 July 1942.

11/11

Verslag van oorlogscorrespondent lt. ter zee II C.J.M. Kretschmer de Wilde over de Japanse aanval en de guerilla-strijd op Timor.

Report by war correspondent Navy 2nd Lt. C.J.M. Kretschmer de Wilde on the Japanese attack and the guerilla war on Timor.

11/12

Brief van commandant Nederlands-Indische strijdkrachten te Melbourne nr. 761/NI d.d. 27 juni 1942 inhoudende reorganisatie Nederlands-Indische strijdkrachten op Timor.

Letter from the Commander of NEI forces in Melbourne no. 761/NI, dated 27 June 1942, concerning the reorganization of the NEI forces on Timor.

11/13

Brief van commandant Nederlands-Indische strijdkrachten nr. 1697 d.d. 8 september 1942 inhoudende anti-Nederlandse stromingen, met bijlagen.

Letter from the Commander of NEI forces no. 1697, dated 8 September 1942, concerning anti-Dutch feelings, with appendices.

11/14
Schrijven commandant Nederlands-Indische strijdkrachten in Australië nr. 1269/NI d.d. 30 juli 1942 met betrekking tot sterkte troepen op Timor en aanvulling uitrustingsstukken
Letter from the Commander of NEI forces in Australia no. 1269/NI, dated 30 July 1942, concerning the strength of the troops on Timor and replenishment of equipment.

11/16
Afschrift telegrammen van commandant Nederlands-Indische troepen in Timor betrekking hebbende op berichtenverkeer met commandant Nederlands-Indische legerstrijdkrachten te Australië (gegevens Japanse troepenbewegingen).
Copy of telegrams from the Commander of NEI troops in Timor concerning communications with the Commander of NEI Forces in Australia (information on Japanese troop movements).

11/17
Afschrift telegrammen van commandant Nederlands-Indische troepen in Timor met dagboek betrekking hebbende op berichten bestemd voor commandant Nederlands-Indische legerstrijdkrachten te Australië.
Copy of telegrams by the Commander of NEI troops in Timor with diary concerning messages for the Commander NEI Forces in Australia.

11/18
Schrijven van commandant Nederlands-Indische troepen op Timor met aanbieding gevechtsrapport over de periode augustus tot september 1942 op Portugees Timor.
Letter by the Commander of NEI troops on Timor including a battle report on the period of August to September 1942 on Portuguese Timor.

11/19
Dagboek Nederlandse troepen in Timor over de periode 6 september tot 20 september 1942 met afschrift telegrammen verzonden aan commandant Nederlands-Indische legerstrijdkrachten te Australië.
Diary of Dutch troops on Timor covering the period 6 September to 20 September 1942 with copies of telegrams sent to the Commander of NEI Forces in Australia.

11/20

Brief van commandant Nederlands-Indische troepen in Timor over toestand Nederlandse troepen in Timor, 12 september 1942.

Letter from the Commander of NEI troops in Timor on the situation of Dutch troops in Timor, 12 September 1942.

11/21

Dagboek Ned. Ind troepen Timor, 9 augustus-17 november 1942 door luit. adj. de Winter.

Diary of NEI troops on Timor, 9 August-17 November 1942, by Lt. Adj. de Winter.

11/22

Brieven van lt. kol jhr. B.J.R. Sandberg, liaison officier general headquarters, omtrent de Nederlandse troepen op Timor.

Letter from Lt. Col. esquire B.J.R. Sandberg, Liaison Officer to General Headquarters, concerning Dutch troops on Timor.

11/23

Bundel telegrammen van commandant Nederlands-Indische troepen op Timor aangaande meldingen van Japanse troepenbewegingen, houding bevolking etc.

A bundle of telegrams from the Commander of NEI troops on Timor concerning notifications of Japanese troop movements, the attitude of the population, etc.

11/25

Brief commandant Nederlands-Indische strijdkrachten over reorganisatie Nederlands-Indische troepen op Timor, kasgelden en doorzending dagboek.

Letter from the Commander of NEI Forces on the reorganization of NEI forces on Timor, cash and the forwarding of a diary.

11/26

Brief van commandant Nederlands-Indische legerstrijdkrachten over cijferberichten.

Letter from the Commander of NEI forces on encoded messages.

11/27

Memorandum van S.H. Spoor 'Gegevens omtrent de actie op Timor,' 24 april 1942.

Memorandum from S.H. Spoor, 'Information on the action on Timor,' 24 April 1942.

V. オランダ所蔵史料（Materials in the Archives of the Netherlands）

11/28

Brief van liaison officer general head quarters over verzorging van de Nederlands-Indische troepen op Timor.

Letter from the Liaison Officer of the General Headquarters on maintenance of the NEI troops on Timor.

11/29

Brief commandant Nederlands-Indische legerstrijdkrachten te Australië omtrent sterkte en moreel van Nederlands-Indische troepen op Timor in afwachting beslissing evacuatie of herovering Timor.

Letter from the Commander of NEI Forces in Australia concerning the strength and morale of NEI troops on Timor awaiting a decision on evacuation or recapture of Timor.

11/30

Beschouwing omtrent de toestand op Timor door lt. kol. N.L.W. van Straten, eind mei 1942.

Consideration on the situation on Timor by Lt. Col. N.L.W. van Straten, end of May 1942.

11/31

Brief Marine commandant Australië over de toestand in Timor eind mei 1942, met bijlage.

Letter from the Australian Navy Commander on the state of affairs in Timor at the end of May 1942, with appendix.

11/33

Dagboek der N.I. troepen op Timor, 21 september 1942-4 oktober 1942.

Diary of NEI troops on Timor, 21 September 1942-4 October 1942.

11/34

Verslag Commandant Expeditionaire troepen Timor-Dilly aan de Legercommandant, 18 december 1941.

Report of the Timor-Dilly Expeditionary Forces Commander to the Army Commander, 18 December 1941.

11/34
W. Detiger, 'Verslag van de onderhandelingen met den Gouverneur van Portugeesch-Timor op den 17den December 1941,' 18 december 1941.
W. Detiger, 'Report of the negotiations with the Governor of Portuguese Timor on 17 December 1941,' 18 December 1941.

11/34
Brief M. de Abreu Ferreira de Cavalho aan W.W. Legatt en W. Detiger, 17 december 1941.
Letter from M. de Abreu Ferreira de Cavalho to W.W. Legatt and W. Detiger, 17 December 1941.

11/35
Stukken betreffende de ondergang van de Australische corvette HMAS 'Armidale.'
Documents concerning the sinking of the Australian corvette HMAS 'Armidale.'

11/36
Geschreven dagboek van N.L.W. van Straten, 7 december 1941-16 september 1942.
Written diary by N.L.W. van Straten, 7 December 1941-16 September 1942.

11/37
Relaas van J.B. Denu over zijn gevangenschap, ontvluchting en strijd in 1942-1945
Account by J.B. Denu of his imprisonment, escape and fight in 1942-1945.

11/38
Verslag van onderhandelingen met den gouverneur van Portugeesch Timor op den 17 December 1941.
Report of negotiations with the Governor of Portuguese Timor on 17 December 1941.
Collectie 'Nederlands-Indië 1945-1950' [*Collection 'Netherlands East Indies 1945-1950'*]

007/1
Bundel brieven over periode april-december 1942 van het Australië archief KNIL o.a. met betrekking tot de strijd op Timor.
A bundle of letters on the period April-December 1942 from the Australian KNIL

[Royal Netherlands East Indies Army] archive, concerning among other things the fight on Timor.

042/5
C.J.M. Kretschmer de Wilde, De Japanse inval en de guerillastrijd op Timor in 1942.
C.J.M. Kretschmer de Wilde, The Japanese invasion and the guerilla war on Timor in 1942.

Ministry of Defense, Central Archives Depot, The Hague

This institution was the main repository for archival collections of the Ministry of Defense. At the time of our survey (2004), the NEFIS archives were still housed in this archive, but as they have been in the process of preparation for a move to the National Archives, they probably can now be found there.

Archief van de Netherlands Forces Intelligence Service/Centrale Militaire Inlichtingendienst, 1943-1949 [*Archives of the Netherlands Forces Intelligence Service/Central Military Intelligence Service, 1943-1949*]

inv. nr. 85
Ingekomen en uitgaande stukken betreffende het zenden van inlichtingengezelschappen (parties) naar bezet Nederlands-Indië onder auspicien van NEFIS III, 1942-1945; "Timor," 1942-1943.
Incoming and outgoing documents concerning the sending of intelligence parties to the occupied Netherlands East Indies under the auspices of NEFIS III, 1942-1945; "Timor," 1942-1943.

Ministry of Foreign Affairs, The Hague

The Ministry of Foreign Affairs has a very interesting collection, but access is highly restricted for even the most mundane materials. These materials include a collection of archival documents originating in NEFIS.

Archief van de Marine en Leger Inlichtingendienst, de Netherlands Forces Intelligence Service en de Centrale Militaire Inlichtingendienst in Nederlands-Indië, 1942-1949 [*1960*]

[*Archives of the Navy and Army Intelligence Service, the Netherlands Forces Intelligence Service and the Central Military Intelligence Service in the Netherlands East Indies, 1942-1949* (*1960*).]

inv. nr. 32

Weekrapporten van de Nederlandse Liaison Officer te Darwin, 1942-1944.
Rapport van 2-8 juni 1944.
Rapport van 23-29 juni 1944.
Rapport van 30 juni-6 juli 1944.
Weekly reports of the Dutch Liaison Officer in Darwin, 1942-1944.
Report of 2 to 8 June 1944.
Report of 23 to 29 June 1944.
Report of 30 June to 6 July 1944.

inv. nr. 63

"Terrain Study," verslagen opgemaakt door de AGS van het SWPA betreffende diverse gebieden in Nederlands-Indië, 1943-1945. "Dutch Timor," (nr. 70), 1943, p. 62, "Portuguese province of Ocussi."
"Terrain Study," reports made by the AGS of the SWPA concerning several areas in the Netherlands East Indies, 1943-1945. "Dutch Timor," (nr. 70), 1943, p. 62, "Portuguese province of Ocussi."

inv. nr. 429

Verslag van het bombardement op de Australische corvette H.M.A.S. "Armidale" in november 1942, opgemaakt door majoor H.J. de Vries, 1943.
Report of the bombing of the Australian corvette H.M.A.S. "Armidale" in November 1942, produced by Major H.J. de Vries, 1943.

inv. nr. 457

Rapporten inzake de inname van Timor door de Japanners, opgemaakt door L.E.I. Brouwer, ex-consul voor Nederland te Dilly en kolonel N.L.W. van Straten, 1942.
Reports concerning the seizing of Timor by the Japanese, written by L.E.I. Brouwer, former Consul of the Netherlands in Dilly and Colonel N.L.W. van Straten, 1942.

inv. nr. 458

Verslagen van de aanval van Japanse troepen op Timor, 1942.

Reports of the attack by Japanese troops on Timor, 1942.

inv. nr. 459

Verslag inzake de gevechtshandelingen op Timor in 1942, samengesteld door HK KNIL, 1943.

Report concerning the actions on Timor in 1942, drawn up by KNIL HQ, 1943.

Archief van het gezantschap in Portugal (Lissabon) (1759) 1888-1957. [*Archives of the embassy in Portugal (Lissabon) (1759) 1888-1957.*]

inv. nr. 132

Correspondentie met het Ministerie van Buitenlandse Zaken inzake het eventueel vestigen van een honorair consulaat te Dilly (Portugees Timor), 1941-1942.

Correspondence with the Ministry of Foreign Affairs concerning the possible establishment of a honorary consulate in Dilly (Portuguese Timor), 1941-1942.

inv. nr. 171

Stukken betreffende Japanse penetratie in Portugees Timor, 1936-1944.

Documents concerning Japanese penetration in Portuguese Timor, 1936-1944.

inv. nr. 236

Stukken betreffende de politieke situatie in Portugees Timor, 1943-1947.

Documents concerning the political situation in Portuguese Timor, 1943-1947.

National Archives, The Hague

The National Archives (formerly the Algemeen Rijksarchief or ARA) houses the major archives of Dutch governmental ministries and related institutions. In accordance with Dutch archival law, documents older than 20 years have to be transferred to the National Archives. However, the Ministry of Defense and the Ministry of Foreign Affairs sometimes house materials in their own archives for substantially longer periods.

2.03.01 Archieven van de ministeries voor Algemeene Oorlogvoering van het Koninkrijk (AOK) en van Algemene Zaken (AZ), Kabinet van de Minister-President (KMP), (1924) 1942-1979 (1989)

[*Archives of the Ministries of General Warfare of the Kingdom and of General Affairs, Cabinet of the Prime Minister, (1924) 1942-1979 (1989)*]

inv. nr. 3380

Stukken betreffende de berichtgeving door vertegenwoordigers van het Ministerie van Buitenlandse Zaken over de politieke situatie in Aziatische landen, gebiedsdelen en allianties. 1942-1945; Portugees Timor 1942-1945.

Documents concerning the reporting by representatives of the Ministry of Foreign Affairs on the political situation in Asian countries, territories and alliances. 1942-1945; Portuguese Timor 1942-1945.

inv. nr. 3411

Stukken betreffende de bezetting van gebiedsdelen in de Pacific door Japan. 1941-1945; 1941-1943.

Documents concerning the occupation of territories in the Pacific by Japan. 1941-1945; 1941-1943.

inv. nr. 3412

Stukken betreffende de bezetting van gebiedsdelen in de Pacific door Japan. 1941-1945; 1944-1945.

Documents concerning the occupation of territories in the Pacific by Japan. 1941-1945; 1944-1945.

2.05.80 Archief van het Ministerie van Buitenlandse Zaken (BuZa), Londens Archief en daarmee samenhangende archieven, (1936) 1940-1945 (1958) [*Archives of the Ministry of Foreign Affairs, London Archives and connected archives, (1936) 1940-1945 (1958)*]

inv. nr. 291

Stukken betreffende politieke, economische en militaire aangelegenheden inzake Portugees Timor, 1940-1945.

Documents on political, economic and military issues concerning Portuguese Timor, 1940-1945.

inv. nr. 751

Stukken betreffende het detacheren van Australische troepen in gedeelten van

V. オランダ所蔵史料（Materials in the Archives of the Netherlands）

Nederlands-Indië, 1941-1942.
Documents concerning the detachment of Australian troops to parts of the Netherlands East Indies, 1941-1942.

inv. nr. 1161
Stukken betreffende het gevangen nemen en mishandelen van diverse Nederlandse hoge officieren en consuls, het torpederen van het ms Tjisalak, alsmede de moord op een rooms-katholieke geestelijke door de Japanners, 1942-1945.
Documents concerning the imprisonment and maltreatment of a number of Dutch high officers and consuls, the torpedoing of the m.s. Tjisalak, and the murder of a roman catholic clergyman by the Japanese, 1942-1945.

2.12.26 Ministerie van Defensie. De marinecommandant Australië tot 27 oktober 1943 tevens onderbevelhebber der strijdkrachten in het oosten. Archieven en de daarbij gedeponeerde archiefbescheiden 1942-1947
[*Ministry of Defense. The Navy commander Australia until 27 october 1943 simultaneously Vice Commander of Forces in the East. Archives and therein deposited archives 1942-1947*]

inv. nr. 122
Ingekomen en minuten van uitgaande stukken, kenmerk Int(elligence); 1/11 Timor 1943-1944.
Incoming and minutes of outgoing documents, reference Int(elligence); 1/11 Timor 1943-1944.

2.12.27 Ministerie van Defensie. Koninklijke Marine in de Tweede Wereldoorlog. Collectie archiefbescheiden (1936-1939) 1940-1945 (1946, 1948, 1950-1951, 1953)
[*Ministry of Defense. Royal Navy during the Second World War. Collection of archives (1936-1939) 1940-1945 (1946, 1948, 1950-1951, 1953)*]

inv. nr. 19
Stukken betreffende overleg met Portugal inzake het zogenaamde Timor-incident, een landing van geallieerde troepen in Portugees Timor tegen Japanse agressie, 1941-1942.
Documents concerning negotiations with Portugal about the so-called Timor-incident, a landing of Allied troops in Portuguese Timor against Japanese aggression, 1941-1942.

inv. nr. 49

Dagboek van de Nederlandse troepen op Timor van 5 oktober-11 december 1942, [1942].

Diary of the Dutch forces on Timor from 5 October-11 December 1942, (1942).

2.12.37 Ministerie van Defensie. Bevelhebber der strijdkrachten in het Oosten, 1942-1946

[*Ministry of Defense. Commander of the Forces in the East, 1942-1946*]

inv. nr. 194

Stukken betreffende rapporten van verrichtingen, patrouillerapporten en uittreksels oorlogsdagboeken, 1942-1946; Dossier SB 15/6, 1942-1944.

Documents concerning reports of activities, patrol reports and excerpts from war diaries, 1942-1946; File SB 15/6, 1942-1944.

inv. nr. 259

Stukken betreffende de toestand in Nederlands-Indië, samengesteld uit officiele bronnen, met name over de guerillastrijd op Timor, 1942-1943.

Documents concerning the situation in the Netherlands East Indies, composed from official sources, especially about the guerilla struggle on Timor, 1942-1943.

inv. nr. 331

Interrogation reports opgemaakt door NEFIS, 1944-1945; mei- juni 1945 [Compilation of Nefis interrogation reports nos. 1807-1838 and 1840-1847, 4 June 1945].

Interrogation reports compiled by NEFIS, 1944-1945; May-June 1945 [Compilation of Nefis interrogation reports nos. 1807-1838 and 1840-1847, 4 June 1945].

Netherlands Institute for Sound and Vision, Hilversum

This institute holds a marvellous collection of Dutch newsreels, TV documentaries, and movies. It holds the archives not only of Dutch public television, but also of Polygoon, a governmental institution which made short films about important news, which were shown in movie theatres before the main feature, and the Rijksvoorlichtingsdienst (The Government Information Service).

V. オランダ所蔵史料 (Materials in the Archives of the Netherlands)

RVD [Rijksvoorlichtingsdienst] Filmarchief
[*Films made by the Rijksvoorlichtingsdienst.*]

1755
Vrij en onverveerd [acte 7], 1943.
Zevende deel van een compilatiefilm over Nederland in oorlogstijd.
00.00-01.46: De guerillastrijd van Nederlanders tegen de Japanners op Timor.
Free and fearless [act 7], 1943.
Seventh part of a compilation film on the Netherlands during World War II.
00.00-01.46: The guerilla war of the Dutch against the Japanese on Timor.

2530
Decorations for Timor heroes, 1943.
Een reportage over de met militair ceremonieel gepaard gaande uitreiking van de MWO, het Bronzen Kruis en het Timorkruis aan de Commandant en Nederlandse, Indonesische en Australische Militairen, die tot december 1942 op Timor het verzet tegen de Japanse invasie hebben volgehouden.
A film report on the military ceremony in which the MWO, the Bronze Cross and the Timor Cross ware granted to the Commander and Dutch, Indonesian and Australian soldiers who until December 1942 resisted the Japanese invasion of Timor.

2573
Door duisternis tot licht [acte 2], 1945.
Tweede acte van een legerjournaalfilm over de Tweede Wereldoorlog in Oost-Azie en rond Australië.
00.36-01.10: Op Timor voert een groep Nederlandse en Australische militairen een guerilla. Patrouillerende soldaten en soldaat in loopgraaf.
Through darkness to light [act 2], 1945.
Second scene of an Army newsreel on the Second World War in East Asia and Australia.
00.36-01.10: On Timor a group of Dutch and Australian soldiers fights a guerilla war. Soldiers on patrol and soldier in a trench.

3804
Wederzijds [acte 8], 1941.

Achtste deel van 12-delige filmreeks over gebeurtenissen in binnen- en buitenland tijdens de regeerperiode van koningin Wilhelmina van 1898 tot 1948.
02.32-02.59: Beeldenreeks van Australische en KNIL-soldaten die als guerilla's op Timor Japanse infanteriegroep op bergweg met geweren en bren beschieten, waarna de Japanners van de wegeen lager gelegen ravijn inhollen.
Mutually [act 8], 1941.
Eighth part of newsreel in twelve parts on domentic and foreign events during the reign of Queen Wilhelmina from 1898 to 1948.
Images of Australian and KNIL-soldiers who as guerillas on Timor shot at Japanese infantry on a hillside road, after which the Japanese ran off the road into a ravine.

Netherlands Institute for War Documentation (NIOD), Amsterdam

Originally the Royal Institute for War Documentation (RIOD), from 1945 this institute was charged with documenting the war years in both Europe and in the Netherlands East Indies, and accordingly it collected a large number of documents in the immediate postwar era. With most documents numbered individually, this archive has been relatively accessible.

The conditions and document numbers may have changed during a recent reorganization of the research collection.

Indische Collectie [*Indies Collection*]

collection 407
Onderzoek Timor-guerilla, 1942 , 6 dozen.
Collectie van (copiën van) archiefmateriaal en literatuur over de Nederlandse guerilla tegen de Japanners op Timor van maart tot december 1942. Het materiaal vormde de basis voor het artikel 'Op Timor wordt nog gevochten' van P. Romijn (zie Literatuur). De collectie is toegankelijk via een beknopte inventaris.
Research Timor-guerilla, 1942, 6 boxes.
Collection of (copies of) archival documents and literature concerning the Dutch guerilla war against the Japanese on Timor from March to December 1942. The material was used as the basis of the article 'Op Timor wordt nog gevochten' by P. Romijn (see Dutch publication list). Access to this collection is facilitated by a short inventory.

V. オランダ所蔵史料（Materials in the Archives of the Netherlands）

000548-549
Brief van P.J.G. Walter betreffende Timor-guerilla, 18 september 1946.
Letter from P.J.G. Walter concerning the Timor-guerillas, 18 September 1946.

010495-508
Notes on Portuguese Timor by L.E.I. Brouwer, former Dutch consul Dilly.

010509-511
Statement by T. de Winter on the Japanese occupation of Portugese Timor, 6 June 1946.

010512-514
Affidavit by M. Borges Olivera, 24 June 1946.

010515
Summary of examination of Francisco Tilman de Ataide, 29 June 1946.

010516
Summary of examination of Ansilmo Bartolemou de Almada, 1 July 1946.

010517-519
Statement of Japanese atrocities in Portuguese Timor against Chinese, 2 July 1946.

010520-521
Verslag over de periode 21 januari tot 20 februari 1946, Conica Timor, 5 maart 1946.
Report on the period 21 January to 20 february 1946, Conica Timor, 5 March 1946.

017523-528
Statements concerning war crimes on Timor, 26 October 1945.

032344 II
Archief commissie Verzetsster Oost-Azie, betreffende de Timor-guerilla, pp. 39-40 en 47-54.
Archives Commission Resistance Decoration East Asia, concerning the Timor-guerilla war, pp. 39-40 and 47-54.

030357-414n
Archief commissie Verzetsster Oost-Azie, Rapport De Voogt, Anti-Japanse en guerilla aktie op Timor.
Archives Commission Resistance Decoration East Asia, De Voogt Report, Anti-Japanese and guerilla activity in Timor.

036722
Krantenknipsel, 'De evacuatie van Nederlands-Timor' in: NRC, 13 december 1952.
Newpaper clipping, 'The evacuation of Dutch Timor' in NRC, 13 December 1952.

047314
Brief van de Japanse commandant in Dilly aan kolonel van Straten, 12 april 1942.
Letter from the Japanese Commander in Dilly to Colonel van Straten, 12 April 1942.

047315
The heroes. lt. Col N.L.W. van Straten.

047316-223
Verslag van de verrichtingen van het Detachement Atamboea gedurende den oorlog met Japan (9 december 1941-20 augustus 1942), 16 juni 1946.
Report of the actions of the Atamboea detachment during the war against Japan (9 December 1941-20 August 1942), 16 June 1946.

063931
Brief M.J. Kommer aan FIWI (Federatie van Illegale Werkers Indië) betreffende Timor guerilla, 16 januari 1947.
Letter from M.J. Kommer to FIWI (Federation of Illegal Workers in the Indies) concerning the Timor guerilla war, 16 January 1947.

075571
Tijdschrifsartikel 'Guerilla op Timor' in: Legerkoerier, januari 1967.
Magazine clipping on 'Guerillas on Timor' in Legerkoerier, January 1967.

編　者　紹　介

後藤　乾一 (Gotō Ken'ichi)

1943年生まれ
早稲田大学大学院アジア太平洋研究科教授
主要著書
 『昭和期日本とインドネシア』（勁草書房、1985年）
 『日本占領期インドネシア研究』（龍溪書舎、1989年）
 『近代日本と東南アジア』（岩波書店、1995年）
 『＜東＞ティモール国際関係史』（みすず書店、1999年）
 Tensions of Empire: Japan and Southeast Asia in the Colonial and Post Colonial World（Ohio University Press、Singapore University Press、2003年）

高橋　茂人 (Takahashi Shigehito)

1968年生まれ
アジア太平洋資料センター自由学校　テトゥン語講師
早稲田大学大学院アジア太平洋研究科　国際関係学専攻博士後期課程在籍
学歴
 信州大学　農学部農芸科学科　農学士（1990年）
 信州大学大学院　農学修士（1993年）

ホートン、ウィリアム・ブラッドリー (Horton, William Bradley)

1967年生まれ
拓殖大学商学部講師
学歴
 University of Michigan-Ann Arbor, Rackham Graduate School
  歴史学　Master of Art（1994年）Ph.D. Candidate（1997年）
主要論文
 "Pieter Elberveld: The Modern Adventure of an 18th Century Indonesian Hero"（*Indonesia*、2003年）
 "Sexual Exploitation and Resistance: Indonesian Language Representations Since the Early 1990s of the Japanese Occupation History"（*Asia-Pacific Forum*、2005年）
 "Ethnic Cleavage in Timorese Society: The Black Columns in Occupied Portuguese Timor (1942)"（『国際開発学研究』、2007年）
 "Comfort Women in Indonesia: A consideration of the prewar socio-legal context in Indonesia and Japan"（『アジア太平洋討究』、2008年）

山本　まゆみ (Yamamoto Mayumi)

早稲田大学文学学術院講師
学歴
 University of Michigan-Ann Arbor, Rackham Graduate School
  人類学専攻 Master of Art（1992年）
 University of California-Los Angeles　Ph.D. Candidate（1994年）
主要論文
 "Spell of the Rebel, Monumental Apprehensions: Japanese Discourses on Pieter Elberveld"（*Indonesia*、2004年）

吉久　明宏 (Yoshihisa Akihiro)

1940年生まれ
元国立国会図書館司書

南方軍政関係史料㊶
第二次世界大戦期東ティモール文献目録

2008年7月初版発行　　　　税込価格 16,500 円
　　　　　　　　　　　　　　　（本体価格15,000円）

　編　者　　東ティモール日本占領期史料フォーラム
　編集担当　後藤　乾一（代表）
　　　　　　高橋　茂人
　　　　　　ホートン、ウィリアム・ブラッドリー
　　　　　　山本まゆみ
　　　　　　吉久　明宏

　発 行 者　　北 村　正 光

　発 行 所　㈱龍 溪 書 舎
　〒179-0085　東京都練馬区早宮２−２−17
　電 話　03(5920)5222・振替　00130−１−76123
　FAX　03(5920)5227

ISBN978-4-8447-0021-0　　　　　　　　印刷　勝美印刷
ⒸPrinted in Japan 2008　　　　　　　　製本　高橋製本